FEELINGS OF STRUCTURE

Facing South, Molly Jarboe, 2008.

FEELINGS STRUCTURE OF

Explorations in Affect

EDITED BY
KAREN ENGLE AND
YOKE-SUM WONG

McGill-Queen's University Press
Montreal & Kingston | London | Chicago

ISBN 978-0-7735-5451-1 (cloth)
ISBN 978-0-7735-5452-8 (paper)
ISBN 978-0-7735-5571-6 (ePDF)
ISBN 978-0-7735-5572-3 (ePUB)

Legal deposit fourth quarter 2018
Bibliothèque nationale du Québec

Printed in Canada on acid-free paper that is 100% ancient forest free
(100% post-consumer recycled), processed chlorine free

This book has been published with the help of a grant from the Canadian
Federation for the Humanities and Social Sciences, through the Awards
to Scholarly Publications Program, using funds provided by the Social
Sciences and Humanities Research Council of Canada. Funding has also
been received from the School of Creative Arts, University of Windsor.

Funded by the   Financé par le
Government   gouvernement   Canada   Canada Council   Conseil des arts
of Canada   du Canada   for the Arts   du Canada

We acknowledge the support of the Canada Council for the Arts, which
last year invested $153 million to bring the arts to Canadians throughout
the country.

Nous remercions le Conseil des arts du Canada de son soutien. L'an
dernier, le Conseil a investi 153 millions de dollars pour mettre de l'art
dans la vie des Canadiennes et des Canadiens de tout le pays.

Library and Archives Canada Cataloguing in Publication

Feelings of structure : explorations in affect / edited by Karen Engle
and Yoke-Sum Wong.

Includes bibliographical references and index.
Issued in print and electronic formats.
ISBN 978-0-7735-5451-1 (cloth). – ISBN 978-0-7735-5452-8 (paper). –
ISBN 978-0-7735-5571-6 (ePDF). – ISBN 978-0-7735-5572-3 (ePUB)

1. Affect (Psychology).   2. Emotions.   I. Engle, Karen, 1974–, editor
II. Wong, Yoke-Sum, editor

BF588.F44 2018   152.4   C2018-903893-4
                                              C2018-903894-2

Set in 10.5/13.5 Sina Nova with Trade Gothic Std
Book design & typesetting by Garet Markvoort, zijn digital

THIS BOOK IS FOR THE GIANT PRAIRIE SQUID

CONTENTS

FIGURES

ACKNOWLEDGMENTS

This collection emerged out of multiple workshops and informal meetings about how academic writing could be approached differently. At a certain point, we decided discussion was simply not enough and we ought to do something about it – and thus *Feelings of Structure* was born. We, the editors, are grateful to all the contributors who committed to the project, but we are indebted to the editorial team at McGill-Queen's University Press, in particular, Kathleen Fraser – and to our editor, Jonathan Crago, for taking a chance on this experiment. Jonathan has been incredibly supportive, offering advice and guidance when necessary. To Molly Jarboe, our gratitude for her generosity with the use of her image as a prelude to the volume of writing. This book would not exist in this form without the support of Dr Vincent Georgie at the University of Windsor School of Creative Arts and of the Federation for the Humanities and Social Sciences Awards for Scholarly Publications Program.

Karen Engle acknowledges the University of Windsor for its research support and thanks Brenda Francis-Pelkey for the time she generously spent looking through photographs.

Yoke-Sum Wong would like to thank the Alberta College of Art & Design for resource support, the Noguchi Foundation and Garden Museum, and the Eames Office.

FEELINGS OF STRUCTURE

Figure 0.1 Untitled, Derek Sayer.

Thinking Feeling

**KAREN ENGLE AND
YOKE-SUM WONG**

Feelings of Structure has its provenance in the desert town of
Marfa, Texas, at a gathering for an experimental workshop that
involved participants committing to expressing or writing a
journey in three days.[1] Marfa is also where Donald Judd's site-
specific concrete structures prowl the deserts. It is a town more
connected to London, Paris, Berlin, and Tokyo than to the rest
of America – or indeed even to Texas. A visitor to Marfa might
possibly check into the Hotel Paisano, where some rooms are
named after the actors in the movie *Giant* (shot in Marfa).
The Rock Hudson suite apparently has a wet bar and a brick
fireplace.

There is an uncanny presence in Marfa – a town that is
everywhere and nowhere at all. Time ebbs and flows here.
Out there, in the desert, some say you can see the extraterres-
trial Marfa lights dancing in the mysterious dark. If you wait
patiently throughout the night, you might catch a glimpse of
these eerie glowing bodies. In the summertime, the heat builds
rapidly, and in the middle of the town lonesome tumbleweeds
roll across the few main thoroughfares, dragging dust in their
wake. The buildings almost resemble those in an Edward
Hopper or Charles Sheeler painting, except in starker fading
colours. Their clarity against the often blue and untroubled
skies is unreal. The air is dry, arid, parched – the occasional

The head was removed after hanging

and taken door to door

Figure 0.2 *Hanging* (1998), Brenda Francis Pelkey.

welcoming breeze picks up the dust – it is as if you have become part of the modernist landscape, and the rest of the world is far away, fades away. You dissipate.

The farther you come from, the more you belong here, ex situ – the more you feel an odd sense of place and belonging. Marfa is an un-place. Marfa is also a place-in-making. Many residents in the main townsite came from elsewhere; more than a few had long ago settled in Marfa with their own journeying stories. The town welcomes the wealthy ranchers nearby who mingle with the literati, attending music and book events and especially artist gatherings. Some long-time residents came with Donald Judd, carrying with them the cherished utopic vision of a bohemian artistic community away from the grasp of capital, and yet today it is not so easy to draw these distinctions. More than ever, Marfa has been braided into global capital as the art world descends upon its core for the big-name openings. This expanse of space promises so much to work from and in. There is the dynamism of youth here, alongside the aged aesthetic energies that have poured into this town. But the sense of belonging does not always commit – people move in and out. Some return from faraway cities, from across the seas. Some dream of returning.

Harsh realities scrape against aesthetic vision here. It is the point where your feelings jar, where structures dissolve, emerge, cohere as if through the sudden jerk of contact with a concrete object, and your being is lacerated – unseen, but felt inside, and it lingers.

By the courthouse, in the searing heat of the afternoon sun, you notice men in orange jumpsuits carrying out their yardwork, their faces bent towards the ground while an officer stands nearby in the shade, watching them. Prison labour exists here amid the stark desert modernism and artist studios. Not too far away, the border police have their office, from which they surveil every car that comes from the south, ever wary of the illegal stowaway. The magnificent Rio Grande is what divides and enables – forbidding terrain that inspires perilous and desperate crossings. Already imaginary walls are being built, and they are hardening. Away from the main townsite, you encounter more of the Hispanic community – the locals will tell you the best tacos and huevos rancheros are found at the edge of town, heading west on the US 90 to El Paso. Keep driving south on US 67 to the town of Presidio and your cellphone will welcome you to Mexico, though you're still in America. The weirdness, the fantasy, the violence, and the patrolled boundaries all meet up in Marfa to generate the particular feeling of this place and this time.

"It has exercised me greatly." This was Raymond Williams's initial response to the question of how his concept of *structures of feeling*, as described in *The Long Revolution*, can possibly "be articulated to a plurality of classes" if it is indeed meant to indicate the as-yet unarticulated experience of an entire cultural generation.[2] Williams's response to this very specific question captures precisely the reaction that several generations of writers and critics have had to this evocative and difficult concept. What on earth is a structure of feeling? Countless critics have grappled with this question. To name just a few influences for this volume: Patricia T. Clough, Stuart Hall, Ben Highmore, Kathleen Stewart, Sara Ahmed, Susan Lepselter, and Lauren Berlant have all spent time grappling with this phrase. Even Williams himself continued to refine and rework the idea he first put forth in *Preface to Film* all through his critical work. While he affirms that his site of application for this concept is "the work of art," we wondered what might happen if we removed those limits and asked anthropologists, cultural historians, social theorists, art historians – in short, writers from a variety of academic disciplines – to reflect upon the diverse relations of these terms: *structure* and *feeling*.[3]

We understand *structure* and *feeling* as entangled, relational, and shifting terms rather than fixed binaries. This volume is, at its core, an experiment. We do not claim to provide the final word on what a feeling of structure *is* or to identify the "proper" methodology for its articulation. Our inversion of Williams's phrase from *structures of feeling* to *feelings of structure* privileges the intangible, ineffable, and evocative aspects of the complex feelings we glean from structures. At the same time, we want to retain Williams's emphasis on "tension" as a crucial nodal point in this collection. As he describes: "structures of feeling … initially form as a certain kind of disturbance or unease, a particular type of tension."[4] While we are not seeking to identify the emergence of a new generational period, we do seek to apprehend the situatedness of the tensions and unease infusing the ex situ: the *feelings* of structures that range from an imagined post-apocalyptic world to American Modernism, to the relations we develop with furniture, to the twentieth-century Canadian prairies and beyond. We do this partly as a response to the emergence and strength of affect studies in academic writing, but also – and perhaps more purposefully – as an acknowledgment of how things that are felt (rather than known) break apart, reinforce, build up, or bring into focus the various structuring frames of our lives.[5] Like gravity, feelings are invisible but absolutely determining. We intend this volume as an opening into further discussions of how *feelings of structure* might help us to take seriously the gravitational pull of feeling as we attune to various scenes of everyday and extraordinary life.

Our deliberate inversion of Raymond Williams's phrase is also an invitation to ludic provocations. Feelings of structures are themselves mutable – they are attuned to changes of presence, sensitive to the waves of intensities of emotions that rise and fall, disperse, accrue, take shape, diffuse in response to the structural forces. Feelings may even threaten to dissolve the certainty of structure. The threat of dissolution, however, offers a way of recognizing difference and building insight. Karen Barad's deployment of Donna Haraway's use of *diffraction*, a concept from quantum physics, as methodological reading offers an interesting dimension to thinking about the formation of feelings.[6] Rather than reading diffraction as encountering interfering obstacles, we read it as intra-active entanglement. To read feeling and structure diffractively is to read them not via causality but as a complex interacting relation. The structures themselves – including institutions and systems – are not inert singular forms, reducible to a monolithic presence and meaning, separated as object from subjective engagement. To read diffractively is to read not only for the narrative bends but for heterogeneities and things in flux and to be aware of feelings in formation. Form breaks down, reconstitutes, abates. Rather than thinking about the *form* of feeling, we might consider feeling as dynamic and in process – and in particular, *formlessness* as creative attention to structural engagement – as feelings find a way of becoming.

Here we engage with Georges Bataille's *informe* or *formless*, to treat feelings and affects as formless. Bataille's writing on the informe is no more than a short dictionary entry found in the surrealist journal *Documents*. For Bataille, the informe is an operation that displaces. And what it displaces, when Bataille wrote it in *Documents* (published 1929–30), is the certainty of meaning and the necessity of form.

"Formless," Bataille writes, "is not only an adjective having a given meaning but a term that serves to bring things down in the world."[7] Bataille uses the word *déclasser* to mean the bringing of things down in the world; the word also operates as *declassification*. For Yve-Alain Bois it is "in the double sense of lowering and taxonomic disorder."[8] Not a thing in and of itself, the formless has only an operational existence; it is performative, like obscene words, the violence of which derives less from semantics than from the very act of their delivery. In translation, the informe is often conveyed as "formless" but the *feeling* is more of an ambiguous conjoining of "to un-form/de-form."[9] Bois contends that the dictionary entry under informe in *Documents* remains one of Bataille's most effective acts of sabotage against the conventions of the academic world, societal structures and institutions, and the spirit of the system.

For Bataille, the very will to give shape is the ultimate problem, for it always tends towards hegemonic form. Structures solidify and ossify. The urge for resemblance demands too much of a priori experience and treats it, to recall Raymond Williams, as a finished product. Social experiences are considered as "formed wholes rather than forming and formative processes."[10] The key words in Bataille's piece are "resemble" and "something like": "everything that resembles something, everything that is gathered into a unity of a concept" is dismantled by the "informe."[11] While the essays in this volume take a variety of *forms*, we do not seek to concretize these forms into a new system or methodological category for "doing writing." We seek instead to embrace the radicality, alterity, and impropriety of Bataille's informe; to embrace the librarian, the pornographer, and the sometime surrealist by inviting the reader to consume without regard for use-value. In this way, we also wish to remain within the zone of Williams's structure of feeling – that zone we sense but cannot shape through language.

We understand Williams's conceptualization of structures of feelings as processual, one of forming and formative processes, very much in the spirit of formlessness. Any eventual materialization of the inchoate – that is, feelings and affects – takes time to emerge and find coherent language and form. If, as Karen Barad explains, "materiality itself is always already a desiring dynamism, a re-iterative reconfiguring, energized and energizing, enlivened and enlivening,"[12] the affects evoked will be similarly fluid. In a sense, the feelings and affects that we have in relation to structure (physical, institutional, texts, conventional language) are themselves in ever-overlapping, ever-evolving relationships – we are grasping to make sense into being. Structures, however, also evoke – even as they *affect* – and generate feelings that are just as ambiguous and indefinable. We cannot fit them, the "all that is present and moving," easily into language or a finished product. We think of Wittgenstein's impossibility of language that leaves one in silence to reflect on that which has no linguistic description yet. We seek to convey these affects in ways that take us beyond our conventional forms of writing.

This is where we turn to Susan Lepselter, who brilliantly navigates the uncanny landscapes of Area 51 with sensitivity and empathy in her book *The Resonance of Unseen Things*. What does it mean to resonate? Lepselter directs us to resonance particularly through the deployment of the concept of apophenia. Apophenia, she explains, is a way of perceiving connections between random and unrelated objects. Resonance is not "exact reiteration" or resemblance, but a resemblance that is partial and fluid. Most of all, it is *felt*. "Resonance," she writes, "itself becomes another story. The story of uncanny resonance becomes an expressive modality, a vernacular theory, a way of seeing the world, an intimation of the way *it all makes sense*."[13]

To feel a structure is a way of making sense – whether it is a tangible built concrete entity or space, or an impermeable institution of clustering power in defiance of language. It is difficult to express the "something being there" but there is "something going on" or something that gets to us. Resonance shimmers as *feelings*: intensities that emerge in a point of contact resonate and are acted upon immediately or linger in the passing of time. These feelings are also powerfully mnemonic and can summon experiences from elsewhere, connecting time and space. They are not necessarily located in the realm of the rational, and sense-making comes only gradually, after we have processed the contextual narratives. They are unformed at best – emergent in their meaningfulness. Resonances make sense for us, and our feelings for them, in whatever configuration, are how we enfold them and attempt to make them mean something for us.

The intensities that are evoked by a specific presence of structure or structures are unformed and mutable even as they find ways of articulation in whatever formation or fabulation. They give our stories content and purpose. There is no necessary clarity and focus. Anger, frustration, confusion, helplessness, longing, happiness, jubilation – all lived emotions are expressed. As Sara Ahmed reminds us, for those who suffer oppressive experiences, the structures get under your skin, operating below the surface of things. They are encounters of struggle and are not shaken off easily, and they stir us into agency.

The temporality of feelings – this here and now that is the formative living present – is also the contemporary present mixed up with the social experience that is defined by the past and future. The living present of experiences does not necessarily recede. Experiences and their residues, sometimes not immediately contextualized, accumulate into mnemonic affects. One gets tangled up in time. Feelings do not go away – they draw on the well of the past in imperfect fragments that cohere with experiences of the present. We should pay more attention to them, rather than to grand statements or capacious declarations. Feelings direct us to the nuance, to the presences of silences and the incommunicable. They lead us to forms of articulations that urge us to read with more care and consideration. They are emergent expressions that operate in the liminal, skirt the edges of language. The density of feelings, even confused and unclear feelings, speaks volumes; they are attunements into the other unseen worlds that form part of everyday experiences – the press of things to come.

The aim of this collection of writings is to further highlight the forms that are not fixed, that are impossible to reduce to the explicit and the physical yet in themselves do exert palpable pressures on our being and stir us to "set effective limits on experience and on action."[14] These emergent feelings and affects are texts in process, have no categorization, defy the rational. They are also social experiences in the making. In their performativity lies their significance. We take inspiration from Teju Cole's *Blind Spot*, whose images and text resonate with each other, leaving us to feel rather than to urge for explanation. He explains his unconventional approach to his book: "I see it as a unified story ... but one in which each fragment of prose is dense in the way that a poem is dense. There are thematic breadcrumbs scattered throughout the text, but, yes, it is oblique. It's not meant to be obvious, but a more psychologically resonant series of fragments that detonate on some deeper level."[15] We are also inspired by the atmospheric attunements (to borrow a phrase from Kathleen Stewart) of

Brenda Francis Pelkey's photography, the way image and text mediate each other, but only obliquely. She leaves the viewer with the distinct feeling that *something happened here*. Her scenes never explain; they just point to some past violence, fear, or ebbing of life. Feeling is Pelkey's province, a feeling that haunts without enlightenment and without release.

Our intent here is not to create a binary of feeling and structure as oppositional but to comprehend the emergent in our various affectual interactions. The writings we are fortunate to assemble here are obviously eclectic in their form and subject matter. We do not offer brief summaries of each paper in this introduction, since we do not wish to pre-structure the encounter with these texts. We want to avoid what Kathleen Stewart refers to as the "prefab concept that happened somewhere else."[16] Readers should know, however, that not all the pieces in this volume are conventional academic writing. Feelings evoke, and at times demand, a different kind of narrative form, perhaps one more visually attuned and sensitive to the poetics of words, a kind of "writing that is open to the world [and] takes what it lights upon: the tendons of a scene, the elements of an actual field forming up."[17] We aim to show how words as a form of text evoke rather than serve as explanatory tools. The essays here address a range of topics from the extraordinarily mundane to metanarrative concerns but approached from different angles – sideway glances, scenes through the mist of rain while in a moving vehicle, a squinted eye peering through a microscope. They emphasize connections and unintended juxtapositions. We think of the Shandean mood, a mood of detours and digressions, "continually reinforced by what one was serendipitously finding en route,"[18] and of unsettled reverberations that come from irreconcilable differences. They should be treated as allusive fragments and conceptual starting points for place, environment, memory, objects, race, dreams, and more. They are all in their own ways fragmented, yet they form a unified collection of structures of feelings in themselves. We have not grouped them in sections or ordered them according to theme, style, or length. Instead, we have opted for a thoroughly randomized sequence in order to encourage what Milan Kundera has called "the density of unexpected encounters."[19] Readers may start anywhere in the volume and assemble their own connecting references and constellations of meaning as they go. We wish to emphasize the aleatory and the unforeseen, immersion and exploration over explanation. Let us enjoy getting lost, in the way Michel Serres urges us to do: "lose your balance, leave the beaten track, chase birds out of hedges. *Débrouillez-vous*, muddle through,"[20] ramble.

NOTES

1 This took place on 9–12 April 2014 and was hosted by the University of Texas at Austin. The workshop was co-organized by Craig Campbell and Yoke-Sum Wong.
2 Williams, *Politics and Letters*, 156.
3 Ibid., 159.
4 Ibid., 168.
5 Stewart, "Atmospheric Attunements."
6 Dolphijn and van der Tuin, "'Matter Feels, Converses, Suffers.'"
7 Bataille, "Formless," in *Visions of Excess*, 31.
8 Bois and Krauss, *Formless*, 18.
9 Ibid.
10 Williams, "Structures of Feeling," 128.
11 Bois and Krauss, *Formless*, 79.
12 Dolphijn and van der Tuin, "'Matter Feels, Converses, Suffers.'"
13 Lepselter, *Resonance of Unseen Things*, 4.
14 Williams, "Structures of Feeling," 132.
15 Sean O'Hagan, "Teju Cole: 'My Camera Is like an Invisibility Cloak. It Makes Me More Free,'" *Guardian*, 25 June 2017, https://www.theguardian.com/books/2017/jun/25/teju-cole-blind-spot-my-camera-is-like-an-invisibility-cloak-interview.
16 Romero and Locke, "Words in Worlds."
17 Ibid.
18 Merton, *On the Shoulders of Giants,* xx. Also see Sayer, *Making Trouble,* for expansion on the method of chance encounters and serendipity.
19 Kundera, *Testaments Betrayed*, 50.
20 Serres, *The Five Senses*, 271.

The Sofa's Objection: Troublesome Things and Affective Emplacements

KIMBERLY MAIR

Imagining Raymond Williams's concept *structures of feeling* in its reverse, as *feelings of structure*, this essay will explore feelings of obligation to furniture and the affective spatial arrangements of relocation that remedy or transfer these intractable feelings and bring new habiliments[1] into being. It will give particular attention to displaced furnishings, items that are ambivalently abandoned and yet entrusted to others. These impedimenta that are given asylum from the anonymity of the flea market or the despair of the town landfill may be cherished or abject things, compulsory burdens of affectionate and resentful obligations, emplaced in the built environments of which they become a part. John Plotz, in a review playfully titled "Can the Sofa Speak?," cautiously grants that there are "anatomizing places where the strict rules for classifying and comprehending phenomena seem suddenly no longer to apply";[2] however, the problem in this essay is not the meanings of objects – in this case furniture and other small things that furniture organizes – but the connections or felt structures that are informed by sensorial emplacement and affect tucked into the interstices of furnishings, much like coins and bric-a-brac that fall between sofa cushions.

Tracking the placement of uncherished gifts in people's homes, Julia Keyte observes that furniture is used to support, but also to hide, an object deemed a troublesome thing. Nicky

Gregson et al. describe troublesome things as those that invoke feelings of un-certainty and bring "an anxiety of possession; a sense that someone, somewhere else, could be a more appropriate keeper or custodian of such things."[3] Keyte observes that, by offering "mini-peripheral zones within and around [it], beyond the parts of it that are accessed the most,"[4] furniture participates in the tactical arrangement of things that produce ambivalent, even negative, feelings but must be kept. Furniture colludes with the built space in the makings of "undesignated spaces"[5] between a wall and a bedside table or at the bottom of a drawer, "gaps between and behind furniture" that can "contain or store objects whose value is ambiguous or uncertain, or that we would rather not think about for a while."[6] Those things with which we have a "secret dialogue,"[7] whether of love or aver-sion, can evoke an intense ambivalence that makes them troublesome. They may be objectively valuable or they may stand apart from the generally appreciated, perhaps something "apparently more insignificant, like a piece of string, a bit of fabric or a newspaper cutting."[8] Between us and these things, feelings of struc-ture, like strings of significance, are laced.

Imagine the roll of rice paper that a friend bestows on you in lieu of a good-bye, insisting that only you appreciate it. It requires that from time to time you consider how to keep from bending, ripping, or puncturing this roll of twice-over precious paper that can never be used. Or a once-beloved chair handed down through three generations, upon which you never sit without knowing why, might have a connection to the reverence performed towards chairs even in the absence of the persons expected to occupy them. As Constance Classen has noted, "simply looking at a nineteenth-century chair, for example, cannot tell us that a dutiful daughter in the eighteen-hundreds might curtsy to her father seated in that chair, and even to the empty chair when her father was absent."[9] The frequent neglect of the spatial, sensorial, and emotional arrangements of things lends implicit support to the heavy attribution of agency to human sub-jects that commonsense understandings offer, yet these arrangements call upon and prohibit certain sensibilities and the possibilities of movement that accom-pany them.[10] The effects of accumulated cultural instruction applied to the sen-sorium are playfully illustrated by the ambivalence produced by surrealist artist Meret Oppenheim's 1936 *Object* (fur-covered cup, saucer, and spoon) and more evocatively by the interactive sculpture *Zizi the Affectionate Couch*, designed by Robert Davy, Kerry Richens, Linda Davy, and Stephen Barrass in 2003. Zizi, a couch that is designed to provide both physical and emotional support, provokes a mixture of visceral reactions, not necessarily all pleasant, as it responds to touch and makes audible objections when ignored.[11]

Drawing from a range of sources – from literature to scholarship, but also from the uncertain itineraries of furnishings – what follows will acknowledge the relation of obligation to furniture as a sensorial and affective predicament wrought with tensions between comfort and discomfort that are at once material and social, despite the opacity of their communication. To do this, I will offer a provisional inventory of feelings of structure organized around a small number of items, some of them real, some of them fictive: sofas, tables, a suitcase that no longer travels, and a credenza that inters a sub-collection of ashes that were sent for safe-keeping – perhaps illicitly – via Canada Post.

THE AESTHETICS AND AFFECTS OF COMMUNICATION

Raymond Williams's concept of structures of feeling intervenes into fixed forms that render "living" experience as a solidified "past tense"[12] and points towards undefined yet present "elements of impulse, restraint, and tone; specifically affective elements of consciousness and relationships."[13] Hence, Williams's proposal of structures of feeling has been accused of opacity. One solution to its seeming lack of instant exportability has been to try to distill it or to reduce it to something like ideology plus more complexity.[14] In contrast, Ben Highmore embraces the ambiguities of the concept. He suggests that the concept of structures of feeling is *"necessarily* vague"[15] and that it opens to the senses, such as feeling and taste, as historical agents in the processes of worlding[16] (or world-making in Lauren Berlant's characterization)[17] that need to be worked out in the contexts of the concept's use. It is perhaps no accident that feeling implicates touch, that most proximal and connective of the senses.[18] These mutual articulations between structures of feeling, as a concept, and their contexts must be attuned to intersensorially. Such mutual articulations must give attention to emplacement, a concept whose force extends beyond and corrects the dominant mind-body tension to entail a unity with spatial and environmental surroundings,[19] as well as with a peripheral and distracted "knowledge that," for Michael Taussig, "lies as much in the objects and spaces of observation as in the body and mind of the observer."[20] Highmore observes that "the felt world is often experienced in something like a synaesthetic mode where feelings of social flourishing and struggling take on particular flavours, sounds, colour-schemes and smells; where hope and nostalgia, melancholy and exuberance have sensual forms that are sometimes durable and sometimes fleeting."[21]

Perhaps Walter Benjamin was attuned to something like this when he insisted upon the significance of the hand in storytelling. For him, the story is tied to the sites upon which it is crafted, where it "twines about a happening like ivy around a wall."[22] The hand brings with it the association of touch, but Benjamin does not give touch to a bound subject as its primary agent. This touch is connective, and it implicates surroundings too, even in a wordless communication. Benjamin also drew a distinction between storytelling and information. His distinction rests upon the place of explanation in the mode of communication. While the storyteller's art is one that gives no explanation, Benjamin considers information to be inseparable from the explanations it intends to deliver.[23] After explanation, memory is also significant to the distinction. Benjamin remarks that the listener is primarily concerned with remembering: "'No one,' Pascal once said, 'dies so poor that he does not leave something behind.' Surely it is the same with memories too – although these do not always find an heir."[24] Information's triumph confirms for Benjamin the claim that "experience has fallen in value" since information is bereft of the "amplitude" of storytelling, "an artisan form of communication" that bears the fingerprints of the tale-teller.[25]

Emphasizing tactility's intersensorial accomplishment in communication, Benjamin observes that the prints are inseparable from the story that the teller crafts in the telling. The wear on a piece of fabric or furniture is inseparable from an accumulation of meetings – direct contacts – in affective arrangements between persons and things. Alex Wilkinson describes something like this accumulation of contact in reference to a shoulder bag he received as a "kind of gift" that he carried across his right shoulder regularly: "it grafted on to me, plastically, like a talisman," for four years until it was beyond repair. "Nowhere was this more evident than on the left side of the reverse, the side which must have brushed my leg thousands of times. My leg had opened up a hole, which consumed me and swished me round, like mouthwash, before spitting me out. It cost me €18. The left hand side of my new bag has those first bobbles of wear, like tears of fatigue rolling down the face of a marathon runner."[26] Before this passage, the reader of Wilkinson's text already has the feeling that the bag was carried neither merely for convenience nor out of positive affection, as he has suggested that the bag was abhorrent to him.

Another instance of the prints or traces left by accumulated contacts comes from the novel Care of Wooden Floors. After spilling copious amounts of wine, not to mention some blood, all over the fine French oak floors in his friend's flat that he is charged with caring for, Will Wiles's protagonist thinks that if only he could hide the stains, perhaps by overturning the floorboards, it would also be a way "of reversing all that had happened."[27] In this novel, the wooden floors to be cared for, like the furnishings that the protagonist also inadvertently damages in several unfortunate occurrences, constitute the substrate of communications between friends who have not for a long while been in each other's presence. One of several notes of minute instruction left by the flat's meticulous owner anticipates irreparable damage to the floors during this act of caretaking and further presumes that both time and the scenes that envelop things leave their marks, whether these are made by the wrong note struck on the piano that he demands no one play or by a spill on the floor. "You will always know,"[28] the instructions insist, and, what is more, you cannot correct it even though "when something goes wrong, you can trace back to a moment when it could have happened differently, a moment when a word, or silence, or an act, or a stillness, could have changed everything. I am thinking now of the floors."[29] He is, of course, not just thinking of the floors, and yet, as his note pleads, the floors are "important to me in many ways."[30]

I wish to consider *feelings of structure* as a matter of aesthetic communication between and with things and, to begin, I wonder if information (as communication) fully deserves its devaluing designation as unfeeling and uncritical. Notwithstanding Benjamin's significant distinction that establishes the storyteller's aura outside of advancing communications technologies that erode it, information has feelings. I am not just being playful in saying so. Information is tied to *the interesting*, which is one of three minor aesthetic categories that Sianne Ngai argues best illustrate aesthetic transformation under late capitalism. Operating representationally through realism, the interesting, as Ngai observes, "marks a tension between the unknown and the already known and is generally bound up with a desire to know and document reality"; in this way, it is tied to information and its novelty or "small surprise."[31] Ngai notes that the epistemological compulsion underpinning the interesting often takes the form of serial comparison and meetings between the idiosyncratic and systemic that emerge in postwar conceptual art, which has used exhaustive devices to detail and systematize information: "specimen cases, list structures, notarized certificates, graphs"[32] – and not to forget *tables*. The interesting is, as Ngai shows, a feeling-based aesthetic, which needs to give no more reason than itself. It – whatever it is – is just interesting, and usually we need not say more. It is tied to temporality as duration in "ongoingness or sequential progression" and repetition as we return to what captures our interest, and thus it has multiple temporalities rather than the singular "sublime as a kind of thunderbolt"[33] of classical aesthetics. This ambivalent attraction of the interesting, according to Ngai, invokes postponed references. Working as a replacement for "a judgment conspicuously withheld," Ngai observes, it is connected to a feeling whose temporality is "anticipatory as well as recursive (what is anticipated is precisely a return)."[34] While it is feeling-based, the feeling of the interesting is difficult to name due to its indecisiveness: "This affective uncertainty is clearly the source of the association of the interesting with ambivalence, coolness, or neutrality – affects not only associated with irony but with the modern scientific attitude."[35] But information and its relays – the phenomena of the minor aesthetic of the interesting – are usually granted neither the status of the aesthetic nor recognition of their feelings, as uncertain as these may be.

Ngai identifies another tension that resides in the aesthetic of the interesting. The difference upon which the interesting depends has – since the nineteenth century and the emergence of shared media points such as "newspapers, advertising catalogs, encyclopedias, novels" and so on – stood in relationship to typicality and given rise to the interesting as "an aesthetic of *typical* difference"[36] from a general sort. While Benjamin's attachment to the storyteller's handprints on a tale incited him to direct at least a little bit of scorn and suspicion towards information, the genre of the novel, and the medium of print, Roland Barthes later wrote of the stinging pinprick that something not quite discernable in a photograph can make.[37] It's not just a matter of the prints that the teller leaves but the potentially (sometimes simultaneously) cherished or abject injury that a thing can enact. Amid and from the relentless circulation of things – images, texts, serially produced objects – our paraphernalia are the "pleasurable burden" we must carry around.[38] Steven Connor reminds us that paraphernalia refers to carriage or porterage. Our paraphernalia, he says, "are important to us, because our lives are lives of porterage, importing, exporting, transporting, reporting, disporting."[39] Unconvinced that being a subject is anything other than having the ability "to come up against the objectness, the objection of things to our dreams of infinite self-enlargement,"[40] Connor insists that "we and our things provide support to each other." Feelings or rather "all feeling involves and demands the intercession of things."[41]

SOFAS

I realize that, of all my furniture, only five items are ones that I selected myself. Of these selections, I regret only one: a sofa that so stubbornly fought against being taken past the turn in the stairs that it made two dents and a scratch on the walls, and I have determined that it can never come back down the stairs again. I am stuck with it or it is stuck, I am not sure which. Although I was drawn to the pale blue floor model, I chose charcoal, a more pragmatic fabric colour. But now, in its place, it seems dreary. I had wanted it to be as impervious to staining as possible. The feeling of its apparent dreariness is the cost of my implicit wish to leave no visible traces in rooms. The fact that I have not spilled anything on the sofa does not mean that the traces of presences are absent, though. This is also where I try to sleep when I am not feeling well or have too many unfinished thoughts on which to ruminate. Most sofas are designed in a way that is more favourable than beds to lulling an unsettled person into sleep. Beds may be soft but they are flat and endless, like a prairie with a seeming eternity of linens in a uniform colour that changes in the cyclical turning of laundry rather than seasons. Beds are prairie deserts lacking the embrace that a sofa is always prepared to give. Thus, Jean-Luc Nancy's handling of the forlorn image of Alcyone waving her arms in sleep to embrace only the air[42] resonates with my criticism, even though he used it in illustration of the mystery of sleep. My bed does not deserve mention in this essay only because it has this poor design that beds generally have; I only purchased mine to silence expressed social pressures from friends. This is a costly expenditure for otherwise unprescribed space. I have learned that the presence of this type of furniture is critical if you want to invoke an impression of normalcy. Thus, I have been more or less socially and sensorially disciplined back into this uncomfortable arrangement, and so, while the bed may be undeserving of mention, it matters.

Nancy's philosophical consideration of the fall into sleep emphasizes indistinction. It is not just that things become indistinct to the sleeper – and here linguistic and social syntaxes fail, as the noun, the sleeper, suggests that sleep is something we do rather than fall into. In sleep, one is indistinct from oneself and surroundings. Nancy writes: "Removed from the bustle of time, from the obsessions of the past and future, of arising and passing away, I coincide with the world, I am reduced to my own indistinctness, which, however, still experiences itself as an 'I' that goes along with its visions without, however, distinguishing itself from them."[43] The indistinctness and simultaneous co-presence that sleep ensures transforms the prairie desert of the bed's social architecture into a warm sea of dedifferentiation, "the abyss and the plunge, the density of deep water and the descent of the drowned body sinking backward."[44] The fall into sleep allows the senses to spill in ways that wakeful and linguistic distinctions prevent, while also wresting from vision the privilege over other senses that it enjoys during wakeful hours. Nancy writes, "In my own eyes, which no longer look at anything, which are turned toward themselves and toward the black spot inside them, 'I' no longer distinguish 'myself.' If I dream of actions and words of which I am the subject, it is always in such a way that this subjectivity does not distinguish itself or distinguishes itself poorly, *at the same time*, from what it sees, hears, and perceives in general."[45] In wakefulness we cannot see behind us and depend upon the perceptual coordination that prepositions describe and instruct; we are nevertheless emplaced with other things in mutual distributions. Awake, we swim in language, our things arranged and arranging in accordance with grammars that impose breakers upon the spill of indeterminacy invited by both water and skin differently socialized.

Beyond culturally specific social organization of the senses, things designated inanimate have the capacity to order the sensorium too. In Mel Y. Chen's discussion, dedifferentiated intimacies attributed to metal poisoning render the embrace given by a loved one and the embrace given by the household couch indistinguishable: "This episode, which occurs again and again, forces me to rethink animacy, since I have encountered an intimacy that does not differentiate, is not dependent on a heartbeat."[46] Whereas my appreciation for the comforts my sofa gives can stand apart from any attribution of social character to it, for Chen, the effects of metal poisoning render a kind of sociality that departs from inculcation so that the epistemological insistence that capacities be located in discrete units is undermined by a lively transcorporeal sentience at the interstices of the meeting of body and couch.[47] This provokes Chen into guilty self-interrogation about "lively" intimacies experienced with things assumed to be inanimate: "Have I performed the inexcusable: have I treated my girlfriend like my couch? Or have I treated my couch like her, which fares only slightly better in the moral equations?"[48]

But, this inexcusability or moral violation is entangled not only with the animacy hierarchy that Chen critically targets but also with, for instance, actor network theory's challenges to the "moral order of representation,"[49] as well as with the warnings given by critics of biopolitics. Roberto Esposito, for instance, examines the distinct and porous categories of persons and things inherited from ancient Roman law, Christianity, and modern philosophy. These have organized Western knowledge via a dialectic that tends towards the personalization of things and the depersonalization of persons.[50] A paradox resides at the intersection of this "great division," as he calls it, between persons and things, since "a legal order founded on the frontal opposition between persons and things produced a continuous slippage from one to the other, thrusting some humans into the sphere of inanimate objects."[51] Of crucial significance is Esposito's observation that this dialectic excludes the body, which is, from the point of view of Western knowledge, neither a thing nor a person.[52] The conceptual distinction between mind and body in modern philosophy is one of Esposito's illustrations of the body's exclusion. He notes that, even in Merleau-Ponty's phenomenological gestures to render the senses and body necessary to the potential for objects and their extension of the body, there is an emphasis on or return to the primacy of consciousness, as inner experience, over the body.[53] The exclusion of the body from this conceptual ordering of persons and things enables the exploitative use of bodies as objects.

Esposito argues that the body is crucial to reimagining our politics and, while he does not fully unpack this, he posits the technological prosthetic body as the one that will deconstruct the divides between subject and object, internal and external, thought and living body. While prosthetic bodies are becoming common, I'm not sure that the effects of this conceptual divide are eroding. To illustrate this potential, however, Esposito gives emphasis to the constellation of bodies, concrete common space, and the senses. He has less faith in the digital commons, for it does not establish these corporeal connections. I discern the senses as critical to Esposito's speculations at the end of his book *Persons and Things* primarily from his indirect invocation of the voice when he writes, "every linguistic act that seeks to have an impact on the political scene requires a mouth and a throat,"[54] which I take to be implicating not only sound but touch (to feel the breath of close bodies) and, if you will accept it as a sense, the perception of proximity and scale: "Even before being uttered their words are embodied in bodies that move in unison, with the same rhythm, in a single wave of emotion."[55] If the mingling of bodies, senses, feelings, spaces (in other words, their intertwinement in emplacement), and new political vocabularies may intervene into the processes of depersonalization that have organized our experiences, Esposito makes some brief gestures towards de-realized things, and these turn back to emplacement and to the atmospheric-bodily ties to which Chen is attuned. Esposito connects things to the body through a literary move from Jean-Luc Nancy's heart transplant to the heart of a stone, in which he observes "experience is concentrated, still palpable, visible, and recognizable."[56] So, while Gaston Bachelard wrote that "things become crystallizations of sadness, regret or nostalgia,"[57] it might be inadequate to assume that their affective formations are static and impervious to the relations of which they constitute an active part.

TABLES

Musing about the non-existent interdisciplinary field of "archiviology," Jacques Derrida imagines its potential immobilization presented at two levels by psychoanalysis. First, it would be immobilized because psychoanalysis is already intertwined with the archive as the science "of everything that can happen to the economy of memory and to its substrates, traces, documents, in their supposedly psychical or techno-prosthetic forms"[58] as its subject. Second, he anticipates archiviology's fall under psychoanalytic authority and unremitting self-interrogation. The intractable problem for Freud was to give an account of memories whose inscription could not be placed in an originating situation, and this is intrinsically tied to Derrida's second expectation,[59] but it is also implicated in emplacement and the sensoriality inherent to it. In this piece, I have only begun to linger on this aspect of emplacement in the ordinary scene of the home and its furniture (a kind of archive). Reluctant to assign to memories singular originating events or to give them over to the brain or biology proper, Freud instead emphasizes the processes of condensation, displacement, and parapraxis as the effects of contradictory intentions that leave their indistinct prints entangled with the living presences of objects, surroundings, movements, and speech.

Foucault, drawing upon Nietzsche's use of three different words to denote origin, is instructive here but particularly for his elaboration of Herkunft as a domain that entails the body's manifestation of "the stigmata of past experience."[60] Herkunft tracks the descent of *common* experience written on bodies: "It inscribes itself in the nervous system, in temperament, in the digestive apparatus; it appears in faulty respiration, in improper diets, in the debilitated and prostrate body of those whose ancestors committed errors."[61] This is the matter of practices and histories, not of crude genetics. Thus, the claim in "Nietzsche, Geneal-ogy, History" that history destroys the body turns inside out the assumption that origins arrive before bodies. What we have been ordered to know –"the origin always precedes the Fall"[62] – is reversed, and the meaning of the word *origin* is more textured.

Michel Serres makes a similar critical inversion of de Condillac's statue as the device in *Treatise on the Sensations* that enables the strict demarcation of senses experienced singularly and for the first time to form the statue's ideas.[63] Lin-gering on the various bottles of wine that have sat on influential dining tables that organized Western culture – from the Last Supper to the *Symposium* to Don Juan – Serres imagines the conversations and sensations of fictional statues seated around these tables. We should not be weighed down by the claims of this other statue that would propose to stand, indeed to be endowed with some-thing we might call spirit, in advance of sensorial emplacements. In any case, its discrete senses can do nothing with the bottle of Sauternes that Serres finds "mimics the world." What it gives is "coloured, luminous, radiant, tactile" – I am abbreviating this passage with editorial coldness, even arbitrariness, because it is nearly endless with description – "Body and world: agrarian, *floréal, prairial, vendémiaire*, wooded." It gives Time and Space, terms he elaborates so that they can evade their usual abstraction, before noting: "Gifts or the given invade the sensorium, leaving tongues behind, travel down arteries and muscles, nerves and bones all the way to the fingernails. The bottle contains the entirety of the sensible, all at once; contains bottomless common sense. Left on the table for a week, open and empty, the course of the emanations never runs dry."[64] Before saying any more about that empty but nevertheless full bottle on the table that held the wine, it makes sense to return to Foucault's discussion of origin as Nietz-sche gives it. The other word of significance here is *Entstehung* as episodes, rather than culminations or completions, of emergence as the "eruption" or "entry of forces,"[65] contrary to and in struggle with each other. If Entstehung is the erup-tion of adversarial forces, then *Entstehungsherd* in the *Genealogy of Morals* is the scene in which this drama of "rituals, in meticulous procedures that impose rights and obligations," plays out continuously. But, as Foucault insists, this place of the scene is really a "non-place," according to Nietzsche. There is no word for this negative: it is given in the text as a "void through which" adversaries "exchange their threatening gestures and speeches," a field without borders, an "interstice," "a pure distance" of uncommon space[66] where these rituals tie with rules.

SUITCASES

I spent the evening clearing up some of the papers accumulated in my bedroom. For about six weeks from mid-July, I spent much time setting my worldly affairs in order; i.e. turning out every drawer and cupboard to see there was nothing there that would inconvenience me by being blown into the street by a bomb. I have destroyed bundles of old letters. On the bedroom table there has grown a bigger and bigger pile of paper that I did not want to lose which were altogether unclassified. When the Russo-German Pact was signed I stopped this job so as to get on with sewing the new lingerie for I want plenty of clothes on hand in case there are laundry difficulties.[67]

Sometimes, precious things need to be abandoned in order to be protected. On 16 September 1939, two weeks after Chamberlain's declaration of war, Mass Observation diarist 5390 commits her cherished old letters to her own method of destruction. While this diarist was destroying her private papers and cultivating a network of objects – new lingerie and butter substitutes – as a homefront defence in a seemingly detached anticipation of air war in Britain, I imagine that another woman may have been carefully packing her treasured letters and documents as she prepared to go abroad to join her new husband in a home recently built according to his specifications. Departing for Canada just before the war, she carried some of her possessions in a tan leather suitcase with a red satin-lined interior, secured with brass clasps. As was common then, the suitcase is monogrammed with the woman's initials: K.C. This suitcase is not a direct inheritance or hand-me-down from her. We are not related, and I never met her, but I know that her name was Katherine and that she passed away in the 1980s. I may have stolen this suitcase. I used to live in the house that was built for her arrival in Western Canada. By that time, at least three or four other inhabitants had come and gone after her departure. When I lived there, a stranger frequently appeared at the front door. The first time, she explained that her father was a close friend of the C. family and that he had many of their belongings in his possession. Whenever she arrived, always unanticipated, she would tell a story about the family or about the house. She usually brought along an object that she would leave behind, insisting that "it belongs in the house." The woman – I do not recall her name – initiated these visits as her father was dying, and again after his death. He had been the keeper of these objects, but now she was obligated to them and with her visits and stories she returned them one by one to the house, naming it as their rightful keeper. Among these were Katherine's suitcase and Clifford's bible, which he must have received in young adulthood. I imagine that it was a gift, as with the bible that Freud received as birthday gift from his own father. Derrida makes a point of quoting the inscription in Freud's copy at length, but I'll abbreviate it here to the phrase "I have presented it to you as *a memorial and a reminder*." For Derrida, this contains "the whole of archival law."[68] The interior cover page of this bible bears the rehearsal of Clifford's signature in repetition but with slight variations in script as though in ink he posed a series of questions about the future rather than making an announcement. These things, the woman said, belong in the house. Or did she say *to* the house? For some reason, that phrase resounded for me.

Once, upon returning to the house after I myself had moved out, I took the suitcase. I do not know why but sometimes it is possible to have the bad feeling that a thing has been left in the hands of an indifferent host. When I moved to where I live now – and I didn't know for certain then that I wasn't coming back – it was my books that I was desperate to move and, for reasons I cannot explain, I took this suitcase. After some time, I am left wishing that I had taken the magnets from the refrigerator door. Both mobile, because they could fit in a pocket, and anchoring, since they fixed those photographs and small mementoes that I couldn't take because they weren't just mine. The magnets would be the metonymic short hand for everything I left behind. Instead, I have this suitcase of someone else's memories. No longer viable as a carrier for travel clothes and necessities, it sits immobile in substitution for a nightstand since it is too beautiful for storage. Set upon it is a tea-light candle that has never been lit. I keep special clothes in it that I plan to alter in some way. The left clasp sticks a bit but opens if you try to correct its alignment just slightly. You have to be careful, though, because when it finally springs open, it will snap against your finger with so much force that it hurts quite a lot. Even though I don't open it very often, I have learned to pull my hand back as quickly as possible. More accurately, my hand remembers to move even if I haven't consciously thought of it. Perhaps Luis Buñuel's attempts to illustrate affect as "a quality of the inanimate,"[69] whose complexity has not been adequately explored, seem purely coincidental. Take, for instance: "I know of a pipe that was picked up from a friend's table by a hard-hearted man, who abducted it without compassion. Well then, when the vile abductor went to light it, it singed his nose. That infuriated pipe spew burning ash from its only eye."[70] But then perhaps this is why the suitcase's clasp aims to injure my fingers.

CREDENZAS

A provisional inventory of troublesome impositions would include a credenza towards which I feel ambivalent. It is one of many furnishings that were given to me by relatives willing neither to keep nor to part with them. It is now my responsibility to care for it. While the top of it retains a nearly perfect finish and thankfully seems impervious to injury from bottles and glasses that are placed on it, the front is severely sun-faded and dons the white streaks that are characteristic of the kind of sunburn that threatens furniture. I appreciate its capacity to hold a number of cherished things, from glassware to large sheets of fabric that can go in with only one or two folds. The second drawer's interior compartments are designed for silver cutlery and are lined with green synthetic velvet. I use these partitions for utensils but I also keep special things in those spaces according to an indeterminable logic that governs this collection. Due to the collection that it keeps so well, I have some affection for this credenza that is otherwise in the way of other things. Much like how Bachelard has described the depth of imagination and memory that can be stored in wardrobes ("Every poet of furniture – even if he be a poet in a garret, and therefore has no furniture – knows that the inner space of an old wardrobe is deep"),[71] this credenza manages a gridless cartography that defies and stretches its physical proportions. An absent fragrant object, perhaps a candle, has left its scent behind like a second body that touches and fills the glasses so that, like Serres's empty bottle of Sauternes that never runs dry, the fragrance resides within each of them so that they need to be washed of their invisible contents before every use.

Perhaps the strangest imposition made by a troublesome thing is the most recent addition to my collection. It arrived several months ago by federal post. In an ordinary envelope, a small collection of ashes – human remains – is carefully packaged. The package arrived without warning, but I am asked – in case of fire or another form of loss that could threaten the ashes of this loved one's departed loved one – could I take this small sub-collection of ashes for safe-keeping? I don't know how I feel about this new inhabitance twice partitioned, first by cremation and then by portioning. I have placed the envelope in the credenza in the only compartment in which I keep paper.

OBJECTIONS

What might appear to be private and purely individual is always constructed by way of cultural formations that furnish social experience and that continue to arrive, intrude, and bend. Highmore notes that a piece of furniture can share with someone anecdotes and memories particular to the place that they mutually inhabit, but its "embodied sociality" extends beyond these particularities.[72] The task is to recognize the social handprints or feelings of structure in what otherwise appears to be individual and specific.

After his mother's death, Marcel Proust cocooned himself amidst his family's supposedly hideous furnishings capable of filling such a large catalogue that his biographer, George Painter, compared it to "the *Iliad* of ships,"[73] and Diana Fuss described his apartment as "a family monument."[74] Consistent with the line "in this cult of grief for our own dead, we pay an idolatrous worship to the things they loved,"[75] Proust had his mother's piano and his father's chair moved into his "precisely arranged, heavily insulated, and carefully managed"[76] bedroom. Oscar Wilde's unfiltered evaluation of the furnishings as "ugly" upon his arrival for a visit to Proust's apartment, which was apparently punctuated by his immediate exit, is often recounted to illustrate the suffocating ambience of the apartment's interior weighted down by Proust's attachment to things.[77] Proust provides insight into the raw feelings he had for (and in fact sought in) the objects he kept. For instance, he once declared in a personal letter that "any picture that one hasn't coveted, bought with pain and love, is horrid in a private house."[78] Could the compulsion to weave about oneself objects so heavy with obligation and attachment inform Bachelard's insistence that above all we prize the experience of immobility, that which is promised and amplified in the "negativism" of a corner, that "sure place, the place next to my immobility"?[79] Immobility can take many forms. After all, Barthes once insisted that Jules Verne was not, as it would appear, a travel writer but "a writer of claustration."[80]

Avery Gordon's methodological intervention into the "reified asocial abstractions"[81] of concepts, the tendency to arrest shifting and living processes into completed wholes, and the treatment of "the social as if it were a hard-edged immobile past" separated from that which is supposedly subjective, personal, and private[82] aptly invokes the image of the seemingly "inert furniture" of ordinary experience to advocate constant movements "between that sad and sunken couch that sags in just that place where an unrememberable past and an unimaginable future force us to sit day after day and the conceptual abstractions because everything of significance happens there among the inert furniture and the monumental social architecture."[83] Painful and pleasurable obligations to troublesome things cannot be fully articulated in vocabularies that render these things idiosyncratic and personal. It is for this reason, as much as for the material weight and dimensions of furnishings, that they are also somewhat inert. Such obligations are intertwined with relations that are social, sensorial, and shared: "the synaesthesia of being at home," as Kathleen Stewart remarks, "is always already afloat in the circuits of the prevailing public winds – privatization, sensible accumulation, family values, or some kind of identity or lifestyle or something."[84]

BTW, can you let me know when it is finally okay to let these things go?

ACKNOWLEDGMENTS

The author wishes to express gratitude to Jake Vinje and to the Trustees of the Mass Observation Archive, University of Sussex.

NOTES

1 This word is used figuratively in anticipation of this chapter's emphasis on the tie between the trappings one "wears" and a way of living.
2 Plotz, "Can the Sofa Speak?," 118.

3 Gregson, Metcalfe, and Crewe, "Identity, Mobility, and the Throwaway Society," 685.
4 Keyte, "Objects in Purgatory," 328.
5 Ibid.
6 Ibid., 329.
7 Esposito, *Persons and Things*, 125.
8 Ibid., 126.
9 Classen, "Museum Manners," 896.
10 Pringle, "Scampering Sofas and 'Skuttling' Tables," 226.
11 For a brief discussion of Zizi, see ibid., 222–3.
12 Williams, *Marxism and Literature*, 128.
13 Ibid., 132.
14 Simpson, "Raymond Williams," 21.
15 Highmore, "Formations of Feelings," 147.
16 Ibid., 145.
17 Berlant, "Structures of Unfeeling," 194.
18 Connor, "Michel Serres' Five Senses," 320.
19 Feld, "Places Sensed, Senses Placed," 185.
20 Taussig, "Tactility and Distraction," 267.
21 Highmore, "Formations of Feelings," 145.
22 Benjamin, *Illuminations*, 108.
23 Ibid., 89.
24 Ibid., 98.
25 Ibid., 83–4, 89, 91–2.
26 Wilkinson, "All Things Thrown and Wonderful," 587.
27 Wiles, *Care of Wooden Floors*, 267.
28 Ibid., 211.
29 Ibid., 210.
30 Ibid., 209.
31 Ngai, *Our Aesthetic Categories*, 5.
32 Ibid., 158.
33 Ibid., 134.
34 Ibid.
35 Ibid., 135.
36 Ibid., 141.
37 Barthes, *Camera Lucida*.
38 Connor, "Taking Pity on Things," 4.
39 Ibid.
40 Ibid., 2.
41 Ibid., 3.
42 Nancy, *The Fall of Sleep*, 8.
43 Ibid., 7.
44 Ibid., 5.
45 Ibid., 7–8.

46 Chen, *Animacies*, 203.
47 Ibid., 204.
48 Ibid., 202.
49 Woolgar, "Configuring the User," 65–6.
50 Esposito, *Persons and Things*, 6.
51 Ibid., 26.
52 The tracing of this exclusion falls outside of the scope of this essay. See Esposito for his detailed explication.
53 Ibid., 123.
54 Ibid., 146.
55 Ibid.
56 Ibid., 124.
57 Bachelard, *Poetics of Space*, 143.
58 Derrida, *Archive Fever*, 34.
59 Ibid., 34–5.
60 Foucault, "Nietzsche, Genealogy, History," 148.
61 Ibid., 147.
62 Ibid., 143.
63 Connor, "Introduction," 4.
64 Serres, *The Five Senses*, 182.
65 Ibid., 149.
66 Ibid., 150.
67 D 5390, Diary for 16 September 1939, Mass Observation Archive, The Keep, Brighton, UK.
68 Derrida, *Archive Fever*, 23.
69 Buñuel, *An Unspeakable Betrayal*, 13.
70 Ibid., 12.
71 Bachelard, *Poetics of Space,* 78.
72 Highmore, *Ordinary Lives*, 66.
73 Painter, *Marcel Proust*, 63.
74 Fuss, *Sense of an Interior*, 162.
75 Proust quoted in ibid., 164.
76 Ibid., 153.
77 Ibid. and Mavor, *Reading Boyishly*.
78 Mavor, *Reading Boyishly*, 303.
79 Bachelard, *Poetics of Space*, 137.
80 Barthes, *Roland Barthes by Roland Barthes*, 83.
81 Gordon, *Ghostly Matters*, 199.
82 Ibid.
83 Ibid., 4.
84 Stewart, *Ordinary Affects*, 52.

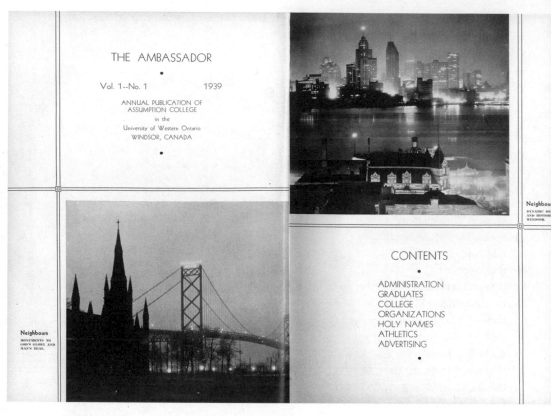

THE AMBASSADOR

•

Vol. 1--No. 1   1939

ANNUAL PUBLICATION OF
ASSUMPTION COLLEGE
in the
University of Western Ontario
WINDSOR, CANADA

•

Neighbours
DYNAMIC DETRO
AND HISTORIC
WINDSOR.

CONTENTS

•

ADMINISTRATION
GRADUATES
COLLEGE
ORGANIZATIONS
HOLY NAMES
ATHLETICS
ADVERTISING

•

Neighbours
MONUMENTS TO
GOD'S GLORY AND
MAN'S ZEAL.

Figure 2.1   These images of Detroit at night appeared in the first issue of *The Ambassador*, the Assumption College High School yearbook, in 1939.

CHAPTER 2

Imagining
Nighttime Detroit

MICHAEL DARROCH

INTRODUCTION

A city's nighttime is part of its signature, tied to our capacity to imagine the scale of activity or stasis that it fosters. As Detroit has emerged from bankruptcy proceedings since 2013, competing images of urban illumination and darkness have been resurrected in debates about the city's possible futures. Nostalgia for its history as a city of technical innovation – one of the first North American cities to be illuminated by electric light – has been set into relief by representations of shifting daytime and nighttime activities and city spaces plunged into darkness as its finances and infrastructure collapsed. These shifting atmospheres of illumination have evoked a range of emotional and sensual reflections on the ways in which Detroit's night is imagined and experienced.

I first experienced Detroit at dusk, from a different country. I had arrived by train at the terminal station of Windsor, Ontario, which struck me as a kind of outpost or lookout, a small Canadian border city perched on the southeast bank of the Detroit River opposite the dominantly lit skyline of downtown Detroit. Its peculiar location on the edge of the southwest Ontarian peninsula tucked into the middle of the Great Lakes – a point that is both terminal within Ontario and central within the American Midwest – left me with a feeling of simultaneous connection and dislocation. Invited for a job interview at the University of Windsor the next day, I sat in my "full riverfront view" hotel room, peering out over the panorama of Detroit's nighttime skyline. This first encounter with nighttime Detroit deeply engraved itself into my subsequent appreciation of both cities.

The experience of urban nighttime has come under increasing scrutiny in cultural and historical analysis.[1] I am concerned in this essay with the ways in which perceptions and understandings of nighttime in Windsor and Detroit are wrapped up with the cities' divisions, with the borderline condition of this urban region, brought to light (as it were) most recently by the renewed debate in Detroit regarding urban illumination. To consider this, I must in part rely on my own experiences of these cities, as a resident of Windsor for nearly a decade and a frequent visitor to Detroit. (As a Caucasian dual Canadian-US citizen, I have had the opportunity to cross this border.) The borderline condition of Windsor-Detroit encompasses a series of cultural disjunctions that only become apparent when one has been immersed in these environments and their histories.

From the vantage point of Windsor, Detroit's downtown feels as if you could reach out and touch it, yet it remains perpetually removed from Windsor's urban imagination. My goal in this paper is to explore how this urban structure, Detroit's presence beside and in Windsor, feels in the everyday lives of citizens in Windsor. (As one of the editors of this volume once expressed, Detroit will always be Windsor's Lacanian *objet petit a*.) Drawing upon historical visual documents and contemporary media texts, I consider how Detroit's nighttime feels in, and with, Windsor – a nighttime ripe with the tension between sociable activities (such as its renowned music scenes) and its depiction as a crime-ridden murder capital. One part of my argument is that the fullness of Detroit's self-concept as a nighttime city is deeply involved with how Detroit is seen from Windsor, even if today Detroiters largely ignore the city's status as a border city. Countless glossy coffee-table compendiums of Detroit images, "ruin porn," and popular cultural histories of the city have been published in recent years, in which Windsor is hardly mentioned as a footnote. Yet Detroit's visual self-understanding has always relied upon the possibility of being seen from the outside, from across the river.

We may all be able to imagine nighttime in a city such as Detroit, but our capacity to imagine Detroit is heightened on location in Windsor where we both see and imagine the city simultaneously (I can see part of Detroit's skyline from my kitchen window through the leafy backyards of Windsor's Walkerville district). In so many ways, Windsor is organized around the magnetism of the border. Citizens from both cities have long crossed the river border in search of consumption, entertainment, vice, and fantasy – or to seek asylum from political struggles, originally by ferry, but later via the Ambassador Bridge and the Windsor-Detroit

Tunnel (built in 1929 and 1930 respectively). Windsor's economy tends to thrive or suffer depending on the free circulation of cross-border traffic, shifting patterns of industrial prosperity, shifting currency relations, and passport regulations. On Windsor's current skyline, one of the few notable features is the urban screen on Caesar's Casino, facing Detroit. Citizens of both cities converge on their respective riverfronts for recreational activities, summer music festivals, carnivals, and other fairs. But the view is nonetheless asymmetrical: Detroit's entrancing skyline beckons to Windsor to participate in an imaginary urban sphere, in a big-city good life that, within Windsor, is only available in limited forms. Yet the skyline itself simultaneously masks Detroit's internal divisions, its histories of segregation and racism, deeply tied to the impoverished and distressed state of vast areas and neighbourhoods in contrast with its resurging downtown and midtown districts. These tensions are equally tied up with the shift from day to night in Detroit, an atmosphere that is palpable to the population across the river.

With thickening border regulations since 9/11 and Detroit's recent emergence from bankruptcy, downtown activities and nightlife in each city have taken a turn away from vice and towards planned cultural entertainment. If nocturnal illumination captures our desire for nighttime economies of consumption, entertainment, fantasy, or transgression, then Windsorites have continually been taunted into wondering what kinds of cultural scenes are welcoming and accessible, or obscured and hostile, on the other side. Since the early 2000s, Detroit has capitalized on its identification with techno and electronica music scenes by staging a range of music festivals in the riverfront Hart Plaza, including Movement, an annual electronic music festival on Memorial Day weekend that now draws over 100,000 visitors. Just as downtown Windsor experiences the glow of downtown Detroit's electric illumination, Windsor neighbourhoods near the riverfront are immersed in the sounds of electronic music and accompanying crowds. In 2001, during the second year of the original Detroit Electronic Music Festival, a Windsor city councillor lodged a complaint regarding cross-border noise. The *Windsor Star*'s editorial "Decibels and Curfews" (30 May 2001) lamented Windsor's attitude toward festival cultures and riverfront events in general, arguing that a bit of noise from Detroit only serves to demonstrate the added value in downtown festivals that draw tourists and families. Detroit's recently established nuit blanche festival DLECTRICITY, alongside the Movement Festival, is suggestive of both the city's history of innovation and the desire to provide safe sociability through illumination and sound. Mega-events such as these absorb the expressive energies of clandestine parties and raves in Detroit's abandoned spaces, recirculating a feeling of transgressive behaviour to populations for whom these activities may be otherwise inaccessible. For Windsorites who experienced the rise of Detroit rave culture, the sensation of vibrations emanating from Movement is powerfully evocative. The thicker border has also allowed Windsor to challenge its own dominant place-image as a nighttime playground for escaping Detroiters – a hub for underage Americans to frequent bars, nightclubs, and strip clubs – and reimagine itself instead as a safe downtown cultural and university campus district.

ILLUMINATION

The capacity to observe one city from another in an environment such as Windsor-Detroit invites us to reconsider the relationship between illumination, darkness, and visualization in North American cities. Vision has long dominated collective representations of urban nighttime – our capacity to see through the darkness.[2] We experience and remember nighttime in the city predominantly through imagistic and cinematic aesthetic forms. Artificial street lighting has extended the day and provided a sense of safety, yet one now accompanied by the possibility of increased observation. Cities worldwide have increasingly sought to transform nighttime into planned cultural environments and economies, encouraging activities of night and day to interpenetrate in the twenty-four-hour city.[3] Yet even in cities where nighttime is saturated with amenities, the night also evokes an aura of violence, danger, or unruliness.[4] Tensions between our sense of the nocturnal city as a space-time that is sometimes hospitable and comforting and our sense that it is sometimes hostile or distressing pervade representations of Detroit and are magnified from the vantage point of Windsor. Detroit stands for both a celebration of urban illumination and a history of obscurity and negligence – a desire to look away.

It is remarkable that in Detroit, among the first cities to experiment with tower street lighting,[5] as much as 40 per cent of the city's streetlights were defunct in 2013. A city that celebrated the dawn of urban electrification in the late nineteenth and early twentieth centuries – street lights and electric trolleys – was in 2017 celebrating a massive LED overhaul of its municipal lighting system and the launch of a new downtown tram route. In his 1888 review, *Municipal Lighting*, Fred H. Whipple noted that "Detroit is the only large city in the world lighted wholly by the tower system. The city limits comprise about 21 square miles, the whole of which is thus lighted. There are 122 towers of 153 feet each."[6] With a population of some 230,000, Detroit's one-square-mile business centre boasted twenty light towers about 1,000 feet apart, with towers in adjacent residential neighbourhoods and suburbs spreading out to 2,000 and 3,000 feet apart (see figures 2.2 and 2.3). Gesturing to its reputation as a Paris of the west, Whipple remarks that the "press of the country has uniformly conceded the city to be the best-lighted of any in the world. All its streets, yards, alleys, back-yards and grounds are illuminated as effectually as by the full moon at the zenith. The blending of light from the mass of towers serves to prevent dense shadows."[7]

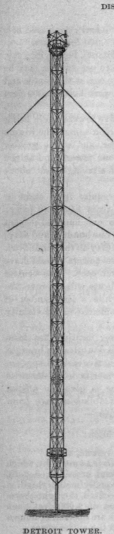

DETROIT TOWER.

wire cable, passing over a sheave wheel at top and bottom, and a heavy weight is connected into the cable, in proper position, to nearly counterpoise the elevator and its load. The towers have two sets of four one-half inch galvanized wire cable guys. One set leads from a point sixteen feet below the upper platform. The other from a point a few sections lower.

The towers are erected by first putting together the top section, then hoisting up and building on the next beneath it and so on until completed. The weight of a complete tower, elevator, etc., including guy ropes, is about 7,200 pounds. The entire wind surface, including lamps, hoods and mechanism, is calculated at eighty-three square feet, but this should probably be increased fifty per cent. for oblique and indirect exposure.

In the matter of the proper height, 150 feet is the most satisfactory. Increasing this height impairs the illumination near the foot and does not perceptibly increase the total lighted area, while diminishing this height diminishes the illuminated area and affords unnecessary brilliancy at the base.

The towers should, so far as practicable, be arranged in a triangular system. The distance apart in business sections may be 1,200 to 1,500 feet; in the best residence sections, such, for instance, as may be found at a distance of half to three quarters of a mile from the business centre, and a greater distance in the large cities, the towers

Figure 2.2 A Detroit light tower depicted in Fred H. Whipple's *Municipal Lighting* (1888), 161. Whipple was president of the Detroit-based electric compilers and publishers Fred H. Whipple Co. and secretary of a special committee convened by the Common Council to determine "the feasibility of the city owning and operating its own electric lighting plant" (Whipple, *Municipal Lighting*, 26).

Figure 2.3 A Detroit light tower can be seen on Detroit's Campus Martius.

In nearby Flint, Michigan, the city council argued that "in rendering our streets safe to all who traverse them at night; in largely preventing crime of every kind; in aiding us to attain that degree of peace and quiet which commends itself to every order-loving citizen, the benefits of this system of light can hardly be estimated."[8] Detroit's mayor, H.S. Pingree, stated in his message to the Common Council of 14 January 1890 that "lighting the streets is as much a public matter as street paving and cleaning, sewer building, maintaining and improving the

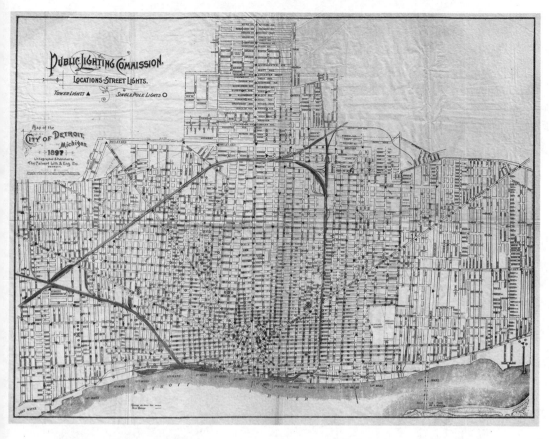

Figure 2.4 This 1897 map published by the Detroit Public Lighting Commission details the extent of public tower lights and single-pole lights in Detroit.

parks and boulevards, supplying water or providing protection against fire."[9] A map of Detroit's street lights in 1897 depicts the widespread distribution of light towers and poles (figure 2.4). Street lights were lit "every night from one half hour after sunset to one hour before sunrise, the time being somewhat extended on very cloudy or stormy evenings and on dark mornings."[10] Urban electrification brought not only greater visibility but also increased mobility within and between the cities. Electric trolleys were implemented in Detroit in 1892, as depicted in figure 2.5 in 1910. Across the river in Windsor electric streetcars had been introduced in 1886 (often claimed to be among the first in North America) to bring residents from Sandwich Town through downtown Windsor to the foot of Devonshire Road in what was then the separate town of Walkerville, where they could catch the Walkerville ferry to Detroit. By 1913, a plan was in place to connect Windsor's electrical system to the Detroit Edison Company. Cables

Figure 2.5 Electric railways and nighttime lighting are captured in this 1910 image of Detroit's Campus Martius square.

would cross the Detroit River from Detroit's Delray district to Sandwich Town, at the time a separate municipality adjacent to Windsor, and would be extended east to join Walkerville's Power & Light Company (although local councillors were concerned that "the lines will be a menace to life, as the power supplied by the Edison company is of much higher voltage than those of the local company").[11]

The visual culture of the border cities since the early 1900s has been asymmetric, a century-long infatuation with the ways in which Detroit appears to Windsor. During the years of Detroit River ferry traffic, the cities' hectic ports and ferry docks were vibrant spheres of economic and cultural interpenetration. Billboards and painted commercial signs on buildings communicated across the river as passengers trundled over on the fifteen-minute ferry ride. Nancy W. Barr, writing for the Detroit Institute of Arts' recent exhibition *Detroit after Dark*, notes that "electrification helped accentuate grand and dramatic views of the city at night," in reference to a photograph of the "impressive Detroit skyline at night as seen from Windsor."[12] Detroit's skyline is historically implanted in Windsor's visual identity (a University of Windsor student once offered me the comment that Windsor "owns" the Detroit skyline). Detroit tour guides almost universally display the skyline as an entry into understanding the city, suggesting the only way to gain perspective of Detroit as a whole is from Windsor.[13] This was also the scene when Kevin Orr, Detroit's emergency financial manager, appointed in 2013, held a press conference regarding the city's bankruptcy filing in front of a podium labelled "Reinventing Detroit" depicting a view of the Detroit skyline from Windsor.[14] Postcards from the first part of the twentieth century depict Detroit's nighttime luminosity as seen from downtown Windsor. Other images offer a snapshot of one city's lit-up downtown, with the other cross-border city in the shadows.

In each of figures 2.6 and 2.7, the beams of Detroit's Penobscot Building reach across the river to inundate neighbouring Windsor. Each of these images gestures to Detroit as an immersive atmosphere for Windsorites. There is a sense of enchantment in figure 2.6, where an interiority to Windsor's cozy streetscapes is accentuated by the grandiosity and phantasmagorical character of Detroit's electrification. In figure 2.7, Detroit is pictured in an oneiric state, the shapes of buildings illusory and undefined. Tim Edensor offers an apt description of such illuminated landscapes, arguing that "distances are difficult to fathom, illuminated buildings appear to float, areas of darkness are impregnable to sense-making, and scale and proportion may be illusory, factors which combine to produce the oneiric dimensions of illuminated, nocturnal space, particularly in the city."[15] In other images from the 1920s and 1930s depicting the "Heart of Detroit," represented from a position above Detroit's brightly lit Campus Martius square, part of Windsor's built environment is visible in the background as integrated cityspace. In figure 2.8, nighttime lighting seems to merge Detroit and Windsor, erasing the river/border – a rendering taken from a photograph of a *Graf Zeppelin* visit to Detroit in 1929 in which the dots of lights of Windsor in the distance are in fact less visible. In figure 2.9, Windsor is clearly a separate cityspace on other side of the river, shrouded in darkness, illuminated only by moonlight just as thunderclouds threaten to obscure the moon. These postcards capture again the atmospheric and at times oneiric quality of Windsor's relationship to Detroit, cities at once connected and separated, a tension that permeates the emotive tone of Windsor. In keeping with the long history of nighttime visualization, illumination and darkness have also been key features in imagining these cities' connection or separation. Ferry services eventually fully halted in 1942, more than a decade after the addition of both the Ambassador Bridge and

Figure 2.6 Detroit's Penobscot Building glows over Windsor in this postcard, ca. 1930.

Figure 2.7 The same view acknowledges Windsor as the viewpoint but omits the city.

The Heart of Detroit at Night.

·THE HEART OF DETROIT BY MOONLIGHT.

Figure 2.8 This postcard rendering is based on a 1929 photograph of the *Graf Zeppelin*'s visit to Detroit, in which the string of lights on the Windsor side are less dominant than in the postcard.

Figure 2.9 Windsor is visible as an unlit urban environment in the background.

View of Ambassador Bridge at Night, Sandwich, near Windsor, Canada.—26.

AMBASSADOR BRIDGE AT NIGHT. BETWEEN DETROIT. MICH. AND WINDSOR. ONT.

Figure 2.10 This postcard features a common iconic view of the Ambassador Bridge from the vantage point of Sandwich Town, in Windsor, circa 1930s, a desirable image for cross-border tourists and travellers.

Figure 2.11 The clear majority of postcard views of the Ambassador Bridge depict it from the vantage point of Sandwich Town or Windsor. Many, such as in this case, feature a low-flying airplane from which, one can imagine, the view of the Detroit skyline would be spectacular.

the Windsor-Detroit tunnel in the years 1929–30.[16] As befits the asymmetrical relationship between the cities, the majority of nighttime images of the bridge – an iconic feature relating the cities' ambivalent relationship and offering a brilliant view of Detroit's nighttime skyline – depict it from the perspective of Windsor, looking across to Detroit.

The bridge tower sign was installed at the outset of construction, but only in 1981 did the Detroit International Bridge Company agree with both cities to add a "necklace of lights" to the suspension cables.[17] The lighting of the bridge at dusk brings an intriguing distinctiveness to the bridge, while the electrification of downtown and the city's skyline become less distinct during the transformation from day to night. Writing in 1960 of the potential of complex lighting for urban environments, the designer György Kepes captured a mood that resembled Windsor's view of Detroit: "Few people would deny that it is a rewarding esthetic experience to perceive the first stages of transformation at dusk. In this first phase, the major forms and spaces of the cityscape are still clearly indicated, but a new system of space is superimposed on this form world through the change of the dark window holes into bright sparks of electric light. Streets once marked by the boundaries of buildings receive their new outlines in street lights."[18] While the bridge's brightly lit cables have been a staple of nighttime imagery since the 1980s, the tunnel has been less frequently depicted in the visual culture of the cities. It seems ironic that the bridge currently deposits a traveller either directly onto a freeway leaving Detroit's city centre or in dilapidated southwest city neighbourhoods, while the tunnel from Windsor propels the traveller into the city's glowing downtown.

DARKNESS

Tim Edensor has written compellingly about the ways in which nocturnal illumination and darkness shape affective atmospheres of experience. The term "atmosphere," he contends, exemplifies a blurring between "discrete emotional and affective geographies."[19] Windsor's borderlands are suffused with the atmospheric moods emanating from Detroit, whether through illumination and darkness, through weather systems that can be seen approaching from southeast Michigan, or through human activity – Windsor's shoreline is inundated with the rhythms and sounds of car traffic, the "People Mover" monorail that makes an occasional riverfront pass, and downtown festivals and events. These environmental conditions and cultural energies lend themselves to the mood of Windsor's urban space, at times shaping warm atmospheres of proximity, integration, and neighbourliness, and at other times cooling off to generate feelings of anxiety, disconnection, and even fear. The need to imagine nighttime Detroit thus penetrates deeply into Windsor's emotional state of mind, particularly in the imagination of its youth and artistic communities, which have long participated in Detroit's nocturnal music and art scenes. Marcel O'Gorman recounts his experience of growing up in Windsor: "When I was a kid, growing up in Windsor, my parents forbade me from going to Detroit. It was the dark continent, a place to be repressed. Watching Detroit (d)evolve from across the river was like watching a slow-motion Hurricane Katrina. The waves kept rolling in, but there were no rescue 'copters in sight – not even police choppers."[20] But kids did cross over, most famously techno artist Richie Hawtin, aka Plastikman, who penetrated the Detroit rave scene in the 1980s to become one of Detroit techno's best-known representatives. Nevertheless, for many Windsorites the physical distance across the Detroit River and the security and surveillance that now engulf border politics preclude a full investment in identifying with Detroit, generating a sense of angst and anxiety that may be on the rise with the changing dynamics of border control in 2018. At night, the border beckons to the possibility of transgressing social boundaries, a possibility that finds little cultural expression in Windsor's more conservative urban spheres, but equally forbids such participation.

Even more dominant themes in popular cultural media representations, and in everyday dialogue, are the overladen relationships between race, racialized spaces, and the affective atmospheres of darkness in North American cities.[21] Discussions of vice and crime all too often converge euphemistically with racial prejudice and the ways in which people gesture to the history of racialized space in a city such as Detroit.[22] Before Detroit's bankruptcy in 2013, the proportion of street lighting that required replacing evoked such broad narratives of Detroit's steady, decades-long decline. In 2014, the state of Michigan established a new City of Detroit Public Lighting Authority to embark on an ambitious course of replacing inoperative street lighting, some 40 per cent of the city's street lighting infrastructure. By the end of 2016, 65,000 new energy-efficient LED lights had been installed across the city, allowing Mayor Mike Duggan to brag that Detroit is now the largest US city to install all LED streetlights.[23] The need to provide nighttime lighting (so at odds with its early reputation as a "Paris of the West") invites us to consider the relationship of light technology to our experiences of and emotional responses to specific places and times and a pervasive impression that nighttime danger is generated by the incapacity to see. Detroit's encounter with a lack of illumination resurrected long-held understandings of our emotional response to such technologies in the city. In an interview, Public Lighting Authority chair Maureen Stapleton equates new LED technology with safety, suggesting that people may fear the loss of older light poles, but "we will light this city and people will begin to feel safe again."[24] As J.C. Reindl wrote for the *Detroit Free Press*, "across the city's 139 square miles, tens of thousands of other people are still living in the dark and with all the problems that brings – more crime and traffic accidents and a heightened sense of vulnerability that forces many to plan their lives around the setting sun for fear of getting mugged on their own streets."[25]

Nighttime in Detroit has thus also long been depicted as menacing, and crime-ridden troubled or distressed neighbourhoods become synonymous with the city, a site of endemic crime and arson. Frequent references to the pre-Halloween "Devil's Night" and the city's counterinitiative "Angels' Night," launched in the 1990s, are euphemistic for the city's long-troubled race relations. While Detroit's downtown is experiencing rapid post-bankruptcy gentrification, the portrayal of Detroit as danger city or murder capital circulates widely in media reports and is perpetuated through the circulation of "ruin porn" photography, urban explorer blogging, and amateur videos. (Googling "Detroit night" in December 2017 delivered countless videos with adjectives such as "shocking," "haunting," "eerie," and "terrifying," and titles including "Detroit's Deep Dark Hoods at Night," largely portraying a windscreen cam filming a car cruising through various Detroit thoroughfares and neighbourhood streets, peering at local citizens.)[26] For its part, Windsor has also garnered conflicting reputations, on one hand as a Canadian sin city, beginning with Prohibition-era smuggling and postwar illicit economies tied to a cross-border circulatory landscape of goods and people,[27] and on the other hand as a cleaner and safer urban environment than its border-city neighbour (recall Michael Moore's claim that Canadians do not lock their doors in *Bowling for Columbine*). Indeed, in 2012, the *Windsor Star* reported that "Windsor remains one of the least homicidal communities in the country" while "Detroit continues to earn its dubious title of the most dangerous city in the U.S."[28]

Detroit and Windsor thus each provide an opportunity to consider shifting attitudes towards morality, crime, and nighttime sociability and consumption, and associated attempts to revitalize downtown spaces and foster positive nighttime cultural activities. It is here, I think, that we may usefully draw upon Raymond Williams's notion of a structure of feeling. Windsor's location accentuates and reifies the ways in which Detroit is enmeshed in much larger discourses of US inner cities. In keeping with Williams's claim that "it is in art, primarily, that the effect of the totality, the dominant structure of feeling, is expressed and embodied,"[29] it is instructive to consider instances of creative expression that have engaged with Detroit's nighttime condition. As the Detroit Institute of Arts' 2016 exhibition *Detroit after Dark* made clear, the history of nighttime Detroit photography has accompanied mid-twentieth-century interest in the changing architecture, after-hours cultures, and crime of modern city life. Unlike night photography in other major cities that has remained aesthetically bound up with the experience of walking, however, nighttime Detroit images are often taken from difficult-to-reach vantage points, emphasizing the need to navigate nighttime Detroit by car and the failing state of public services. Scott Hocking's sweeping nocturnal landscapes of industrial sites and decaying buildings lay bare the

Figure 2.12 The Broken City Lab's *Cross-Border Communication* project, during the Great Recession of 2009.

discrepancy between geographies of corporate infrastructure and the increasing reliance in Detroit (before its LED revolution) on single and unpredictable sources of light from private spaces. This is a theme taken up by numerous photographers including Jon Deboer and Dave Jordano, as well as in a recent exhibition by architect and artist Catie Newell at the University of Michigan Museum of Art (2016). Newell's *Overnight* consists of both an installation and photographs from her ongoing series *Nightly* that emphasize the materiality of light and dark as they intersect with and activate the broader architectural environment. The project recalls Kepes's call to reconsider the emotional context of our use of illuminative technologies: "A focused source of light, such as a candle, a lamp, or a fireplace, generates a focused attention, almost a feeling of warmth or nesting. Our interests are so function-centered that such emotional use of light is rarely given thought."[30] Newell's *Nightly* series avoids clichéd ruined landscapes and focuses instead on the city's transformation from day to night and the feeling of nighttime urban spaces in which darkness outweighs illumination, largely in the neighbourhoods around East Grand Boulevard and the Grand Belt. *Overnight* consists of photographs from *Nightly* as an environment for the installation of aluminum and copper wiring, referencing the changing technologies of street lighting currently under way in the city.[31]

Broken City Lab & Life In a Border Town Presents:

Shaping our City: Brainstorm Session at Civic Space, January 3rd - 7 PM

411 Pelissier Street, Windsor, Ontario.

Figure 2.13 During its key period of activity from 2009 to 2015, the Broken City Lab hosted numerous brainstorming workshops to consider creative perspectives on the scale of dynamic change in the border cities.

If artists engaging with the nuances of nighttime Detroit have largely ignored its relationship to Windsor, artists and creative collectives in Windsor have embraced the border condition of this strange urban environment. The Broken City Lab, led by Justin Langlois and students at the University of Windsor and active in Windsor from 2009 to 2015, proposed a series of social practice urban interventions, workshops, and brainstorming sessions to provide spaces to record our emotional and collective responses to the urban condition in these cities. *Cross-Border Communication* (Figure 2.12) was produced in 2009, at the height of the Great Recession, drawing on what the group termed "the desperate need to communicate with Detroit, Michigan, from Windsor, Ontario."[32] *Cross-Border Communication* projected messages including "We're in this together" and "Windsor + Detroit = BFF?" onto buildings facing Detroit at the riverside intersection of Windsor's main street, Ouellette Avenue. The team worked with local high school students to design and implement the projection, calculating the size of the letters to make them visible from Detroit. By reframing the Windsor skyline as spectacle, the project worked as a commentary on the phantasmagorical character of Detroit's skyline and encapsulated a desire to reverse the asymmetrical relationship between the cities – a desire to remind Detroiters that Windsorites were equally implicated in the emotional anxiety of Great Recession political turbulence.

CONCLUSION

I have tried to suggest that Windsor is in a privileged position (as what I have elsewhere called an "intimate onlooker"[33]) to apprehend the affective atmospheres that emanate from Detroit. My goal has been to explore the long-term technological histories but also recent histories of the cities in order to apprehend ways in which Detroit creates and shifts moods that extend spatially and virtually to Windsor in specific forms and contexts. Detroit and Windsor, one of the first urban regions in North America to embrace electricity and technologies of illumination, have long been cities that pride themselves on technological innovation. This history evokes deeply rooted nostalgic reactions among local residents, highlighted by recent histories of Detroit's failing municipal lighting systems, the city's bankruptcy, and powerful commonplace associations between urban decline, darkness, race, and crime. Yet despite these associations and fears, the visual power of Detroit's skyline has always retained its phantasmagorical character, a sense of enchantment and wonder that forever beckons across the border. If Windsorites frequently broadcast their own urban anxieties against the backdrop of their larger US neighbour, then Detroit's nighttime skyline equally works as an illuminated screen that broadcasts and reflects the exhilaration of urban nightlife – vividly imaginable but perhaps always just beyond view or reach.[34] Deeply embedded in the structure of this peculiar cross-border urban environment, illumination and darkness shape the atmospheres through which Windsorites perceive, imagine, and participate in nighttime Detroit.

ACKNOWLEDGMENTS

Initial research for this essay was supported by a Social Sciences and Research Council of Canada Insight Development Grant, "The Urban Night as Interdisciplinary Object" (2012–15), on which I was co-applicant. I wish to thank the project's director, Will Straw, for his comments on the essay. I would also like to acknowledge the University of Windsor, particularly the Faculty of Arts, Humanities, and Social Sciences, for continuing to support the IN/TERMINUS Creative Research Collective.

NOTES

1 See for example Blum, "Nighttime," in *The Imaginative Structure of the City*, 141–63; Edensor, "The Gloomy City"; Straw, "The Urban Night."
2 Zardini, "Toward a Sensorial Urbanism," 19–20.
3 Straw, "Urban Night," 188–97.

4 Schivelbusch, *Disenchanted Night*, 80–143; Blum, "Nighttime," 141.

5 Nye, "Transformation of American Urban Space," 32–4.

6 Whipple, *Municipal Lighting*, 157; Schivelbusch, *Disenchanted Night*, 124–7.

7 Whipple, *Municipal Lighting*, 157.

8 Ibid., 163.

9 Public Lighting Commission of Detroit, *First Annual Report*, 10.

10 Ibid., 35.

11 "Walkerville Councillors Served with Injunction," *Windsor Evening Record*, 9 December 1913, 1.

12 Barr, "Detroit after Dark," 8–9.

13 Rodney, "Art and the Post-Urban Condition," 268.

14 Darroch, "Border Scenes," 312.

15 Edensor, "Illuminated Atmospheres," 1107.

16 Al Roach, "Walkerville's Last Passenger Ferry," *Walkerville Times*, 1988, http://www.walkervilletimes.com/lastferry.htm.

17 Mason, *The Ambassador Bridge*, 214–15.

18 Kepes, "Notes," 159.

19 Edensor, "Illuminated Atmosphere," 1105.

20 O'Gorman, "Detroit Digital."

21 See Talbot, *Regulating the Night*.

22 See Bunge, *Fitzgerald*; Sugrue, *Origins of the Urban Crisis*.

23 J.C. Reindl, "Detroit Streetlights Go from Tragedy to Bragging Point," *Detroit Free Press*, 15 December 2016, http://www.freep.com/story/news/local/michigan/2016/12/15/detroit-streetlights-go-tragedy-bragging-point/95483846/.

24 J.C. Reindl, "Why Detroit's Lights Went Out," *Detroit Free Press*, 17 November 2013, http://www.usatoday.com/story/news/nation/2013/11/17/detroit-finances-dark-streetlights/3622205/.

25 Ibid.

26 See "Detroit's Deep Dark Hoods at Night," 21 April 2016, accessed 8 December 2017, https://www.youtube.com/watch?v=66DO3794Kw8.

27 See Karibo, "Ambassadors of Pleasure."

28 Dalson Chen, "A Tale of Two Cities: Windsor and Detroit Murder Rates Show Stark Contrast," *The Windsor Star*, 4 December 2012, http://windsorstar.com/news/local-news/a-tale-of-two-cities-windsor-and-detroit-murder-rates-show-stark-contrast.

29 Williams and Orrom, *Preface to Film*, 21.

30 Kepes, "Notes," 160.

31 Dave Lawrence, "U-M Photography Exhibition Explores a Dark Detroit," *Arts & Culture* (Ann Arbor: University of Michigan), 25 May 2016, http://arts.umich.edu/news-features/u-m-photography-exhibition-explores-a-dark-detroit/.

32 Broken City Lab, "Cross-Border Communication," accessed 8 December 2017, http://www.brokencitylab.org/tags/cross-border-communication/.

33 Darroch, "Border Scenes."

34 Darroch and Nelson, "Windsoria."

CHAPTER 3

Industrialism and the Time of Catastrophe: A Lesson in the Anthropocene

CRAIG CAMPBELL

Here is one lesson I've learned in the Anthropocene: time is profoundly weird. The lesson emerged in research undertaken for a new collaborative project titled The Shadow of a Dam: River Life and Industrial Economies in the Siberian North.[1] This project explores the anticipatory feelings attending the indefinitely deferred construction of a subarctic hydroelectric dam. Since the 1980s, thousands of villagers – mostly indigenous Evenkis – have lived with the threat of displacement from the construction of a hydroelectric project. The dam's reservoir would swell up far past the natural banks of the river to drown their villages. Twice proposed and twice suspended, the idea of the dam – its anticipatory spectre – has produced a coercive temporal orientation where the near future is permanently bracketed off as not only unknowable but potentially catastrophic. Or at least that is our thinking.

The Shadow of a Dam is interested in the collective nesting affects of peoples' prolonged exposure to a suspended future event. It is a study of *anticipation*, which might be a gloss for waiting or expecting and which seems to be a composition of affective labours. In anticipation's composition (waiting, working, putting off, getting ready, forgetting about it) the spectrality of the future is framed as a strange rhetorical construction. It is also component to a larger problematic I call "weird anthropology," the crux of which is built upon a set of claims around divination and anticipation set against temporal compositions and rhetorical tactics that have characterized the discipline. Divination and anticipation are two future orientations with different structures of causality. They point to, but are not exhausted by, a fatalist sentiment and a coordination of terms like fate (in Russian, *sud'ba*) and inevitability (*neizbezhnyi*). The weird chronologies are furthermore reflected and amplified in the figure of the shadow, a phenomenon that complicates conventional temporal arrangements or distributions.

The Shadow of a Dam attempts to describe the enduring feelings of a structure indefinitely deferred within industrialism's political ecologies. Where there is no dissipation of the dominance of one narrative for the future over another, there is a sedimentation of feeling around the experience of not knowing. It is not the emergency of a catastrophic future but a stickiness of expectation, a weird foreclosure on the possible. While Raymond Williams was adamant that a structure of feeling was as "firm and definite as 'structure' suggests,"[2] he also noted its delicacy. If we imagine industrialism not simply as a specific set of technical and material relations but also as a structure of feeling, we might begin to appreciate his sense. It is this latter point that is explored in this chapter that tracks roughly one hundred years, from the 1917 Communist Revolution to the designation of the Anthropocene, which has gripped our attention and rearranged so much thinking in the past decade.[3]

The question is deceptively simple: what does the future feel like for those living in villages located along Siberia's Lower Tunguska river? What does it feel like to live in the shadow of a dam? That question, however, can only be answered through future research. This chapter is an effort to work through the contours of the idea, to fine-tune a description of industrialism and catastrophe that will allow us to undertake the proposed investigation.

In the early 2000s I published research showing that indigenous Siberian peoples[4] living in remote villages and settlements experienced decreasing access to the infrastructures of industrial modernity and thus were suffering from a variety of problems associated with geographical isolation.[5] At the time, I saw this as a peculiar form of rural ghettoization. The patched and reworked matter of Soviet-era settlements and the ruins of their requisite infrastructures constituted vivid material reminders of a built environment that had failed to adapt to the conditions of nascent Russian capitalism. These settlements were poorly suited to the needs of remotely located rural peoples in the first decades of the post-Soviet era – an era defined rather abruptly in the last days of 1991 by the dissolution of the Soviet Union. Calling it rural ghettoization wasn't really accurate; the settlements' structural effects of demobilization were less technologies of containment than by-products of abandonment.

It might be argued that the persistence of the residual infrastructures of the Soviet era (tangible or not) have sustained the relevance of "Soviet" as a naming convention, a quarter of a century after the collapse. In Siberia today, Soviet residues and socialist legacies continue to perform an outsized role in shaping everyday life. The settlements I studied in a region of central Siberia known as Evenkiia were designed to function through state-financed infrastructures, transfer payments, and heavily subsidized commodities. The settlements I visited and studied in the late 1990s struggled to function in the absence of these inputs. More recent reporting suggests that these are enduring challenges. Soviet settlements in rural Siberia can be described as delocalized[6] technological systems, places whose dependence upon transfer payments, non-monetary subsidies, and centralized bureaucracies rendered them precariously reliant on non-local forces. The collapse of the USSR in 1991 animated the effects of this delocalized technological system through successive systemic failures associated with the inflexibility of infrastructures and their inability to respond to dramatic national changes and crises. In my research, I found that the post-Soviet landscape of the late 1990s was also littered with the fragmentary remains of industrial resource-extraction infrastructure, and that delocalized technological systems both crippled remote villages and persisted as impediments to greater degrees of autonomy. In more recent work from the area it is clear that the conditions have not changed significantly.[7] Anemic state financing continues to complicate living in villages located on the taiga and along rivers.

Land tenure for indigenous peoples is essential for cultural continuity and community well-being. Reduced access to hunting territories and reindeer pasture has been exacerbated by economic divestment and a general erosion of support for indigenous peoples in Siberia. Both Olga Povoroznyuk and Natalia Koptseva et al. demonstrate the social violence reproduced in the colonial maze of imposed legal, social, economic, and political structures.[8] Features of the Soviet landscape have endured into the early years of the twenty-first century as dysfunctional industrial artifacts. The dramatic resilience of Soviet Siberia's built environments and landscapes – residual infrastructures of socialist industrialism – is a powerfully structuring experience for both indigenous northerners and newcomers. The predicament of demobilization and isolation in remote villages of central Siberia is a result of enduring dysfunctional landscapes and the difficulty of negotiating mobility within these landscapes. Building on Ann Stoler's work on the material legacies of colonialism, Nikolai Ssorin-Chaikov[9] describes the challenges of navigating the debris of the Soviet project in the language of "performatives" and "constatives" of speech act theory. For Ssorin-Chaikov the "indigenous wilderness" and the "long-term civilizing missions of the Russian state in Siberia" were constatives. On and against these constatives is the performative of "Soviet debris of the period from the 1960s to the 1980s."[10] The specific agency of this debris as a performative that has the capacity to redistribute social reality is clear but why are the so-called "indigenous wilderness" and Russia's civilizing mission constative? When the metaphor is ported from the semantics of linguistic analysis to complex historical assemblages it is put under stress. What happens when we invert this figurative language so that the "Soviet debris," what I am calling residual infrastructures, is the constative upon which an indigenous wilderness functions as a performative? What Ssorin-Chaikov describes as the constative basis for the enduring encounter between the Soviet (now post-Soviet) state and indigenous peoples is premised on the same terms I describe in my own work: profoundly delocalized structures around, upon, and through which people compose their own rich social worlds. Considering feelings of structure urges us to consider a much more dynamic assemblage for understanding the performatives and constatives of everyday life.

Through the imperial Russian era Evenkis (as well as Kets, Dolgans, and Iakuts – other indigenous groups) living in what is now known as Evenkiia enjoyed relative autonomy from tsarist power in their everyday lives. These remote areas of taiga were connected to the Russian Empire through overland trails and river travel, enabling the entangling threads of trade, religion, and tribute to the tsar. The Evenkis were known to Europeans as great travellers – nomads with remarkable technologies and skills for moving through the vast Siberian landscape. These skills are still counted with pride for many Evenkis today. After the 1917 revolution, rapid technological and social change swept through the former Russian Empire. Evenki peoples' extensive travels were coercively recast in terms of Soviet modernity and in the context of industrial mechanization. The Soviet landscape in this part of Siberia was built through the forced sedentarization of reindeer pastoralists and the consolidation of villages into towns more easily governed by powerful technocratically minded managers. Consequently, travels not only followed traditional routes and trails by reindeer saddle and sleigh, but also were undertaken as journeys in the modern Soviet state: on motorboats and barges and then later in helicopters and airplanes.

The most acute points of Soviet violence toward indigenous Siberians, their cultures, and their economies are typically accorded to the state-sponsored programs of collectivization and sedentarization. "[The] tragedy of the Evenkis began with the period of collectivization. At this point the Kolkhozy [collective farms] became the owners of the Tayga lands, later it was the sovkhozy and gosprokhozy. Forest inhabitants lost the basis of life – their clan and family lands."[11] Technocratic managers from centralized rural planning and economy departments outlined the program of collectivization where property that was seized by the state was redistributed among newly formed cooperative entities. Mobile hunters and herders were forced, under programs of sedentarization, to adapt and change their traditional seasonal migrations to fit settled life in villages. The analysis of my earlier work borrowed the idea of a "system of paths" from the Russian anthropologist S.M. Shirokogoroff in order to describe Evenki forms of travel through a known, storied, and "cultivated" landscape. This is a composite term that binds traditional knowledge with ecology, and it allowed me to better describe traditions and legacies of travel against the backdrop of Soviet modernization and sedentarization. "System of paths" was not merely a poetic way of rephrasing the concept of tradition. The anthropologist Robin Ridington notes that it has been "far more attractive for northern hunters to carry knowledge from place to place than to be burdened with carrying material artifacts."[12] I use the "system of paths" to focus on the genius of a technology held in the mind, rather than in the hand. Maintaining these technologies became increasingly difficult in Soviet modernity.

Although most scholars start their analysis of the incursion of state forms of social and economic organization with the civil war that followed the Communist Revolution,[13] others note that the most radical changes to everyday life in remote villages occurred in the 1960s – the era of industrialization.[14] This was an era when the scope of centralized planning and management was matched by depth of application. An important beginning for the establishment of a distinctly Soviet system of mechanized travel was the removal of women and children from the taiga. While organizational changes significantly altered the mobility of many Evenkis, it was not until the state's economists, scientists, and bureaucrats sought to modernize and industrialize the forest economies that the Evenkis' system of paths, maintained by hunters and herders, was more profoundly challenged.[15]

As I've noted elsewhere, the modernization and development of northern regions in the Soviet Union built on industrial expansion, extensive exploitation of natural resources, and the reorganization of local industries.[16] Reindeer breeding, along with all other components of the traditional economy (hunting, fishing, plant and berry picking), was reconstructed, rationalized, and subjected to techno-industrial bureaucracy. Some other scholars, like Kerstin Kuoljok, have made the rather narrowly conceived argument that industrialization did not threaten reindeer breeding in the Soviet North because of a nationality policy that preserved "the specific character of each people."[17] Furthermore, she stated that polluting industrial complexes were not extensively cast upon the Siberian landscape. Their concentration in industrial centres, along with the "shortage of roads and railways in the North,"[18] supposedly protected reindeer industries. In my work I show how industrial reindeer breeding was nominally similar to traditional small-holder and kin-based reindeer herding practices but fundamentally different in practice. Industrial reindeer breeding relied on the erasure of the Evenki system of paths. Regarding environmental degradation, David G. Anderson's ethnography of Evenkis on the Taymyr Peninsula provides evidence of the broad effects of heavy-metal pollution on reindeer herds.[19] Soviet industrialism's other forms of environmental degradation include – among other things – oil development in Yamal as well as nuclear testing on the border of Yakutia (Republic of Sakha) and Evenkiia in the Viliuy basin.[20]

For Siberia in general, the momentum of industrialization accelerated after 1956.[21] Between 1955 and 1956 "the 'land tenure regulation' [*zemleustroitelnaia*] expedition of the Ministry of Rural Economy of the RSFSR gave each kolkhoz concrete recommendations in the use of reindeer pastures" in Evenkiia.[22] The socialist industrial reorganization of Evenki economies was an important part of what Aleksander Pika pointedly referred to as the "marked experiments of social engineering aimed at destroying nomadic ways of life."[23] Undermining Evenki autonomies was meant to produce good Soviet citizens. In the words of Evenki historian V.N. Uvachan, "The peoples of the North, as equals, have entered into a new historic community – the Soviet people."[24]

INDUSTRIALISM WITHOUT THE FACTORY

Components of the Soviet economy were expected to conform to technocrats' new standards of scientific management, including the most "traditional" occupations like wild plant and fruit harvesting, reindeer herding, hunting, fishing, and trapping. Scientific planning and machinery were understood as the backbone of an industrial economy. So-called non-socialist practices were seen as inefficient and "backwards" (un-modern). In the industrialization and mechanization of northern "agriculture," the capacity of Evenkis to resist and creatively interpret state forms of social organization diminished under the massive weight of socialist central planning. Soviet institutions and cultural organizations cultivated new sensibilities and affinities that promoted a properly Soviet way of life. Traditional modes of being in the world were put under great tension and scrutiny. Such challenges can be seen as a labyrinth of colonial experience, where indigenous peoples were required to navigate a complex and shifting territory of images set within another shifting disciplinary grid.

The era saw some Evenkis increasingly enfranchised through the mechanisms of the multi-ethnic state and what Terry Martin has retroactively labelled affirmative-action[25] policies. One might say that it was through education, travel, war, prison, and employment that Soviet identities became available to Evenkis. These identities compromised, to some degree, solidarities and shared experiences among those who continued to practise more or less traditional land-based activities (hunting, herding, fishing). The compartmentalization of professions gave the state greater control over mobility. Self-determination in the traditional economies of hunting and herding was undermined by the conflicting scientifically legitimated strategies for herd management, hunting, and fishing introduced by the new "experts" from urban universities and colleges.

Land tenure regulation and "scientific management" marked the beginning of new socialist-technocratic and industrial management strategies that came to dominate in the 1970s. Aside from ideological motivations, the two main incentives for collectivization were the need to produce surplus foods and other goods for growing urban populations in the Russian North[26] and the creation of industrial employment in regions that were previously undeveloped.[27] The notion of cultural and economic "backwardness" (*otstalost*) was explicitly implicated in this effort, a lingering irritation from the earliest days of revolutionary planning. Overcoming Russian backwardness and illiteracy was central concern of Stalin's first five-year plan. The persistence of traditional northern economies was seen by some as an embarrassment and by others as an opportunity. Herding and hunting brigades were pushed to expand their herds and provide ever greater quantities of meat to feed growing administrative centres like Tura. A report entitled "Development of the Technology for Producing Reindeer in the USSR"[28] outlines the industrial approach to reindeer herding in Siberia: "The prospects for development in this field [of reindeer breeding] are determined by important economic goals such as strengthening northern economy, improving the prosperity of indigenous peoples, [and] establishing a local food supply ... Thanks to Lenin's national policy which is being carried out by the Soviet government, reindeer breeding is developing successfully."[29]

Throughout the Soviet era, the traditional system of paths was sustained by Evenkis where possible in the cycle of production herding and hunting activities. In most cases the maintenance of a system of paths was frustrated and undermined by the impingements of Soviet management for industrial culture. This, for example, is evidenced by the increasing difficulty of regular access to taiga life for many women and children. Geographic shifts from forest to settlement and then to consolidated settlement "served to decrease the range of a woman's activities, her cultural and economic options and flexibility, and to channel younger women increasingly away from any level of involvement in such traditional activities."[30] Once again, the system of paths becomes a useful tool for thinking about cultural practices tied specifically to dwelling in and moving through the taiga.

Evenkis have told me one particular story that exemplifies the state's botched attempts to manage hunting practices. In the mid-1980s Gospromkhoz Turinski, with the assistance of the Evenki Okrug Department of Agriculture and the Scientific Institute for Rural Economy (based in Noril'sk), set up long drift-net fences across the tundra to funnel wild herds of migratory caribou (known locally as *morskiye*) to convenient stations where they could be shot en masse and "efficiently" harvested. The project was eventually abandoned but the nets were left strewn across the tundra, altering caribou migration routes. Authorities in Taimyr, an arctic territory north of Evenkiia, in fact put considerable energy into the commercial hunt. Leonid Kolpashchikov et al. report that this massive commercial harvest was undertaken principally by non-indigenous Russians and that the "cost of transporting meat, largely with helicopters, was low because of state subsidies."[31]

K.B. Klokov corroborates my own ethnographic reports on this method of harvesting mass quantities of migrating deer as they tried to cross rivers.[32] "Significant efforts began in the early 1970s to actively promote commercial harvest of Taimyr's wild reindeer in response to concern about overexploitation of the range by a growing wild population."[33] Evenki hunters who, prior to that time, were able to hunt the wild herds of caribou without travelling great distances have since had to range hundreds of kilometres north to encounter the migrating caribou. The logistical difficulty of making such a trip, given the failure of mechanical transport (due to the inaccessibility of the machines, the parts, and the fuel to run them) and limited access to domestic reindeer, keeps many Evenki within much more limited bounds and forces them to rely on scarce moose and non-migratory forest caribou for meat.

The most recent research on mobility in the Arctic regions of Siberia demonstrates "several contradictory mobilities: out and in for emigration/immigration flows; south–north in terms of economic flows between regional centers, traditionally located in southern Siberia, and Northern cities; north–north if we follow the professional trajectories of those Northerners building their career in several Arctic cities over the years."[34] What Marlene Laruelle and others in that collection fail to note is the lack of mobility of many who have neither the means to travel nor the social capital to navigate distant places. Of course, there are also those who would simply rather not leave, who prefer to live life according the familiar, grounded system of paths inherited as part of their cultural heritage – even where their status on the land is largely reliant on the goodwill or inattention of the central Russian government and where they navigate the residual infrastructures of socialism.

Geographical and social isolation and the failure of transport networks were central problems that came about after the disintegration of the Soviet system and the inauguration of new and chaotic temporalities. Modes of transport and travel on the land, on the river, and in the air – in addition to the built environments and social landscapes – contextualize Evenki people's rural experience.

Each of these modes was integral to the Soviet projects of northern industrialization and professionalization. They have also been integral to the collapse of what is understood as a manufactured separation between hunting and herding camps and village settlements.[35] More generally, these projects of socialist reconstruction were integral to the displacement of the traditional system of paths and have had the effect, in the post-Soviet era, of demobilizing Evenkis – isolating rural settlements in east-central Siberia and locking people in a kind of suspended state. This brings us back to thinking about life in the shadow of the dam and its strange arrangement of temporal affects. The anthropologists Tim Choy and Jerry Zee describe a sense of powerlessness and suspension as a distributed condition of being in the world today. This is a concept that Zee further develops in his use of the idiom of the holding pattern – a kind of affective repertoire of ordinary life waiting for something big to happen; the kind of feeling that seems likely to pervade Evenki villages on the Lower Tunguska River.[36] Anticipation, as Vivian Choi notes, is productive; by reorganizing and structuring the lives of individuals (but also economies and nations) it draws together "new regimes of fear, hope, and governance."[37] There is a compelling story to explore here, not only about indigenous people and ethnic Russians living in precarious states, not only about life in the aftermath of socialist industrialism and the face of new Russian industrial forms, but about general future orientations as well.

MYTHOPOETICS OF THE ANTHROPOCENE

The term *Anthropocene* has become remarkably generative, not only in the geological sciences but across the spectrum of academic scholarship as well as for the general public. For many years it has been a proposed name for a proposed epochal succession to the twelve-thousand-year-old Holocene. While Anthropocene is a specific term defined by geologists, it has also come to be used as a shorthand for talking about anthropogenic global warming, mass extinction, and innumerable other environmental catastrophes associated with the doings of humans. Gerardo Ceballos et al. state, "The number of species that have gone extinct in the last century would have taken … between 800 and 10,000 years to disappear. These estimates reveal an exceptionally rapid loss of biodiversity over the last few centuries, indicating that a sixth mass extinction is already under way."[38] While the Anthropocene has yet to be ratified as a geological "event," its import has already muddied temporal and semantic frames. In 2016 the International Commission on Stratigraphy delivered a proposal that framed the Anthropocene as a formally defined and bounded epoch within the geologic time scale.[39] This is a chronologically framed scale of time, naturalized as a linear narrative of progression. While sensitive instruments and methods allow us to imagine on this scale, it has no analogy in the lived experience of the everyday world. As Ian Baucom argues we must learn not only how to scale time but, even more critically, how to scale effect.[40] In his call for a revived and retooled labour imaginary, McKenzie Wark has identified this as a struggle between the molar and the molecular.[41] His account, like everyone else's, is dire.

What fascinates me about the frictions and failures of imagining, knowing, and feeling scalar shifts, and what connects these perturbations to my research in Siberia, is the way in which the Anthropocene structures time, how it organizes and configures the world. I'm less interested in the science of the Anthropocene, which non-specialists must accept at face value; it marks the territory of a geologically recognizable epoch but more and more it becomes another way of thinking about the rapidly unfolding crises associated with global warming, extinction, ecological pollution, and human displacement. It is becoming, regardless of accuracy, an epochal name for the processes we call global warming, shorthand for anthropogenic climate change and loss of global biodiversity. While the mark in geologic time may not be our collective doom, the production of it has delivered us to the crisis. Any boundary-making event is a challenge and this one is rightly circumscribed by its own disciplinary obligations.

A creative and experimental endeavour launched by the journal *Cultural Anthropology* called the Lexicon for the Anthropocene describes this moment as "a time to test, engage, and experiment with new ways of being in the world and with the world. We may yet have the chance to reverse-engineer ourselves toward a less imperfect humanity. This lexicon is meant as a site to imagine and explore what human beings can do – have already been doing – differently with this time."[42] Doing differently *with* this time and *in* this time paints the contours of the contemporary, of time on a very human-biographical scale. I am compelled to ask: what is the feeling of that scale? How do such scalar shifts constitute a sensorial and affective regimen, a vague threat and sustained sense of dread whose pervasive signal is registered in a range of feelings as banal unease, political theatrics, and anxiety for imminent catastrophe? This is the anticipatory force of slow violence,[43] which instead of framing the neoliberal state as the villain distributes culpability much more broadly and personally.

For many anthropologists (and indeed following Bruno Latour's address to the American Anthropological Association in 2014) the Anthropocene has become an opportunity to engage the discipline in a much broader dialogue that is happening with or without us. The Anthropocene names anthropology's anthropos but it is also a short step to the humanities' human. Rob Nixon reminds us that the Anthropocene "began as a provocation, an exhortation, a shock strategy of a kind that we are attuned to in the arts and the humanities."[44] The shock: that anthropogenic marks on the earth have become so deep, so profound, and so widely distributed as to constitute an entirely new geological epoch. This news fits well with that of global warming, reinforcing what we all fear is true as natural disasters are reclassified simply as disasters and so-called "acts of God" are revealed to have mortal authors. Indeed, it seems as though all disasters might now be understood – in "man's" own geological era – as having a kind of species specificity.[45] There's much more to say here but for now let me bracket this off and move on to the principal controversy of the Anthropocene for the humanities and how it relates to my work on the catastrophes of socialist industrialism.

The Anthropocene has catalyzed a host of challenges collectively, though unevenly, faced by earth's inhabitants. The stability of the identity figure that is the Anthropocene, which some imagine as self-evident, is revealed to be much more troubled through a proliferation of pseudonyms – Cthulhucene, Capitalocene, Plasticene, Anthro-Obscene, Misanthropocene – each with its own angle and critique. Without the burden of committing to a universal naming event, the generativity of pseudonyms has become a powerful locus of activity speaking back from the place of the cultural critic rather than the scientific expert. Critics, unbeholden to a fuller understanding and disciplinary framing of climate and earth science, come to the subject from a wild diversity of positions. So it is that *Anthropocene* has exploded in the hands of the geologists – they did after all give it to us, so what did they expect?

Donna Haraway insists that we don't re-inscribe the divisions of nature and culture when undertaking this naming event. She writes: "No species, not even our own arrogant one pretending to be good individuals in so-called modern Western scripts, acts alone; assemblages of organic species and of abiotic actors make history, the evolutionary kind and the other kinds too."[46] But Haraway also agrees with so many others who decry the erasure of history in the inclusive "we," the anthropos, of the Anthropocene. If the Anthropocene succeeds in naming the geological agency of the species, critique informed by the humanities very quickly reminds us that it was indeed not the species who did this thing any more than it was nature that put us here. Some people and some forms of social organization are more culpable than others.

With that critique in mind, let me register my discontent with the moniker *Capitalocene*, one of the "cenes" described by a number of different authors. Andreas Malm writes: "Ours is the geological epoch not of humanity, but of capital … the fossil economy is coextensive with the capitalist mode of production – only now on a global scale."[47] The author concedes that communism had its "own growth mechanisms connected to coal, oil, and gas"[48] but asserts that they are now gone. Lest the spectre of communism suggest a plausible alternative to capitalism, or lest capitalism be allowed in all its totalizing and abstract horror to function as the singular bogeyman, let me playfully suggest an alternative grounded in a different historical and technical specificity: the Prometheocene.

The Prometheocene is that moment when the undoing of man by his own arrogance finally becomes generally true. Prometheus, you might remember, was the Titan who gave man fire, and through it the arts. For this he was punished by Zeus, though humans too were cursed: "I will give men as the price for fire an evil thing in which they may all be glad of heart while they embrace their own destruction."[49] So it was that Zeus sent Pandora to bring suffering to mankind by tricking Prometheus's brother, Epimetheus, into marrying her and accepting her dowry of suffering. According to the logic of these ancient Greek myths, humans as *inheritors* of fire, recipients of the gift,[50] bear some responsibility for its original theft – they too pay a price. A vessel full of troubles brought by Pandora was their curse, though we are told that the last of the items in Pandora's box was *elpis*,[51] a term that might be translated as either hope or expectation. The evident ambiguity of the word resonates mightily with the earth's current predicament.

David Landes's famous 1969 economic history, *The Unbound Prometheus*, might lend credence to the naming of the Prometheocene. Reading the figure of Prometheus as a metaphor for industrial modernity has been common: "Prometheus has often been viewed as a metaphor for human enlightenment and the disasters that can come from overreaching our limits."[52] Consider Mary Shelley's 1818 novel titled *Frankenstein; or, The Modern Prometheus*. While there was both enthusiasm and apprehension for such technological developments, there is no denying that the logics of industrial development – enabled by the transference of carbon to the atmosphere – enjoy a hegemonic and thoroughly naturalized position. The age of industry was inaugurated with the invention of the steam engine in the mid-eighteenth century. Since that moment the demand for energy has increased dramatically, leading, most economists will tell you, to an equally dramatic increase in "comfort" ... at least for some. "The long-standing debate on the transition from feudalism to capitalism sought a clear pathway through stages of economic transition to an ultimate goal of industrialization."[53] Industrialism is the engine of modernity with the mine and mill, as much as the factory, the icons of promethean ambition.

A LITANY OF CATASTROPHES

The spectacular eventfulness of catastrophe organizes history. How is it that thousands more pages of research and speculation have been written about the Tunguska event, a mysterious cosmic explosion in 1908 that seems to have killed no one, than about the chronic, mundane, and slow violence that grips the fortunes of many indigenous peoples in Siberia? I have mobilized the language of catastrophe to critique its aesthetics and explore its contours for in it I see a vital connection to the politics of urgency and deferral that threaten to be enacted once again in the moment of anthropogenic crisis. The danger in naming the

Anthropocene is that this naming could re-inscribe flawed (racist and inequitable) epistemologies. There is old magic in the power of a name to conjure a beast: to utter its unspeakable name is to give it force.[54] By the urgency of politics, the horizon of act, expectation, and planning is shortened dramatically. The crisis of the Anthropocene produces an urgency that will be predicated on a pernicious forgetting of injustice. If we're not careful, the Anthropocene may simply inaugurate a(nother) grand deferral of justice. Certainly, one can imagine a dystopia of climate sustainability. Green militaries that go to war against carbon polluters; technocrats insulated from the difficulties of abject life as they make centralized decisions on behalf of humans, for the sake of the world-for-us.[55] "To allow plutocrats to deputize for the species would represent a new twist in the sorry history of government for the people without the people."[56] The obscenity of industrial economics witnesses the seemingly unstoppable rise in income inequality: "What does it mean, in terms of the history of ideas, that the Anthropocene as a grand explanatory species story has taken hold in plutocratic times, when economic, social and environmental injustice is marked by a deepening schism between the uber-rich and the ultra-poor, between gated resource-hogs and the abandoned destitute?"[57] Does the name of the Anthropocene naturalize inequality? Does it mark the obscene site of injustice?

And we all know that the crisis is real and terrifying – though for most I suspect it is also being swiftly accommodated by an adaptive human response to vicissitudes; it becomes background noise to gradual change amidst the barely ordered chaos of everyday life. Because of inertia, we're told by climate scientists, even if we manage to stop ourselves from putting CO_2 into the atmosphere today, the earth's temperature will continue to warm for at least fifty years: this is the future perfect of climate science. This matters in the Arctic where ice is melting at a catastrophic rate. In the boreal forest the permafrost thaw is not only disrupting traditional trade and travel routes but also releasing carbon into the atmosphere in the form of methane, one of the most troubling greenhouse gases. This is known as a positive feedback loop: more carbon in the atmosphere traps more heat and warms the planet more, melting more of the permafrost. More than enough trouble to go around – even those most insulated must sense danger. Plants as well as animals migrate in response to warming temperatures, which leads to stressed ecologies, tumultuous and chaotic from so much change. Recently it was reported that larch trees and other conifers of the boreal forest were unable to migrate quickly enough to match the speed of climate change. It is easy to imagine the compound challenge of this for people who rely on hunting, herding, and fishing in the north. We might see this as a social feedback loop where people who are already vulnerable due to economic modernization find it increasingly difficult to practise those marginal economies to sustain themselves.

THE SPEED OF VIOLENCE: TWO HUNDRED YEARS OF CATASTROPHE IN THE CENTRAL SIBERIAN TAIGA

I'm a little uneasy writing a litany of catastrophes lest it come, for my readers, to define life in the central Siberian Arctic. So I offer a rhetorical gesture designed to establish the remarkable resilience and persistence of Evenki people. In the face of an often corrupt, duplicitous, unloving, and belligerent state it is a celebration and an indictment, not a eulogy. The little struggles of everyday life persist alongside bigger struggles. Children write poems about the seasons in their schools, the sun slipping up over the horizon illuminates golden larch trees – my friend who worked at the nursing station commented that the luminous scene was breathtaking. The new snow of late fall covers the taiga and begins to freeze rivers and lakes ... I think my Evenki acquaintances find a grounding happiness in the seasonal round. The structure of repetition is powerfully enforced through the annual hyperbole of light and dark, warmth and cold. On the winter solstice in Tura, Evenkiia's capital, the sun appears only for a few hours before tumbling behind the hills. And it is cold. But Evenkis gather around fires and stoves, drinking tea and telling stories; or when they're in the village they watch hockey, news, or serials on television. Kids agitate to play Grand Theft Auto on the computer. They do all this while land is arbitrarily partitioned and managed by a distant state; while mining concerns appear out of nowhere; when sociologists deliver questionnaires asking your opinion about a hydroelectric dam that will flood your village; when the treasury gives a hollow apology for salary payments that are months overdue; when Russian hunters kill your deer and there is no real way to get recompense.

Catastrophe, like falling stars, ought to be a chance incident. In central Siberia, catastrophic events related to external agents have been a troublingly regular recurrence for hundreds of years. The language of slow violence is one of catastrophic regularity, a suspension of chance – hope and expectation. Walter Benjamin's state of emergency is a description of both this world and the being in it. It is a unity enforced by the Anthropocene thesis – even if the proliferation of emerging worlds under generalized and redistributed crises is not equitably shared.

The great catastrophe of Europe after the Second World War is often thought of as a world unable to sustain its own myths of and hopes for cohesion. Paul Harrison, following Maurice Blanchot, writes that the "underlying unity and orderliness which the word 'world' implies ... had been revealed as an illusion."[58] Catastrophe is a transit point marking violent dissolution – it may also threaten to naturalize the states and identities on either end. My typology of catastrophe works well enough if we are to maintain a foundational blind spot in "Western" or Euro-American ethnocentric thought: the dualism of nature and culture. If we choose not to, though, if we take a weird path, what are we left with? I'm just teasing out the significance of this, so I offer less a revolutionary reading of catastrophe than an itemization of catastrophic events toned with speculative gestures towards a weird anthropology.[59] It strikes me as a weird theory and a weirding of theory, one that takes the temporal strangeness of the world as its constituent modality.

THE GRANDIOSE PERSPECTIVES THAT OPEN UP BEFORE US

Will we become connoisseurs of catastrophe? Perhaps we are already. Extinction events, habitat loss, trees unable to migrate quickly enough out of warming zones: these compound the catastrophes of inequality in the world. We don't need to rehash the profound failures of capitalism in the United States with its increasing poverty and disenfranchisement compounded by growing income inequality. But we must also consider the failures that gather capitalism's great Other under the name of industrialism.

Maxim Gorky, Soviet Communism's premier literary propagandist, developed a concept he called geo-optimism. "With the advent of socialism, he averred, chaos would be banished forever from the world. Swamps, predators, drought, snakes, deserts and other 'unproductive' lands, 'sleepy forests,' Arctic ice, hurricanes, and earthquakes would all be eliminated."[60] How troubling that we're now seeing this weird prescience, the success of geo-optimism in leaving a mark on the world. What it would ultimately mean to leave a mark on the world was clearly not understood. Socialist marks on the world were mobilizations of force and power to re-arrange the supposedly limitless resources of the earth. This geo-optimism is now replaced by a geo-pessimism (and maybe a nostalgia for geo-optimism, too). And we should not be surprised to learn in the Anthropocene that those who benefited most are mostly dead or bankrupt or have snuck away to islands of leisure and entitlement.

The legacy of the Soviet rhetoric of triumph over the depredations of nature was inscribed in the bodies and identities of indigenous minorities in Siberia. There continues to be a commonly held belief (among both ethnic Russians and many indigenous peoples) that the life of northern natives was essentially nasty, brutish, and short. That before socialism, they suffered not only from exploitation by villainous traders but also from starvation and disease. The promise of the Soviet project was stability; it was to be a bulwark against exploitation, starvation, and sickness. Whether this was a truth is questionable. I've heard Evenkis argue both positions (that "precolonial life" was brutal or that it was not). Crucially, though, the temporality of this is unresolved. According to the weird temporality of the Communist imaginary, indigenous people had to traverse a mountain of one hundred years: from the stone age, passing over feudalism and capitalism, to arrive at the joyous garden of communism. This remarkable temporal imaginary was built on a chauvinist and racist ideal. Remarkably, though, it seems that such an imaginary produced as its by-product a very real compression of "normal" time. The technological accelerationism of the twentieth century is undeniably evident in the accelerated destruction of habitat and biodiversity, which has led us on this path to the sixth great extinction. This same technological accelerationism, which Wark has called the "carbon liberation front,"[61] brings us global warming resulting in the unprecedented melting of glaciers and polar ice. What would normally have occurred in the span of hundreds or thousands of years has been compressed into decades. The central irony is that the accelerationism and technological progressivism were seen as evidence of mastery – promethean feats: liberating humans from a state of dependency and vulnerability. Indigenous peoples in Siberia, as elsewhere, were dressed up as "our common ancestors" – living anachronisms and parables meant to teach that the precarity of human life could only be overcome through technological mastery.

Thus, I am with the critics who wish to serve a restraining order against "the runaway hubris of technocratic Anthropocene expertise by resisting the political logic of [technocrats], whereby those who crunch the numbers are first in line to engineer the new worlds."[62] Administrative efficiency and organization went hand in hand with industrialization. Indeed, we're blinded by machines and shop floors when we think of industrialism without social organization, when the tangible eclipses the intangible. My use of the term *industrialism* in this expanded sense, which includes not just gas-belching machines but managerial technologies of organization, is key to understanding the central Siberian social and economic landscape in this century of residual infrastructures.

In the historian Douglas Weiner's environmentalist histories of Soviet Russia, he uncovers many remarkable tales of arrogance and hubris. One academic in the late 1920s wrote that the goal of socialist industrialism is no less than a "profound rearrangement of the entire living world – not only that portion which is now under the domination of humanity but also that portion that has still remained wild. Generally speaking, all wild species will disappear with time; some will be exterminated, others will be domesticated. All living nature will live, thrive, and die at none other than the will of humans and according to their designs. These are the grandiose perspectives that open up before us."[63] This shocking text is not an example of prescience; rather it is testimony that the Anthropocene was produced by design, not accident. While Weiner and others detail historical protests, as well as little victories against the industrial leviathan, these were minor notes in the prometheanism of Soviet modernity.

Working with this insight and critique of the magisterial thinking of industrialism, I return finally to my new collaborative project on river life. The vast territory and relatively small population have made the Evenki region a tempting

site for Soviet and Russian administrations to develop resource extraction economies and dump unwanted waste (hosting at least five nuclear waste sites). Our
study will be looking at a proposed hydroelectric dam (called the Evenki Hydroelectric Station) to be constructed along the Lower Tunguska River. If the dam
is built as planned, its massive reservoir would inundate the site of the administrative capital (Tura) along with six other centralized villages comprising the
children and grandchildren of those forcibly settled by communist planners.[64] It
would also flood two nuclear waste sites (Babkino and Blodekit) with unknowable results. The total number of people displaced would be over six thousand.
While our project will explore the potential impact of the proposed dam, our
primary interest is in producing a socio-cultural snapshot of everyday life along
the Lower Tunguska River with a special emphasis on understanding Evenki
peoples' attitudes toward the future.

This project aims to engage and collaborate with local indigenous communities while exploring more generally the idea of sacrifice in this time of global
warming. Major hydroelectric dams are described as ecologically friendly re-
newable sources of electricity by their proponents, yet the displaced are rarely
counted among the beneficiaries. There is considerable scholarly literature dem-
onstrating that the negative environmental impact of major industrial projects
like this is not reasonably classified as ecologically sustainable. Quite the opposite. While looking at the particular experience of thousands of potentially displaced people we also consider the situation of the earth more generally, where
vulnerable communities face devastating futures of melting ice, animal extinc-
tions, and ecosystem collapse, among myriad other dire and likely irreversible
processes. The big question for those living in the shadow of the proposed dam
is one that is shared by humanity in general, living in the shadow of climate
catastrophe: what is the future and how can we live with it?

ACKNOWLEDGMENTS

I would like to acknowledge the Atkinson Center for a Sustainable Future and the Society
for the Humanities at Cornell University for their support of this work.

NOTES

1 My colleague Anatoly Ablazhey (of Novosibirsk State University) and I are co-investiga-
   tors on this project.
2 Williams, *The Long Revolution*, 64.
3 Elements of this paper are heavily informed by my collaborations with Vasilina Orlova.

4 The current designation is translated as "Native small-numbered peoples of the North, Siberia, and the Far East of the Russian Federation" (*Korennye Malochislennye Narody Severa, Sibiri, i Dal'nego Vostoka Rossiiskoi Federatsii*), also called native small-numbered peoples of the North (KMNS). I also use "indigenous peoples of Siberia" in this paper, which is a term used by the Russian Association of Indigenous Peoples of the North (RAIPON).

5 Campbell, "Contrails of Globalization."

6 Cf. Pelto, *The Snowmobile Revolution*.

7 See, for example, Koptseva and Kirko, "Post-Soviet Practice," and Ssorin-Chaikov, "Soviet Debris."

8 Povoroznyuk, "Belonging to the Land"; Koptseva et al., "Political Struggle."

9 Ssorin-Chaikov, "Soviet Debris."

10 Ibid., 717–18.

11 Grigorevna (1992) quoted in Fondahl, *Gaining Ground?*, 57.

12 Ridington, "From Artifice to Artifact," 57.

13 Fondahl, *Gaining Ground?*; Pika and Grant, *Neotraditionalism in the Russian North*.

14 Anderson, *Identity and Ecology in Arctic Siberia*, 37.

15 Ibid.

16 See also Kuoljok, *Revolution in the North*, 51–2.

17 Ibid.

18 Ibid.

19 Anderson, *Identity and Ecology in Arctic Siberia*, 62–3.

20 Golovnev and Osherenko, *Siberian Survival*; Crate, *Cows, Kin, and Globalization*.

21 Kuoljok, *Revolution in the North*, 52.

22 Kovyazin and Kuzakov, *Sovetskaya Evenkia*, 96.

23 Pika and Grant, *Neotraditionalism in the Russian North*, 96.

24 Uvachan, *Put´ Narodov Severa K Sotsializmu*, 292.

25 Martin, *Affirmative Action Empire*.

26 Fondahl, *Gaining Ground?*, 58.

27 Anderson, "Property Rights and Civil Society."

28 Koshelev and Mukhachev, "Development of the Technology."

29 Ibid., 341.

30 Fondahl, *Gaining Ground?*, 69.

31 Kolpaschikov, Makhailov, and Russell, "The Role of Harvest," 8.

32 Klokov, "Northern Reindeer of Taymyr Okrug."

33 Kolpaschikov, Makhailov, and Russell, "The Role of Harvest."

34 Laruelle, *New Mobilities and Social Changes*.

35 Kwon, "Maps and Actions"; Povoroznyuk, Habeck, and Vaté, "Introduction."

36 Choy and Zee, "Condition – Suspension"; Zee, "HOLDING PATTERNS."

37 Choi, "Anticipatory States."

38 Ceballos et al., "Accelerated Modern Human-Induced Species Losses," 1.

39 "Working Group on the Anthropocene," Subcommission on Quaternary Stratigraphy, International Commission on Stratigraphy, last modified 9 March 2018, http://quaternary.stratigraphy.org/workinggroups/anthropocene.

40 Baucom, "History 4°."

41 Wark, *Molecular Red*.

42 Howe and Pandian, "Lexicon for an Anthropocene."

43 Nixon, *Slow Violence*.

44 Nixon, "The Anthropocene," 3.

45 There seems to be a kind of liberation of obligation in an act of God. No one is at fault. This has probably been used for generations to sidestep responsibility (for example in the case of Hurricane Katrina). In some ways, the naming of the Anthropocene might diminish that argument. The last acts of God must be cosmic in origin, the only things that have no geography.

46 Haraway, "Anthropocene, Capitalocene, Plantationocene, Chthulucene," 159.

47 Malm, "The Anthropocene Myth."

48 Ibid.

49 Hesiod's *Works and Days* in Zillman, *Prometheus Unbound*, 724.

50 We might also remember Marcel Mauss's gift or Bataille's accursed share. With Bataille's general economy, industrialism has produced an excess that if not "spent" in a harmless and wasteful manner gets turned to war.

51 The dominant interpretation of classical mythology translates it as *hope*. cf. Detienne et al., *The Cuisine of Sacrifice among the Greeks*. See also O'Gorman, "Bernard Stiegler's Pharmacy."

52 Van Bryan, "Prometheus the Creation of Man."

53 Berg, "Skill, Craft and Histories," 130.

54 Lonsdale, "Attitudes towards Animals."

55 Cf. Eugene Thacker's *In the Dust of This Planet*.

56 Nixon, *Slow Violence*, 18.

57 Ibid., 11.

58 Harrison, "Corporeal Remains," 434.

59 Weird anthropology might be an anthropology "beyond nature and culture" (Descola, *Beyond Nature and Culture*). It offers different techniques for the identification of *things* in the world that apprehend them in relationality and in permanent states of becoming. Furthermore, it does this without coming through its own teleology to declare it has discovered indeterminacy. Weird doesn't end in indeterminacy; rather, it begins there.

60 Weiner, "Predatory Tribute-Taking State," 288.

61 Wark, *Molecular Red*.

62 Nixon, *Slow Violence*, 5.

63 Kashchenko in Weiner, "Predatory Tribute-Taking State," 290.

64 Noginsk, Tutonchany, Uchami, Nidym, Kislokan, and Iukta.

Figure 0.1 Untitled, Derek Sayer.

Figure 2.6   Detroit's Penobscot Building glows over Windsor in this postcard, ca. 1930.

Figure 2.7 The same view acknowledges Windsor as the viewpoint but omits the city.

The Heart of Detroit at Night.

Figure 2.8 This postcard rendering is based on a 1929 photograph of the *Graf Zeppelin*'s visit to Detroit, in which the string of lights on the Windsor side are less dominant than in the postcard.

Figure 2.9 Windsor is visible as an unlit urban environment in the background.

View of Ambassador Bridge at Night, Sandwich, near Windsor, Canada.—26.

Figure 2.10 This postcard features a common iconic view of the Ambassador Bridge from the vantage point of Sandwich Town, in Windsor, circa 1930s, a desirable image for cross-border tourists and travellers.

Figure 2.11 The clear majority of postcard views of the Ambassador Bridge depict it from the vantage point of Sandwich Town or Windsor. Many, such as in this case, feature a low-flying airplane from which, one can imagine, the view of the Detroit skyline would be spectacular.

AMBASSADOR BRIDGE AT NIGHT. BETWEEN DETROIT. MICH. AND WINDSOR. ONT.

Figure 2.12 The Broken City Lab's *Cross-Border Communication* project, during the Great Recession of 2009.

Figure 2.13   During its key period of activity from 2009 to 2015, the Broken City Lab hosted numerous brainstorming workshops to consider creative perspectives on the scale of dynamic change in the border cities.

Figure 4.1 Untitled (freeze-frame), author video.

Figure 4.3 Untitled (freeze-frame), author video.

Figure 6.1 Sky cinema, Instagram image, 3 March 2017.

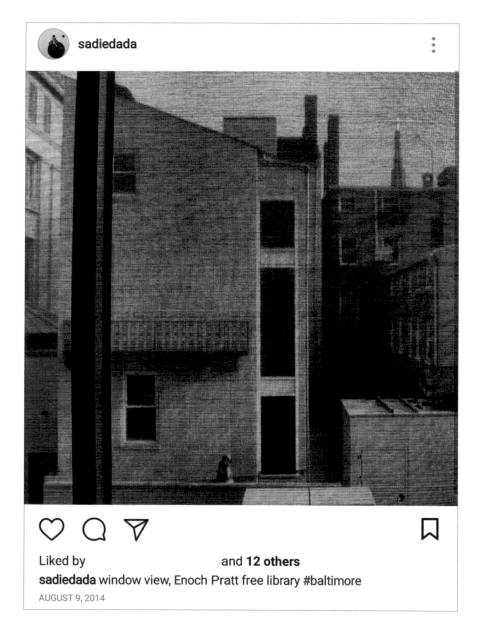

sadiedada

♡ ◯ ⊽   ⊓

Liked by   and **12 others**
sadiedada window view, Enoch Pratt free library #baltimore
AUGUST 9, 2014

Figure 6.2   Window view, Enoch Pratt free library #baltimore, Instagram image,
9 August 2014.

Figure 6.3 #luxury, Instagram image, 2 June 2017.

sadiedada

Liked by   and **7 others**
sadiedada library window view #toronto
AUGUST 19, 2014

Figure 6.4   Library window view #toronto, Instagram image, 19 August 2014.

Figure 9.2 Interior of Eames House, Case Study #8, Pacific Palisades.

Figure 9.3   Tumbleweed.

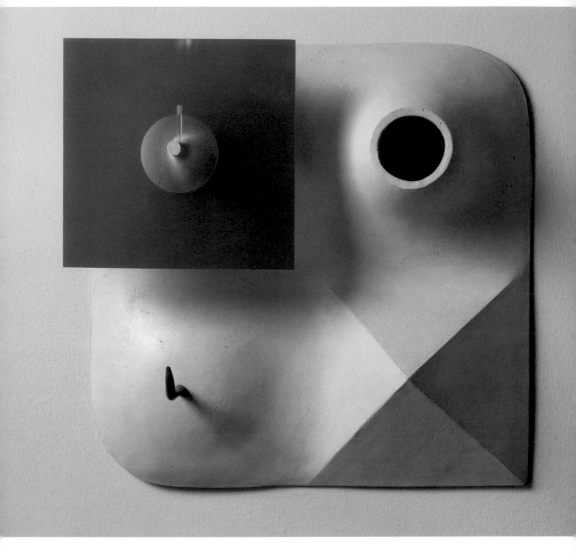

Figure 9.4 (above) *My Arizona.*

Figure 9.6 (opposite) *Kouros*, 1944–45.

Figure 11.1 (overleaf) Missing and murdered women window display, Moose Jaw, Saskatchewan, August 2016.

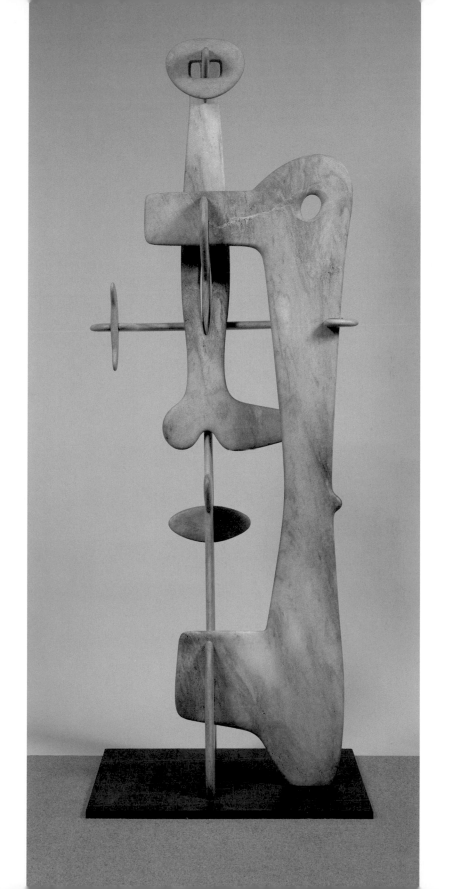

Figure 11.2 Al Capone marks the entrance to the Chicago Connection tour, August 2016.

Figure 11.3 Anonymous Chinese man marks the entrance to the Passage to Fortune tour, August 2016.

Figure 11.4 Power lines, August 2016.

CHAPTER 4

Still

CHRISTIEN GARCIA

The history of the freeze-frame
remains to be written[1]

Figure 4.1 Untitled (freeze-frame), author video.

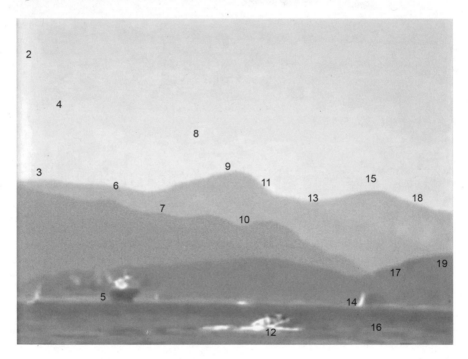

Figure 4.2 Untitled (freeze-frame), author video.

Figure 4.3 Untitled (freeze-frame), author video.

Figure 4.4 Untitled (freeze-frame), author video.

1 Bellour, "The Film Stilled."

2 Roni Horn, *Still Water (The River Thames, for Example)*, 1999, lithograph on paper. *Still Water* is a series of fifteen large lithographs depicting the surface of the river Thames. The water in the images has a frozen-in-time quality, simultaneously conveying a sense of stillness and movement. In some instances, the water is calm and glassy; in others it heaves and ebbs dramatically. Closer inspection reveals small numbers scattered throughout the pictorial frame, corresponding to footnotes running along the lower border of each piece. The notes include personal anecdotes, stories about the Thames, and references to film and literature.

3 Several years ago, one of my sisters gave my family a copy of an old VHS tape she had converted to DVD. It was Christmas and so we watched the video then and there in what we call the family room of the house I grew up in. The video had been recorded during the only real vacation we ever took as a family. The video was difficult to watch. The happy and light-hearted scenes drew into contrast the difficulties I associated with those times. And this discord in turn seemed to rupture the present familial atmosphere in which the video was being screened. The problem wasn't so much that the video brought to the surface a history that had been buried; it was that the video seemed to be demanding an explanation, a narrative account of how I got from "there" to "here," one which I could not and did not want to give.

4 The term *still* is commonly understood to mean not moving or making a sound, but in its adverbial form – in the still of a phrase such as "I still love you" – the term implies not the absence of something, but rather something's endurance through time. It is the relationship between motionlessness and continuance that is the subject of this piece. Is it possible to think of the film still or freeze-frame not simply as a moment frozen and clipped from the continuity of cinematic time, but also as some kind of endurance or ebb rooted in the very disruption of time?

5 A black and red freighter anchored in English Bay, Vancouver.

6 The idea of the photograph being a moment frozen in time is complicated by the idea of the photograph as a testament to the passing of time. As Susan Sontag describes it, "Precisely by slicing out this moment and freezing it, all photographs testify to time's relentless melt" (*On Photography*, 10).

7 In the narrative of the family trip to the sea, it is customary, especially for the child, to take something of the landscape home. A vial of sand, a collection of stones, a pearly shell – little souvenirs that are for keeping but also for losing, so that among the accumulations of the passing years they might, perhaps suddenly, be found and the beach and that vacation taken many years ago recalled.

8 Narrative might be thought of as a kind of movement in time, a means of organizing objects and events under the presumption that what exists can be told. Stillness, then, becomes a matter of disrupting not only the continuous flow of the cinematic image, but also the imperative to produce the self as a kind of narrative sequence in time.

9 "Before film appeared, there were little books of photos that could be made to flit past the viewer under the pressure of the thumb, presenting a boxing match or a tennis match." Benjamin, *The Work of Art*, 52n30.

10 What is the draw of stills in the analysis of the moving image? Laura Mulvey's work on what she calls the "aesthetics of delay" in cinema offers a framework for thinking about the relationship of stillness to film. Mulvey's focus is on the technological sea change from celluloid to video and digital modes of production. She argues that the relative ease with which these newer technologies allow film to be stopped, looped, slowed down, and otherwise manipulated shifts the mandate of cinematic time from the side of the producer to that of the viewer. However, despite Mulvey's invocation of a new interactive mode of spectatorship, it would be wrong to read this as simply a question of relocating the agency of narrative production from one side of the cinematic apparatus to the other – a democratic shift from the producer of film to the viewer of video. There is ultimately a more disruptive element of Mulvey's argument, one that seeks to uncouple the patterns of cinematic form from the structure of horizontal narrative. "The process of delay not only brings stillness into visibility," Mulvey writes, "but also alters the traditional linear structure of narrative, fragmenting its continuities" (*Death 24x a Second*, 26).

11 In *Cinema 1* Gilles Deleuze famously dismisses the conception of cinema as a succession of still images bearing the illusion of motion, insisting that it is the continuity of movement itself that constitutes the medium of film. "In short," Deleuze writes, "cinema does not give us an image to which movement is added, it immediately gives us the movement-image [the image of movement itself]" (2).

12 The aesthetics of the late-twentieth-century home video speak to a technology that is nascent and unsure of itself. Unlike the contemporary idiom of selfies, Instagram stories, and memes, which circulate behaviours and patterns in bite-sized pieces, the home video is frequently rambling and digressive. Its representations hover and jerk about. Objects drift in and out of focus and scenes either are cut short or carry on for far too long. In this light, the home video as a genre of representation seems to demand stories without offering any of its own. The camera doesn't know where it's looking. Just as soon as it begins a general survey of the landscape, it is suddenly distracted or called upon by some person or event. This meandering is redoubled by the fact that the home video is notoriously pervious to its own means of production. "How do I turn this thing off?" we hear someone ask. "Push the red button." Or viewers face ten minutes of nauseating ground gazing as the camera swings from the hand of the person who forgot to switch it off. And of course, the home video is liable to being taped over with the Eskimos–Roughriders game, as indeed the last two hours of the Garcias' West Coast Vacation of 1990 was. In this sense, the home video's production is its story. If you know me, you don't really need to see my home videos to know what they are going to look like. Acknowledging their own specific socio-economic frame of production, all home videos seem to be films about the genre of home videos.

13 "Something abstract, something moving, something calling only for the very slightest help from words or from music to make itself intelligible – of such movements, of such abstractions the films may in time to come be composed." Woolf, "The Cinema," 175.

14 I am interested in how the adverbial *still* connotes "the continuance of a previous action or condition" (*Oxford English Dictionary*), a still against the odds. I think of the phrase "I still love you," which implies the endurance of a love but also, implicitly, all those things

that make that particular love unlikely – so many years gone by, that one time, the distance or boredom that has formed between us, or my love for someone or something else.

15 Footnotes are like stills. Fragmentary, supplementary, residual. Corresponding to a whole yet reminding the reader that there is more besides.

16 Stashu Kybartas's 1987 film *Danny* is a video portrait of the director's relationship with the film's namesake, a man who we learn at the beginning of the film has died of AIDS. Danny is depicted almost entirely in freeze-frames. We instinctively recognize the images as freeze-frames because of their fuzzy, granular quality, yet we never see the running video from which these images are "extracted." As a sign without a referent, then, the freeze-frame becomes a kind of medium in and of itself, independent of any whole. Rather than simply serving as details of some greater representation, they constitute both a lost totality and an ongoing form. This reversal, whereby the freeze-frame becomes the substance rather than merely a subtraction of something else, speaks to the fact that the genealogy of the cinematic still is more complicated than it may appear. As much as they are secondary artefacts of film, stills also represent an idiom in and of themselves. Cindy Sherman's film stills, for instance, are neither extractions from moving image nor photography. Such examples represent the still's emerging taxonomic break from the contrasting categories of moving and still imagery.

17 "The cinema has always found ways to reflect on its central paradox: the co-presence of movement and stillness, continuity and discontinuity. To look back into the cinema's history, out of passing time and refracted through new technology, is to discover a medium in the which these kinds of uncertainties have constantly recurred. In the aesthetic of delay, the cinema's protean nature finds visibility, its capacity to create uncertainty that is, at the same time, certainty because its magic works without recourse to deception or dissimulation. The cinema renders, in Dziga Vertov's words, 'uncertainty more certain.'" Mulvey, *Death 24x a Second*, 12.

18 Five hues of blue rolling in the background.

19 "There is one category of time not considered by Gilles Deleuze in his dynamic taxonomy of images: the interruption of movement, the often unique, fugitive, yet perhaps decisive instant when cinema seems to be fighting against its very principle." Bellour, *The Film Stilled*, 99.

20 To think of the adverb *still* (meaning up to and including the present) as a quality in and of itself, and not simply something that modifies something else, is to consider the rhythms and motions that form within that other, adjectival, stillness. It is a matter of that which lurches and starts only in the absence of movement.

21 A landscape without a horizon. Three men, eighties clothes, and a shared gaze, left.

22 For Deleuze stillness in film is not in any way a contradiction of cinematic form. Rather, it exemplifies the movement of time itself. In other words, for Deleuze cinematic stillness is an affirmation of movement because for him movement is above all a question of time. Stillness, then, is duration in its simplest form.

23 Given their lack of structure, home videos already represent mediations between movement and stillness insofar as they lack the cuts and montage that typically give cinema its narrative flow. Lacking the edited structure of conventional cinema, home videos with

their nostalgic late-twentieth-century hue share with the photographic snapshot an aleatory, open-ended quality. In other words, home videos tend to have a kind of silence and immobility usually reserved for photography.

24 "There is becoming, change, passage. But the form of what changes does not itself change, does not pass on. This is time, time itself, 'a little time in its pure state': a direct time-image, which gives what changes the unchanging form in which the change is produced. The night that changes into day, or the reverse, recalls a still life on which light falls, either fading or getting stronger (*Thai Night's Wife, Passing Fancy*). The still life is time, for everything that changes is in time, but time does not itself change, it could itself change only in another time, indefinitely. At the point where the cinematographic image most directly confronts the photo, it also becomes most radically distinct from it. Ozu's still lifes endure, have a duration, over ten seconds of the vase: this duration of the vase is precisely the representation of that which endures, through the succession of changing states. A bicycle may also endure; that is, represent the unchanging form of that which moves, so long as it is at rest, motionless, stood against the wall (*A Story of Floating Weeds*). The bicycle, the vase and the still lifes are the pure and direct images of time. Each is time, on each occasion, under various conditions of that which changes in time." Deleuze, *Cinema 2*, 17.

25 Danny: "He doesn't refer to me as his son. Instead of saying, 'My son'll be up to get it,' 'The boy'll be up to get it.' Whadaya mean *boy*? It makes me feel like Tarzan and the jungle. *Me boy*." Kybartas, *Danny*.

26 While the world of home movies can be enchanting, the experience of sitting through their minutes and hours can be incredibly tedious. Watching a home video requires a kind of editing process on the part of the viewer. You watch out for certain elements and stitch things together. Perhaps you search yourself out while simultaneously editing others out. Who was that guy? What was his name? The setting in which the video is being watched is likely a more entertaining scene than the one on the screen. The audience – maybe a family gathering during the holidays – fills in the lack of plot with their own live commentary. Perhaps they fast-forward or rewind to the good bits. But in the context of all these strategies to make the home video more consistent with narrative cinema, the technology is frequently uncooperative. The camera misses opportunities to weave elements together. It fails to build suspense. It struggles to establish focus and structure. The camera shows much, but says little. It lingers on something when it should turn elsewhere. Where was *I* in this scene? I ask myself.

27 Two men linger at the end of the pier, between them another man, my father. The three men stare off toward the horizon. This is what you do at the end of a very long pier. The blue water is oil-slicked with the oversaturated colours of VHS. The younger man on the left seems self-conscious. He untucks his baggy t-shirt from his short shorts, pivots and looks to one side, past my father toward the other man.

28 Given the dissimilarity between what I was seeing on the screen and the childhood that I carry with me, the video seemed more inclined to undo the cohesion of the present moment – us sitting around the TV as a family – than to explain how it came to be. Is it possible to speak of the past without either excavating or reconstructing it?

29 "Indeed, the main writings on the freeze frame do interpret these re-developments of stillness within the cinematic flow not only as the mark of an enunciative agency trying to exteriorize a photographic truth typically repressed, hidden in the invisible infrastructure of film, but also as the irreducible trace of a vanished time." Guido and Lugon, *Between Still and Moving Images*, 234–5.

30 We travelled by van about twelve hours from the prairies to the West Coast. This would be my first encounter with the ocean. Nearly twenty-five years later, the hazy, acrid images and the distant-sounding audio mingled with what my memory could scrape together of that time.

31 Desire often confounds conventional, linear accounts of the relationship between the past and present. Rather than a simple understanding of memory as a window onto the past, which now settles us into the present, or in other words, a linear, progressive account of time, I see *still* as evoking some of the more complex temporalities of desire, such as subsisting with, dwelling on, giving in, and letting go.

32 In 1990 a personal video camera was not a luxury that I could claim for my own family. The camera belonged to the family we had been staying with. And it was the father of this family who, for the most part, operated the camera, intermittently narrating the scenes with little observations about the landscape, gags about my dad being a sea monster swimming out in the ocean, and mock-catcalls at his wife and my mother as they strolled along the beach. At the age of six, I rarely hold the camera's gaze. Perhaps I wasn't quite old enough to understand and reciprocate the camera's interpolation, the man's gaze, or my own. Whereas the camera frequently engages my mother and my older sisters in flirtatious banter, I tend to flit about oblivious to the camera and the cameraman. When the camera does capture my figure, I seem to exist as a wobbly part of the landscape. I slip from view easily. I turn my back, or run away. I'm startled by the way my body moves, not quite ordinarily, sometimes violently, faggoty. The stillness of the freeze-frame allows for a kind of reclamation of my image but it also divests it of the qualities of motion that make it particular. When I engage my mother or father, I seem to want to draw them into some world, tugging at their arms or nearly climbing up their bodies – some world not of words along the ocean, the pier, and the beach. These are the images I want to still, the images that still.

33 "To a certain extent (the extent of our theoretical rumblings) the filmic, very paradoxically, cannot be grasped in the film 'in situation,' 'in movement,' 'in its natural state,' but only in that major artefact, the still." Barthes, "The Third Meaning," 65.

34 Whereas Deleuze resists thinking about stillness in film as a kind of interruption of time, Barthes, by contrast, has been accused of just the opposite, of perpetually folding the moving image into the logic of photography. As Garrett Stewart puts it, "when Barthes turns to the motion-picture medium for commentary, he notoriously resists its movements" (*Between Film and Screen*, 341n13). The paradoxical observation that Barthes makes is that "the filmic" is better ascertained in the still than it is in the moving image. However, at the same time as foregrounding stillness to the exclusion of the diegetic flow of film, Barthes also insists on a particular kind of movement that is unique to the still – or as he puts it, "a permutational unfolding" embedded within the fragmentary image

("The Third Meaning," 67). Unlike Deleuze's conception of the cinematic still life as the movement of time itself, the adverbial still that Barthes describes involves a consideration of a paradoxical continuity rooted in the very negation of time.

35 "The desiring anonymous viewer, who has not created the film, lip-reads what the character seems to say. Amateur films, then, evoke silence and opacity. The films consist of moments stretched yet arrested, and so they embed movement and stillness simultaneously, with their unique temporalities." Abraham, "Deteriorating Memories," 171.

36 By engaging the scrub bar on my screen, I track to find the single instance when the two strangers' gazes might have met, across my father and me. The older man with a mullet and tight jeans looks over his shoulder so that we just get a glimpse of his face. The moment of possible exchange seems to be a single frame. One instant I'm in the frame between my father and the man on the right with the mullet. The next instant it's three not four. I run toward the camera in a tipsy burst, disappearing at the bottom edge of the frame from which the pier extends, bleached from the sun, toward the shore. It's a pier built for tourists. An attraction, a municipal project in a suburban town on the coast of British Columbia near the American border. 1990.

CHAPTER 5

The Tremendous Image: Viceland TV's *Abandoned* Series and the Persistence of Ruin Porn

LEE RODNEY AND ADAM LAUDER

Attributing authorship to a neologism can be tenuous, but nearly a decade ago Detroit photographer/writer James D. Griffioen used the term "ruin porn" to describe the popularity of images of Detroit's crumbling Gilded Age, art deco, and prewar architecture.[1] Depending on your perspective, ruin porn – or sublime images of verdant decay in Rust Belt regions – has become either a specialization or a bad habit, in which Griffioen and countless other photographers, filmmakers, bloggers, curators, and publishers have become intimately involved. In the 1990s, Stan Douglas and Camilo José Vergara spent time in Detroit documenting the metropolis at the end of the millennium in spectacular suites of photographs. More recently, Vergara proposed that the city itself be transformed into a veritable museum of ruins – an "American Acropolis" – an idea that captivated the public imagination but didn't take root. By the time globalization came into full force, photographers and filmmakers from around the globe had descended on the city. In retrospect, charging admission might have been a good idea.

The City of Detroit began official bankruptcy proceedings in 2010 amidst a Michigan State–sponsored program offering tax incentives to promote film production between 2008 and 2015. Much of this cinematic activity was situated downtown. During this time, the city became the backdrop to a range of

Hollywood films, from full-frontal disaster spectacles to period pieces dramatizing the failure of the American Dream. A revealing digital artifact of this period, the Detroit Film Office, still advertises on its website that the city "offers beautiful lakefronts, picturesque landscapes and inviting cultural attractions, matched with an urban flare [sic] that can make your project exciting and unique." The didactic orientation of the office's URL is worth quoting in full as it suggests the ambition of a large-scale public works project: http://www.detroitmi.gov/How-Do-I/Find/Detroit-Film-Office.[2] This incentive program unrolled alongside a burgeoning documentary and indie film culture that included French filmmaker Florent Tillon's *Detroit Wild City* (*Detroit Ville Sauvage*) and a profusion of YouTube videos documenting and popularizing urban exploration in the area's numerous abandoned structures.

Viceland TV's ten-part series *Abandoned* (2016) not only traffics in ruin porn, but perfects the celebratory tone of this emergent genre of urban exploitation film. The spectacular character of ruin porn is symptomatic of the scale and ambition of Viceland TV itself: launched in February 2016 as an offshoot of Vice Media, a joint venture between A&E, Disney, and Rogers Media, it is a self-described lifestyle channel for millennials. *Abandoned* is among the first series to run under this banner. It begins outside of Cleveland, Ohio, in the Randall Park Mall, an abandoned seventies-era shopping complex turned ghostly megastructure. The series subsequently shuttles between far-flung destinations ranging from California's Salton Sea to shuttered fishing villages on Newfoundland's northeastern coast before arriving at its final destination of Detroit, the mecca of ruin porn. The decision to conclude the series in Detroit introduces the possibility of closing on a somewhat optimistic note, by showcasing the resilient efforts of long-time Detroiters to establish renewal from the ground up, as an urban ecology propelled by Black history, culture, and activism. However, the final episode, "Two Detroits," opens with nearly ten minutes of ruin porn: empty buildings and depopulated post-urban vistas, including the requisite high-resolution drone footage of the historic Highland Park Packard plant, whose impressive cinematic sweep is a ubiquitous artifact of the mass-marketization of the GoPro HD video camera introduced in 2014. A high-resolution, scorched-earth aerial survey of the Highland Park landmark figures strongly at the end of the ten-part series, following a survey of ruined industrial landscapes across the North American continent.

The *Abandoned* series was also released as the adjective "tremendous" took on new and frightening political connotations during the run-up to the 2016 presidential election. The epic ambition of the series is notable in its desire to map industrial ruins across North America: it captures a shifting picture of post-urban poverty in the US and Canada. That *Abandoned* coincided with the rise of the alt-right and the election of Donald Trump may be a matter of inconvenient timing on the part of its producers. But the series needs to be read in terms of its collision with recent political history in the US as well as the uncomfortable racial divide between the Viceland TV production team and its many urban Black subjects who guide the episodes, from sites in St Louis to Cleveland and Detroit. Like with most *Vice* magazine and Viceland TV productions, *Abandoned* viewers are framed as conventional voyeurs, and we are brought fairly intimately into the interplay between the subjectivity of the series' host, Rick McCrank, and his journalistic interactions with the people he appears to meet along the way. We follow a sensitive, well-intentioned skater from the West Coast, who comes out at the beginning of the series as a victim of family and societal abandonment, as he traverses the continent in the sympathetic guise of an adult-teen misfit (born in 1976), driving a rented Toyota Prius from one liminal site to another.

Abandoned is a skater's adventure that provides an escapist panorama of the creative destruction wrought by twentieth-century manufacturing and resource economies. It tends toward situating its viewers as implicitly and comfortably white and/or male, even though much of its audience may not be. At the same time, it casts about for universal appeal in situating all of us as outcasts and potential victims of late capitalism, by turns offering a redemptive script in visiting the overlooked and anarchic traces of human habitation and self-reliance alive within the ruins. There is much to like in the series, but we are left feeling that it was all done too easily and too fast. Much is left outside the frame, leaving the difficult questions veiled behind an orgiastic series of action shots filmed on location in the hulking shells of structures that once housed and defined the American military-industrial complex. The filmic introductions are smooth, distant, and impressive, often intercut with archival footage to situate the extent of the fall. As such, *Abandoned*'s opening sequences seem to employ ruin porn as a theatrical device from the annals of eighteenth-century landscape painting.[3] And while ruin porn is heir to the long-standing romantic tradition of the grand tour, with its prototypical figure of the peripatetic Englishman in Rome, it has also inherited the unsettled politics of the gaze in contemporary visual culture, which has only intensified as the disembodied eye of drone footage has become a mass-market phenomenon.

Abandoned brings into focus ruin porn's constitutive entanglement of subject matter, camera technology, and political temporality. When we first watched the series in November 2016, Donald Trump's repeated use of the word "tremendous" seemed to resonate in the panoramic opening sequence of each episode. Tremendousness is not normally associated with presidential rhetoric: it belongs to romantic literature, science fiction, and the sublime. Tremendousness conjures images of earth-shattering disruption, or more critically, the short, explosive flash that eclipses the subsequent and enduring awareness of loss and destruction. More recently, Trump has fixated on a far more prosaic use of the term: tremendousness as a special sauce, the key all-American ingredient in an economic action plan that would fire up the Rust Belt's abandoned factories and send men (real men) back to work. Trump's flat, flippant, and empty delivery, his takedown of the word and all of its associations, stuck to the drone-aided opening loop of *Abandoned* like a blowfly shattered on the camera's lens. As Trump's favoured adjective of late 2016, *tremendous* reverberates as a cynical and tyrannical point of view, a favoured aesthetic sensibility manifested by the series' signature hawkish images of industrial abandonment. This is not to suggest collusion between Viceland TV, Team Trump, and GoPro. Rather, we are interested in comprehending the political moment through its emergent aesthetics. Fortress America waits in the wings here, as both aesthetic armature and seductive ideal offering up the absent figure of the immigrant as a scapegoat for the economic woes so brilliantly captured in images of America's abandonment as ruin porn.

Swimming against the tide of disposability that characterizes a post-photographic culture, *Vice* magazine and Viceland TV have continuously made use of high-resolution print media and film to circulate a branded image of disaster for popular consumption. Viceland TV, like the magazine it developed out of, crafts twenty-first-century voyeurism from a formula harkening to the pornographic gaze first explored by feminist film theorists of the 1970s onward, from Laura Mulvey to Linda Williams. The politics of spectatorship woven through Vice Media productions are more complex than might be immediately suggested by this analogy, however. As implied by the title, *Abandoned* implicates its viewers in the trappings of nostalgia for the economic certainties associated with a military-industrial past, one that was largely white and middle class, eulogized through the spectacular zombie sites of late-capitalist and industrial ruination. Viceland TV's cinematic take on deindustrialization, like the photographic precedents of the 1990s, circulates in a specific image economy that bears witness to urban sites that point to the accelerated abandonment of the material remains of twentieth-century planning: its obsolete industrial cultures, its failed infrastructures (both capitalist and socialist), its utopian cities, suburbs, and systems of distribution. But to name ruin porn merely to denounce it would be to overlook both its currency and its impact.

Linda Williams locates the pre-modern origins of the modern pornographic film squarely in the nineteenth century with the proto-scientific gaze of Eadweard Muybridge. Returning to the beginnings of cinema, Williams links the early modern fascination with capturing and measuring bodies in motion with a more general "frenzy of the visible" that propels the ambitions of the cinematic project from the outset: a desire to see what cannot be registered by the human eye unaided by technology.[4] Extending these observations to ruin porn, we might see how the ruin and the proto-pornographic, as twin fascinations of modernity, easily converge in the high-resolution "tremendous image" of recent years.

While touring the Packard plant in Highland Park at the outset of the Detroit episode, host Rick McCrank makes a passing reference to ruin porn, leaving the topic just as casually as it was inserted in the narrative. The disjuncture here between the narrator's recognition of the genre and his nonchalant reproduction of it echoes a much earlier instance of *Vice* magazine's flirtation with the subject. Detroit resident and *Vice* blogger Thomas Morton wrote in 2009 of the then-rising interest in disaster tourism in his hometown: "At first, you're really flattered by it, like, 'Whoa, these professional guys are interested in what I have to say and show them.' But you get worn down trying to show them all the different sides of the city, then watching them go back and write the same story as everyone else. The photographers are the worst. Basically the only thing they're interested in shooting is ruin porn."[5] As a label, ruin porn suggests a prohibition on imaging industrial ruins, a proscription that simultaneously eroticizes and anthropomorphizes the sites themselves. The existing and somewhat limited discussion around ruin porn thus re-enacts a conventionally tautological ethos of the image. Identifying the pornographic in these romanticized views onto the recent past suggests a general ambivalence and uncertainty about what these images might mean. As landscape images they offer a privileged perspective framing the final scene of a long, slow disaster. Like pornography, they script a fantasy encounter without the hassle of experience; they foreclose insight and empathy, each image offering the promise of a paradoxically conclusive action shot. These images are consumed, for the most part, in distant places by representatives of an exclusive "creative class" that has notably displaced the very working class absent from the frame. The characterization of ruin porn and its attendant critical position typically stops short of analysis. Its usage tends to suggest, if not a moratorium on imaging former industrial sites, that there are better ways to represent and mediate the residue of globalization.

While these criticisms are logically founded, they lack the subtlety and complexity of the debates on pornography that characterized feminist theory of the late 1980s and 1990s, where, for instance, the exploration of the gaze was taken up through unpacking the "politics of representation," rather than calling for a corrected representation of politics.[6] By the 1990s, this emphasis on the gaze worked to unpack the role of desire in looking and sought to understand the mechanics of pornographic visuality rather than to prohibit it completely. In attempting to comprehend the popularity of ruin porn, one might ask whether a similar understanding of the pornographic gaze might be proposed, one that takes into consideration forms of alterity and disavowal at work in the global exchange of architectural currency and displaced labour.

Simply naming ruin porn as such also misses the point of pornography as metaphor. It often fails to address why we are drawn to visit, image, and imagine places that stand as the material ruins of late modernity. What do these images suggest in an accelerated culture of globalization that disavows its waste products? Do they trade in the polarized language of financial and real-estate markets, where "winners" and "losers" are held up as moral examples, object lessons of fiscal foresight and grave debt? Or do they serve as a kind of rear-view mirror to the recent past, suggesting that we can never really travel too far from the sites we leave behind without the potential for another encounter in the future? In *Beautiful Terrible Ruins*, Dora Apel writes of the anxious gaze trained on Detroit in this unending stream of photography of the last two decades. She stops short of employing the pornographic metaphor, however: "As faith erodes in a future that promises to exclude the many and privilege the few, the global network of ruin imagery expands and grows denser with a variety of contact or nodal points that connect to social issues." Apel further speculates that Detroit has become the "crucial nodal point" for a global urban imaginary, "the quintessential urban nightmare in a world where the majority of people live in cities."[7]

While romantic painting aligned the classical ruin with the emergent image of the national landscape by the close of the eighteenth century in Europe, theoretical interest in ruins trailed behind, appearing as a recurring obsession in modern aesthetics by the mid-nineteenth century. This interest persisted and returned with regularity throughout the twentieth century and into the twenty-first.[8] Julia Hell and Andreas Schönle observe that the seduction of ruins is "an experience as inescapable as it is old." They note the "manly" rhetoric implied in the various returns of "ruin gazing" that "jolts us into wakefulness."[9] Yet the ruin endures as an aesthetic and conceptual category within modernity that is "uniquely ill-defined."[10] Following on the heels of these conversations, could we see history repeating itself in these returns, first as art and eventually as pornography, as many commentators seem to suggest? Or is there difference to be found in these repetitions?

GOPRO OR GO HOME: THE INTOLERANT IMAGE

Abandoned's camerawork and drone footage, capturing urban displacement and the baroque perspectives offered up by Viceland TV's limitless skate park of industrial ruin, is difficult to distinguish from an extended ad for the GoPro camera, whose mass-market release in recent years, followed by the more recent

GoPro Karma (a drone-mounted version), has defined a subset of participatory observation in the extreme sports and remote adventure communities.[11] The camera became increasingly popular with these consumer groups as an affordable prosumer device that serves to document and legitimize the user's exploits: a $500 selfie stick that provides the promise of instant fame.

Rather than producing new or different perspectives, as the company claims, the proliferation and circulation of this material tends toward the reproduction of familiar tropes from the cinematic lexicon of gazes and their attendant forms of power and objectification. From the early modern god's-eye view of the panopticon to the colonial and masculinist fetishization of control, the perspectival promise of the GoPro brand reproduces the familiar trope of the singular, masculine, controlling visual subject of Western history. Nicholas Mirzoeff examines the trappings of visuality through the writings of Thomas Carlyle, whose texts on hero worship in the nineteenth century cemented gaze as an implicitly masculine position traceable from the battlefield to the plantation.[12] At issue is the marketing of the camera rather than the technology itself. GoPro cameras can enable multiple perspectives and points of view, but they are largely branded as gadgets for appending to eagles and Roombas alike, vehicles for capturing the polar ends of the spectacular and the banal, the animal and the robot.[13] Like Viceland TV, the GoPro Hero and the GoPro Karma are marketed to appeal to the ambitions of a generation of emerging millennial filmmakers, yet they fall short of producing anything inherently new. Rather than a departure from traditions of visuality that have been unfolding since the nineteenth century, Go Pro cameras establish a subject position that reinforces the same circuits of desire and control that have been in play for centuries.

If the tremendous image generated by the GoPro Hero can be said to exist, it does so in conversation with the "poor image" Hito Steyerl critically identified in 2009. The poor image emerged as a by-product of global, mobile networks, proliferating rapidly and cheaply as cell phone coverage expanded in the first decade of the twenty-first century. "Poor images," she writes,

> are the contemporary Wretched of the Screen, the debris of audio-visual production, the trash that washes up on the digital economies' shores. They testify to the violent dislocation, transferrals, and displacement of images – their acceleration and circulation within the vicious cycles of audiovisual capitalism. Poor images are dragged around the globe as commodities or their effigies, as gifts or as bounty. They spread pleasure or death threats, conspiracy theories or bootlegs, resistance or stultification. Poor images show the rare,

the obvious, and the unbelievable – that is, if we can still manage to decipher it.[14]

Ruin porn and the tremendous image, by contrast, can be distinguished from the cheap, low-resolution, and often muted narratives hinted at through digitally devalued pictures that fuel the conspiracy-laden politics of the present. Steyerl's Benjaminian take on the poor image suggests a kind of post-documentary optical unconscious, one that is simultaneously validated by the over-sharing economy of mainstream social networks as well the exchange value of the dark net. In Steyerl's estimation, the poor image circumnavigates the trappings of documentary and produces its own shifting veracity. The tremendous image, by contrast, flaunts its opulent resolution and seeks to reinstate the power and seduction of the single POV and first-person voice-over. Yet both kinds of image participate fully in the same economies of global violence, dislocation, and displacement that are "accelerated," according to Steyerl, "within the vicious cycles of audiovisual capitalism."[15]

If poor images circulate illicitly, or even outside of proprietary channels as Steyerl suggests, the tremendous image, by contrast, is bound to corporate-controlled formats and privatized media circuits. Viceland TV's *Abandoned* series occupies a mediatic space that parallels Steyerl's metaphor of a "flagship store."[16] Like the flagship store, one of Steyerl's analogies for the modern fantasy of "perfect cinema"[17] as an authorial, masculine trope, the high-resolution image fetishizes the spectacle of display as a cover for reactionary politics. It is worth noting that the critique of perfect cinema's technical mastery was advanced by Third Cinema as a subaltern force.[18] At the end of this metonymic collision, the flagship store emerges as a relative anomaly in the contemporary landscape of abandoned main streets and grey malls explored at the outset of each episode of *Abandoned* – it remains as a single fetish, a slow, experiential shopping amusement that attempts to counter Amazon's accelerated drone-aided forms of consumption. It is notable that *Abandoned* was released at the same time as markets for artisanal goods, like Shinola watches, created new spaces for proprietary capitalism by shuttling luxury goods into Detroit's city centre.

If *Abandoned* unwinds at the slower industrial speed of coal-fired industry it also evokes the spectre of race in contemporary American culture. The series highlights tension between a disenfranchised white working-class subject, one who is rural and suburban, and the Black subject of contemporary urban poverty. To speak of ruin porn without remarking upon the slow violence of geographic discrimination in the US, the many practices of exclusion from redlining to financial expropriation that affected the material and racial fabric of American cities in the twentieth century, is to overlook a central feature of absence and disavowal at work in Vice Media in particular and in contemporary ruin images more generally. Ta-Nehisi Coates has written recently that "elegant racism lives at the border of white shame." While there is nothing empirically racist about ruin porn, it is through its perspectival distance, its sublime "grace," its resolution, and most importantly its tremendousness that we sense an aesthetic margin that has been drawn outside of the frame. Elegant racism is said to be invisible.[19] The post-industrial and possibly post-human absence located at the centre of ruin porn disrupts the ruinous gaze only when one pauses to remember that there are still 700,000 people who inhabit Detroit, most of whom are Black. Seen against the backdrop of the political rise of the alt-right, the images conveyed by *Abandoned* suggest the implicit racialization and fetishization of the ruins themselves, counterposed by the white masculinist gaze of the GoPro that surveys the field for urban exploration as a potential act of conquest or colonization.

The tremendous image, like Trump's media persona, is thus self-consciously and overabundantly "rich" in sharpness and resolution, vying for dominance in a competitive media hierarchy. Where the poor image is strategically impoverished, swapping speed and accessibility for its transparently low status, the tremendous image announces itself as a large, affluent, and slow challenger on the same mediatic turf: the luxury goods flagship store neighbouring the industrial ruins of Highland Park.

ACKNOWLEDGMENTS

The authors would like to acknowledge the support of the Social Sciences and Humanities Research Council and the IN/TERMINUS Research Group at the University of Windsor.

NOTES

1 "Ruin porn" is attributed to Giffioen, who first used it in the late 2000s (Lavery and Gough, "Introduction").
2 Detroit Film Office, "How Do I," City of Detroit, accessed 29 June 2017, http://www.detroitmi.gov/How-Do-I/Find/Detroit-Film-Office.
3 Hell and Schönle, *Ruins,* 2.
4 L. Williams, *Hard Core,* 51.
5 Thomas Morton, "Something, Something, Something, Detroit," *Vice,* 31 July 2009, https://www.vice.com/en_us/article/ppzb9z/something-something- something-detroit-994-v16n8.
6 See Phelan, *Unmarked,* and Burgin, *In/Different Spaces.*
7 Apel, *Beautiful Terrible Ruins,* 6.
8 Garrett, "Assaying History."

9 Heller and Schönle, *Ruins*, 6.
10 Ibid.
11 Chalfen, "Your Panopticon or Mine?"
12 Mirzoeff, "The Right to Look."
13 Alexander, "From Dust till Drone."
14 Steyerl, "In Defense of the Poor Image."
15 Ibid.
16 Ibid.
17 Ibid.
18 Ibid.
19 Ta-Nehisi Coates, "This Town Needs a Better Class of Racist," *The Atlantic*, 1 May 2014, https://www.theatlantic.com/politics/archive/2014/05/This-Town-Needs-A-Better-Class-Of-Racist/361443/.

CHAPTER 6

Frames of Love, or
Love's Perspective

ADAM KAASA

This is something like the interior's
perspective on the window.[1]

Perspective performs a dual meaning. Etymologically, perspective can refer to the science of optics and to tools for seeing. In art and architectural history, it most often refers to the translation of three-dimensional space into two-dimensional representation by various means, tactics, and rationalities.[2] In this sense, it can be the effect of drawing or representing on a planar surface objects in relationship to each other such that on that planar surface they appear as the actual objects do when viewed from a particular point. But it can equally be the representation or the view itself, and not necessarily its translation. In more modern use, its ideational meaning is more pronounced. One gains perspective on a thing or situation by looking at it or into it through close inspection, by gaining distance from it, or by seeing it from multiple (not single) points of view.[3] Perspective can signify "a particular attitude towards or way of regarding something; an individual point of view," but also the ability to measure "the relative importance of things."[4] Finally, it can imply an outlook on the future or an expectation, as when one holds a long-term perspective, adding a temporal aspect to a spatial history.

sadiedada

Liked by **and 63 others**

sadiedada sky cinema

View all 6 comments

Gorgeous

Love!!

MARCH 3

Figure 6.1 Sky cinema, Instagram image, 3 March 2017.

If the definitional quality of perspective involves the dual meanings from its graphic and ideational histories, then I am particularly interested in where the first two notions – the spatial order, and the materiality of the window as that architectural gesture that frames the object of view – meet the mental and cognitive processes of having a perspective on something or, indeed, somebody. How does a physical perspective, out of the window for example, created as a framed perspectival view, change one's cognitive perspective on the world? How are these co-constituted and co-constituting? More specifically, what is considerable in considering the idea of love and the notion of this spatial and ideational perspective? Why do so many lovers look longingly out a window in popular cultural representations? Why do young people climb through a bedroom window in many Anglo-American-produced teenage television and film dramas?[5] Why does one of the most clichéd scenes from Shakespeare involve two tortured lovers and a window balcony? In Western leisure spaces, why is it that the view, from the hotel balcony for example, holds such importance? Is love a frame or a perspective? Is perspective a frame or a view? Is a frame only a means to see? Or is perspective a thing in and of itself? What can one say about love's perspective?

What follows is an effort to consider the relational condition of the window as a condition of and a contributor to love's perspective. Conceptually the chapter works through Erwin Panofsky's notion of perspective as "seeing through," with the "entire picture transformed ... into a 'window,'" alongside the historiography of Le Corbusier and Perret's confrontation regarding the historical change from portrait-style windows to modernist landscape "cinematic" windows, and finally through Wittgenstein's note 115, which reminds us that the propositional "this is how things are" is akin to thinking one is "tracing the outline of the thing's nature over and over again."

I turn to three biographical encounters with the window to think through frames of love. First, my childhood bedroom window, one I return to cyclically on an annual basis and which structures a feeling of homely love. Second, the windows that take centre stage in conversations with immediate family living in different cities (London, Hamilton, Toronto, Edmonton, Fintry, Los Angeles, Mazatlán), and the micro-relational quality of needing to share a view (a perspective) at the beginning of any conversation ("look at the garden," "let's show you what we're looking at right now," "it's dark right now in London, look"). And finally, the window of leisure or the view of rest as a signal of the structure of love's memory (holiday images through windows and views, the placing of these on computer desktops, mobile screens, and apps like Instagram). By thinking through our relationship with what we look out onto, by considering the frames we encounter the world through from specific domestic sites of kinship, I work to examine love's propositional quality and the structures that frame its endurance.

A WINDOW ON MY CHILDHOOD

Landscape is a natural scene mediated by culture. It is both a represented and presented space, both a signifier and a signified, both a frame and what a frame contains, both a real place and its simulacrum, both a package and the commodity inside the package.[6]

In my bedroom growing up, in Edmonton, Alberta, there were three windows facing east. Known as a gateway to the north, its relationship to gold rushes and mining in the early twentieth century, and to tar sands in the late twentieth and early twenty-first centuries, mark Edmonton as a city of trade and exchange, long founded on cycles of boom and bust, and on people coming to seek their fortunes. As with most of Canada, Edmonton is a settler colony, and the city sits on Treaty 6 territory. Out of those windows in my bedroom, I watched the sun rise some mornings from behind small postwar bungalows across the street. Dotted in the snow, or the parched summer grass, these houses and their own large picture windows silhouetted in the morning sun announced the rhythm of sociality embodied in my newspaper delivery job at the age of eleven for the *Edmonton Examiner*, up and down and up and down each curved walkway from the city pavement to the door. Or on Halloween nights, skirting convention, I ran across gardens and lawns to ring more doorbells and get more candy. Edmonton being a northern city in a prairie landscape, the sky was always more than half the view, prickled by evergreen and elm canopies planted by those settler landowners who speculated on dividing the land at the edge of the North Saskatchewan River for real estate.

Out of my bedroom window in London, far from the Belgravia of my childhood but not far from the neighbourhood of Edmonton (UK), a northern suburb within the M-25 circular roadway, I see a brick wall. No sky or trees prickling the sky, rather a wall of cooked earth. Out my other bedroom window, I see the back of a pub, a pub I have seen change over eleven years from "local" to dance club to craft beer and pizza bar. I see the air conditioning and plumbing, and the patio. Growing up with the view that I did, I thought I might always, in some way, have access to that view, something of the sky, and something of the tree. As a fourth-generation immigrant to Canada, with family on both sides who were able to prosper only through the state theft and redistribution of land from First Nations to European and other migrants through various proto-capitalist structures of companies, trade, governance, and war, the idea of sky, of emptiness, of a view, of a perspective, of a relationality with the frame of landscape that desires emptiness as a condition of its fulfillment is, perhaps, a condition of the frame of my childhood. And a violent one. The sunrise over evergreen is somehow framed in blood.

What I and many others grew up looking out onto in many Canadian cities, the view we had, was vastness. Radically empty nature over extended quiet suburbia. What a convenient architectural rendering to frame the conditional perspective generationally necessary to allow the continued settler colony to persist. Sky and trees, and next to them, nothing, or at least the sense of the nothing required to justify settling. The sun always rises, someone once told us. And so it does. And the warm rays wake me, one of my parents yells at me to get up, and something about everyday love happens. I shower (wash my hands of __?) and go to school.

THE "AS IF"

The architecture of perspective is, arguably, the window. As Anne Friedberg suggests, "the window serves as a symptomatic trope in these debates, because it

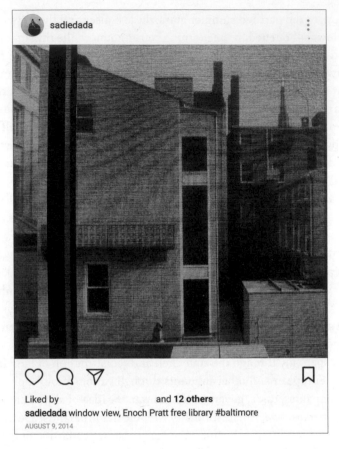

Figure 6.2   Window view, Enoch Pratt free library #baltimore,
Instagram image, 9 August 2014.

has functioned both as a practical device (a material opening in the wall) and an
epistemological metaphor (a figure for the framed view of the viewing subject)."[7]
The window is both an opening and a planar division. It is something associated
in modernity with transparency (and linked with the development of transparent
glass), but equally and earlier as a simple "material opening in the wall" for air
and light rather than as something specifically for vision. Indeed, early windows
did not always use glass; instead they had lattices of lead or other materials to
allow air to flow in, but not to be full openings to the weather, and if they did
use a form of glass, it was often opaque.[8] At the time of early renaissance writing about the rules of optical perspective, windows were not necessarily open in
the sense of framing a view, or even in terms of having a transparent materiality. The idea of the window, the "as-if" metaphoric capacity of the window as

opening, becomes more salient for the frame of a spatial context than the literal representative or mimetic effort of looking out a window and representing it in two-dimensional form. That is, many pictorial representations used the image of the window opening to frame a view, without that view necessarily being an actual view from a window.

This is in part the sense that Albrecht Dürer gave to perspective (made famous in the opening lines of Erwin Panofky's essay *Perspective as Symbolic Form* [1927]), when he references the Latin "perspectiva" or "seeing through." As Panofsky writes, "we shall speak of a fully 'perspectival' view of space not when mere isolated objects, such as houses or furniture, are represented in 'foreshortening,' but rather only when the entire picture has been transformed ... into a 'window,' and when we are meant to believe we are looking through this window into a space."[9] Panofsky is thinking about drawing and a drawerly tradition of creating the frame-like entry point to a view "as if" through a window. One draws, if one were to draw in alignment with Renaissance rules of perspective, "as if" for a viewer who is meant to believe they are not looking at an opaque assemblage of materials like oil, wood, or canvas, but somehow looking through a window. In performing the rules of perspectival representation, deception is the edgeland of truth: a representation can only conform to the "as if" of the actual through distortion.

The "as if" of Panofsky's as if looking through a window finds a correlate in Wittgenstein's note 115 on the question of the proposition's capacity to shift the register from actual to virtual: "'The general form of propositions is: This is how things are.' – That is the kind of proposition that one repeats to oneself countless times. One thinks that one is tracing the outline of the thing's nature over and over again, and one is merely tracing round the frame through which we look at it."[10] The difference between the thing and the frame finds resonance in a rereading of Alberti's 1435 *De pictura* by Anne Friedberg. Alberti's use of the window as a perspectival metaphor was not meant to suggest looking through a window and literally painting what one sees. Rather, as Friedberg writes, "Alberti supplies us with a Renaissance root for the concept of a windowed 'elsewhere' – not a realism of subject matter but a separate spatial and temporal view."[11] What this rereading allows is the possibility to examine the view out the window not simply as a kind of perspectival reference in literal terms – perhaps best represented by Leonardo da Vinci's "perspectival window," which literally puts a glass pane between the eye and the view on which to trace the world behind – instead suggesting that what one sees through the pictorial frame is more ideational.[12] That is, the image of the framed perspective was used to give a painting of a historical scene or view "as if" it were a literal or a real one. The window metaphor becomes a means to consider the relationship between spatial acuity and historical representation.

FRAMING RELATIONSHIPS

The window is the frame, at once near and distant, in which desire waits for the epiphany of its object.[13]

I no longer live in the place where I grew up. I no longer sit at the kitchen island, or in the living room. I no longer see the same things that my parents, siblings, extended family, friends who might be over might see out of the windows. I can remember what was there. I can remember looking out of each of them. The precarity of a foot of snow on the fence top out the kitchen window at night while filling up the kettle for a cup of tea before going downstairs to watch television with my mom and dad, anxious about the boyfriend they didn't know I had down in the basement the night before. The symmetrical darkness of the spruce trees out the front windows and the severe frustration of authority experienced in a domestic setting. The window in my sister's bedroom that I had always imagined the burglar coming in through at night and then coming home alone one day, and a man upstairs makes a noise, and then the police, but no windows broken. And watching the horror film at night and the window is a black pane thick like lead, and on the TV the stillness of the person, clown, murderer standing still, still on the other side of the window, and you see them, but the characters don't, or too late, and you look up and they're gone. And once a year, when I return home, I look out the windows again. But it's when I'm not there that they, the windows, take on a more present frame.

"It's sunny here today," my mother might say when I call in early autumn, and the idea of what she sees out her window makes me think of golden leaves, a wind bristle, the hopefulness of September with warmth and rot in one single breath, momentum hurling toward something like a crystalline blanket, and yet only wearing a sweater for the late-afternoon heat from the sun that's still hard-working, reaching out its warmth even as the earth tilts away as if to say it's time to say goodbye. Melancholy, maybe. Or longing. She's visited me here in my flat in London, and so when she asks what it looks like and I turn my phone to the white skies of my adopted city, I imagine she might be imagining what it means for me to be here looking out the window, and her there looking out, and both knowing what the other is looking out onto. Both of us feeling pleasure, some sort of spatial intimacy in knowing where the other's eyes might be drifting. One might call it love's frame. Literally.

Perhaps the people one loves are those out of whose windows one can imagine them looking. We fall out of love, possibly, when we grow apart, when perspectives change, when the view is just too different, ideationally and spatially. If the windows in the house one grew up in were boarded up or changed, the very structure of the relational perspective would shift entirely. The structure of the feeling of my white, middle-class, central-suburban Canadian homely love might

sadiedada
Echo Park

Liked by   and **37 others**
sadiedada #luxury
JUNE 2

Figure 6.3   #luxury, Instagram image, 2 June 2017.

be the sightlines from wall through couch, blinds to grass to electrical pole, to spruce, to alleyway melting snow, to house across the way, to generic green, to sky. I want to will an image of the mathematical perspectival optical triangles from all the points of view in the home through the windows that extend out to objects, buildings, skies, and other windows. To spatialize the possible views would be a veritable index of transversal perspectives, infinite and equal in number to the ideational perspectives – a spatial network of communicative action linking retina, glass, air, and matter. The matter of the views. The matter of perspective. Perspectives that matter.

FOREGROUND, MID-GROUND, BACKGROUND

Every face, every shop, bedroom window, public-house, and dark square is a picture feverishly turned – in search of what?[14]

In the 1920s an argument erupted between Le Corbusier and one of his mentors, the French architect Auguste Perret.[15] Perret, a pioneering agent in the use of ferroconcrete, and so a progenitor of modern architectural materials and building techniques, criticized Le Corbusier over the shape of the windows in his architectural designs. Le Corbusier introduced and advocated for horizontal windows, elongated through new technological developments in steel and glass production. Perret, on the other hand, defended the traditional vertical French window, or *porte-fenêtre*. In the *Paris Journal* in 1923, Perret suggested that windows were important embellishments for architectural facades, but more primarily that "a window is made to illuminate, to let light into an interior, and this is the reason for its existence, its prime quality."[16] His argument was that the horizontality disrupted both these functions, and also disrupted the scalar relation between window and human body. Le Corbusier, on the other hand defended the new window shape, arguing that the horizontal window was made possible in part through material innovations that Perret was known for, and new industrial techniques.

Architectural historians have interpreted this difference between Le Corbusier and Perret in at least two distinct ways. Beatriz Colomina suggests that the difference between the two is the difference between the space of the canvas and the space of photography.[17] Specifically she suggests that the move from the portrait-framed window to a horizontally elongated one changes the viewer's experience from a single-viewpoint perspectival encounter, a point of view that positions a viewer in front of a static image, to one more akin to photography, or with the panoramic flow or movement of cinema. In effect, Colomina argues that "the horizontal window is an 'architectural correlative of the space of the movie camera.'"[18] Where Colomina focuses on the relational experience of the viewer, the shifting point of view in relation to the shifting structure of the view, Bruno Reichlin expands on the change to the perspectival depth that a shift from portrait to landscape creates. For Reichlin, moving from the "perspectival window" – the traditional French window Perret defends – to the horizontal "cinematic window" that Le Corbusier introduces flattens the perspective.[19] Whereas in a picture window, one would see the full stretch of foreground, mid-ground, and background, the horizontal window effectively acts as a slice that cuts the foreground and the background to provide pure, flattened mid-ground.

Perhaps one way to think about this is in the colloquial phrase *to lose perspective*. But then the place to start is to consider what it means to gain perspective – that is, that perspective on a topic, or ideational perspective, is gained by examining different views on a topic, and in so doing gathering a broader sense of it. Perspective is therefore relational at its core – it requires the other and another, and cannot be enacted on its own. If one loses sight in one's eye, one loses partially, or fully, the capacity to perceive depth. That is, the world flattens into a mere presence – a pure mid-ground. Perhaps this is the core concern between Perret and Le Corbusier: "What does it mean to lose perspective?" Was Perret suggesting in his defence of the *porte-fenêtre* that the architecture of the window frame of modernity – that modernity itself – is a process of losing perspective?

Mere mid-ground presence might not be a loss, but something else. Perspective on a thing is also a distance from it. That is, perspective produces the structure of distance between here and there. Or another way to frame it is that perspective requires a distance to operate in tactile reality, and it requires the image of an "as if" distance in perspectival representation. One can hear routinely said that one needs to get some distance from a thing, or a person, or a relationship, to gain or to get or to have (a) perspective. Become too close to things, and one loses perspective. Attention to detail, cropping, the zoom are technologies of losing one perspective while gaining another. Are love and perspective, then, antithetical structures? Love requires closeness, perspective implies distance. How can love, then, have perspective? And what is being framed in the mid-ground of its pure presence?

MIRROR, MIRROR

Doors, windows, box office windows, skylights, car windows, mirrors, are all frames.[20]

Although I don't make phone calls very often, I do speak with people on my laptop or phone with regularity. Friends call me through WhatsApp, I FaceTime my partner, my brother, and my sister, and I Skype with my parents. My aunt, having now moved to live with my grandparents, takes Google Chats, and so for the first time in a long time, I see my grandparents in the window of the screen, and I see the window of their house in the Okanagan behind them, and the lake behind the window in the screen, itself reflecting the sky. All these relational frames of love trademarked by the capitalized app that intermediates the call, the data flowing through cables and data centres from pixelated screen to pixelated screen captured and rendered of value. Verbs created in boardrooms shift the guttural act of calling out, or making a call, into a mode of connecting through frames within frames, the windows within windows that mark contemporary digital relationships. I FaceTime; you FaceTime; she FaceTimes; they FaceTime; we FaceTime.

The late-1990s stock image of a beach – turquoise blue water, palm tree, wisps of cloud, white sand, and sun – on a PC desktop or screensaver was an early foray into an addictive positioning serviced by the image flow of contemporary social media. The uploading, sharing, tagging, and liking of these image screens announces the convergence of biography, aspiration, and relationship on screens that emit pixelated perspective. Slower than the twenty-four frames per second of celluloid cinema, the frames of Instagram move through the analogue flick of a thumb. But unlike the linearity of cinematic technologies that create the illusion of changing still frame into moving image, Instagram's feed is a constant change of content typologies (selfie, body shot, still life, landscape, urban image, food, pet, fetish, etc.). The frame connects them through its structural repetition.

Figure 6.4 Library window view #toronto, Instagram image, 19 August 2014.

Neither portrait nor landscape, the original square form further sliced the per-spectival possibilities of depth, but it is the movement, the flow through the images that makes the program more like Le Corbusier's horizontal shift than Perret's portrait window.

> "Well, in OUR country," said Alice, still panting a little, "you'd gener-ally get to somewhere else – if you ran very fast for a long time, as we've been doing."
>
> "A slow sort of country!" said the Queen. "Now, HERE, you see, it takes all the running YOU can do, to keep in the same place. If you want to get somewhere else, you must run at least twice as fast as that!"[21]

When Alice steps through the looking glass and into the other side, she is, quite literally, stepping into another perspective. The notions that everything is backward, upended, or turned on its head are routine descriptions of encountering the *other* side. It is the world of the "as if," the virtual. One of the cross-referenced definitions of perspective in the OED is "perspective glass," or a scrying glass often known as a black mirror.[22] Long used for fortune telling and pagan rituals, the perspective glass crystal ball was flattened and polished. Mirror, mirror on the wall. Black obsidian glass objects in our hands. Something opaque, but in looking to and through, visions, visions of the future, perspectives emerge.

LOVE'S PRESENCE

He who looks through an open window from outside never sees as much as he who looks at a closed window. There is no more profound, mysterious, fertile, dark, or dazzling object than a window lighted by a candle. What can be seen in broad daylight is always less interesting than what goes on behind a windowpane. In this black or luminous hole, life lives, life dreams, life suffers.[23]

What is the relationship of the act of looking out a window, being asked to look out the window, staring out the window, or looking through a window, taking a picture of a window, taking a photograph of the view from a window, imagining what it must be like to be looking out the window somewhere else, or with someone else, different either from where one is geographically or in time, to one's relationships, kinships, friendships?

Perhaps love's perspective is more akin to the Le Corbusian mid-ground gaze than to Perret's sense of depth, entrapped in the present, unable in its representational quality to capture what came before or after. Either fated to reproduce unknowingly what just happened, again, or something one never knew one wanted, without ever knowing a time that one didn't want it or couldn't come to think of desiring it. Love just comes there, is framed, has edges but not depth. It's hard to make out in this sense how far from or close to us love is, and how to put it in perspective with other things in one's life.

Love's perspective might be a window into someone's life. Or perhaps it is more like a signal that one sees and likes and recognizes what another or others put/s forward as a framed structure of their feeling of life. Something that they see and capture and share, and another sees it too, and the equal recognition, back and forth, of asking for the view, or of double-tapping and clicking, and liking, and loving, and comments – ";) <3" – and streaming, repetition, and knowing that someone sees another seeing the world and that the world sees things that yet another gets to see.

Love's perspective is, perhaps, to witness. And sometimes we witness through the window.

NOTES

1 Benjamin, *The Arcades Project*, note [EI,I].
2 *Oxford English Dictionary Online*, 3rd ed., s.v. "perspective, n."
3 Anne Friedberg's historiography of the metaphor of the window makes the argument that Alberti's (*De pictura*, 1435) original sense of a perspective being "as if" looking through a window has been misinterpreted as a claim of literal mimetic representation. Using the examples of early Renaissance perspectival paintings, Friedberg suggests there are occasional mono-centric viewpoints in space orchestrating the organization of objects, people, and environment in relation to each other along perspectival rules; however, there are often multi-temporal representations, so that while the spatial point of view might suggest a single viewer, there are in fact multiple temporal points of view existing in the same planar space. Friedberg foregrounds this historic distinction to engage the history of cinema not as a radical break from perspectival tradition, but in fact as an extension of relationships of time and space that have longer histories than are regularly assumed in the literature. See Freidberg, *The Virtual Window*, 25–56.
4 *OED Online*, s.v. "perspective, n."
5 A recent example is the character Jughead from the CW's *Riverdale*, a new televised take on the Archie comic franchise, climbing through Betty's window. Later in the same episode, the two share a kiss, holds hands, and perform the start of a coupled kinship. See *Riverdale* (2017), season 1, episode 7, "Chapter Seven: In a Lonely Place."
6 Mitchell, *Landscape and Power*, 5.
7 Friedberg, *The Virtual Window*, 26.
8 Ibid., 31–2.
9 Panofsky, *Perspective as Symbolic Form*, 1.
10 Wittgenstein, *Philosophical Investigations*, n115.
11 Friedberg, *The Virtual Window*, 32.
12 Ibid., 29.
13 Starobinski and Pevear, "Windows," 551.
14 Woolf, *Jacob's Room*, 133.
15 See Friedberg, *The Virtual Window*, 123–9.
16 Quoted in ibid., 126.
17 Colomina, *Privacy and Publicity*, 128–39.
18 Ibid., 134.
19 Reichlin, "Pros and Cons," 65.
20 Deleuze, *Cinema 1*, 15.
21 Carroll, *Through the Looking-Glass*, 25.
22 *OED Online*, s.v. "perspective, n."
23 Baudelaire, "The Windows," in Starobinski, "Windows," 555.

CHAPTER 7

Touched by a Whale

LESLEY STERN

We are on a small boat in a lagoon. All around: blue water and gray whales. *Eschrichtius robustus*, also called a California gray. Now and then and here and there you can spot whales spouting, spy hopping, flipping their tales into the air. Sometimes there are single whales, but mostly you will see a mother whale accompanied by her baby, they surface side by side, glide gracefully, and then slowly descend again underwater. We all wait with bated breath for the pair to resurface, the mothers can go a long time underwater but the babies only for about a minute and a half. Sometimes there appears to be a rhythm, a dance almost, to the way in which they appear and glide and descend and reappear. But mostly it's surprising – they pop up unexpectedly, far away or on the other side of the boat. We have learnt to look for signs: a footprint, which is a clear pool of water in the sea where the whales have been, or you can see their shapes moving underwater by the boat. You have to peer because the water is murky and shallow, and the whales stir up the bottom.

Sometimes they come close to the boat, or panga. You can see the mother and baby rolling over one another, playing, the mother carrying her baby on her back or nudging it seemingly toward us. And occasionally, just occasionally, a baby (a fourteen-or-so-foot baby weighing a thousand pounds) lifts its nose up right by the boat, and you lean down and touch its face, a rubbery hairy face, and it looks you in the eye, and then sinks down below the water. When it looks you in the eye you feel a wildness entering into you.

Or is it quite the opposite: the instinct for domestication, and for reassurance of our own human capacity for empathy and compassion?

I arrive in San Ignacio, a lagoon in Baja, Mexico, with a thundering headache. My whole skull, including the face, seems like a powder keg, ready to explode. The day before coming to San Ignacio, along with a monthly infusion of immuno-globulin, I had a shot of Neulasta. This was to top up my neutrophil supply, which has run dangerously low, putting me into the neutropenic range. Simply put: very vulnerable to infection. Neutrophils are a particular kind of white blood cell that protects against infection. Among other things they form pus, so if your count is low you don't want to get any cuts. I didn't feel or look neutropenic but the doctors were not prepared to take any risks on the verge of travel. I was warned that bone pain could be a "side" effect of the shot, that the skull is particularly targeted or frequently a locus of pain. It happens because suddenly a torrent of these white blood cells are pumping through the bone marrow, causing pressure. It is like having a migraine. Pain migrating all over your face and head that does not respond to ordinary painkillers.

In San Ignacio, on the lagoon, the pain seemed to disappear. It was there but my being was elsewhere: out on the boat, in the wind, the water, with the whales. Being visited by these whales is indeed like a visitation; they appear to us as though from another universe, although it is they in fact who are in their element and it is we who are the visitors. These mighty creatures from the wild ocean appear and swim around our boat, playfully nudging it now and then, swimming underneath, but never tipping it over. On the last day we saw a young baby, less than a week old still with its fetal folds.

We feel honoured and privileged to be visited by the whales. They have trav-elled nearly 6,000 miles from Alaska's Bering Sea to the Baja lagoons, the longest mammal migration on earth. We are in awe. Also, rather smug. Pleased at our human capacity for reform and betterment, for appreciating nature, for learning to leave a small footprint. And we are well disposed to think that the whales approach us because they are so relieved and happy to know they are safe, that they come to us in love. In *Seven Tenths: The Sea and Its Thresholds*, a magisterially quirky book written in 1992 that savagely describes and poetically mourns the devastation of the ocean by the fishing industry, James Hamilton-Paterson also lobs a few missiles in the direction of the enlightened eco-traveller: the loss of creatures, the changing environment "mobilizes in him a tenderness akin to vulnerability, to a point where a large part of his wistful concern for the whales and the environment generally is displaced fear for himself."[1]

Here we are on a small island, Punta Piedra, deserted except for this eco-camp. Deserted and a desert. Sand stretches in all directions, except for the mangroves, which ring part of the circumference, and through which we kayak. Helen B and I are here with a tour group from San Diego. The footprint of the camp is small – solar energy, simple tents, six chairs along the shore. Helen and I sit here after the morning boat trip with a cup of tea, and after the afternoon trip with a glass of wine, and converse, sometimes with others in the group, though we warm most to the pair from Australia as we can more easily exchange deadpan jokes with them. You can watch the whales and dolphins and sea lions and cormorants and pelicans and other birds appear and move across the view within a hundred feet of the shore line.

An island epitomizes the fantasy of a return to originality, and at the same time it evokes territory, ownership. Our island. Our lagoon. You can walk in the early morning along the Mexican sea shore, see no people, only creatures, assured nevertheless that you can return to safety, far from urbanity. This is my first real exposure to ecotourism, to professional travellers, to people who have been to almost every country in the world and are able to trade country stories like other people trade Jewish jokes. Perhaps I am entering into that realm so bitingly satirized by the Australian writer Murray Bail in *Homesickness*, a novel that describes the global travels of a group of tourists to diverse museums, real and imaginary, around the world.

We are told by the naturalists that splashing brings the whales to the boats, they like the sound. And if they come close enough you should try and encourage them to come even closer by splashing more. We do this with great energy. Six people in this small boat splashing like crazy, screeching with joy, a spectacle of ecstasy. Do whales have a sense of curiosity and humor? This is a question often asked (of whales, not tourists). One whale seemed certainly to be playing with us. In answer to our splashing she raised a fin and thwacked the water resoundingly, creating an almighty splash that engulfed the boat, soaking Helen who was closest and had been splashing most vociferously, but spraying us all. She then went under and almost immediately rose up out of the water, a perpendicular dive into the air, did what appeared to be a 360-degree turn, then subsided into the water and buggered off, out of our lives forever.

You imagine the whale is playing, performing, entering into a jokey exchange with us, but you do not really know. You feel in the presence of something unfathomable, a mammalian like ourselves, but a mighty being, a wild creature that in our consciousness for so long has been threatening. And threatened.

These gray whales have twice been brought back from the verge of extinction. This lagoon was once a killing field. When the mothers came in here to have their babies they were prime targets for hunters after blubber, and in 1857 Scammon's whaling fleet left few survivors. The second severe depletion occurred during modern whaling, when factory ships used to process the entire whale while still at sea. Now the gray whales are an Endangered Species Act success story. Now San Ignacio is a refuge. Not, any longer, from hunters but from other whales, from those toothed beauties: orcas. The gray whales, while birthing, find a refuge here from these mammalian killers.

The island and lagoon are a refuge for us too. For many who are ecologically disposed the natural environment, whether wilderness or an environment like this, seemingly restored to what it once was, provides salvation from the toxicity and pollution of urban living. I am less inclined to consider "nature" as redemptive in this way, more cynical about the tourist slot I fill, but I too have experienced the curiously transportive sense of being touched by a whale. And for an exhilarating hallucinatory moment I believed or rather sensed this experience as curative, imagined the whales might redeem us, cleanse us of cancer and the sins of the Anthropocene. The moment – or moments, for there were more than one – passed, subsided into mere mortal happiness and joyous fun. It does, however, make sense to me that when we touch the whales we are in turn touched, by the whales themselves but also by the way they summon all those other creatures of the sea that have disappeared. As well as joy they open a path to melancholy and grieving and anger for every living being that is threatened today by landscapes and seascapes that are changed in ways that can never be reversed. But if the whales are good at channelling other creatures they, along with those other cetaceans and large mammals (whales, dolphins, elephants, pandas), are so much more televisual, so much better equipped to channel human love than those crabby crustaceans and ugly insects and invisible microbes that too are threatened by disappearance.

This lagoon will never be restored to what it once was, the wild creatures will probably never have the lagoon to themselves again. But a new ecology is evolving. This refuge has been created through long years of environmental activism, negotiations between local and national and international interests, compromises between wilderness advocates and tourism, slow bureaucratic enactment of legislation. Once the gray whales visited the bays in San Diego but in the 1880s the entire herd was destroyed and they never returned. When they were on the point of disappearing from Baja the International Whaling Commission finally protected gray whales from hunting in 1946. They were given additional protection in 1973 under the Endangered Species Act. In 1988 the Mexican government established the El Vizcaíno Biosphere Reserve of which San Ignacio is a part. It is the largest wildlife refuge or sanctuary in Latin America. San Ignacio is now a UNESCO World Heritage Site, declared so in 1993.

A new ecology. The fact that there is no fishing or swimming allowed in the lagoon during the whale season (nor in the two other areas in Baja where the whales come, Ojo de Liebre Lagoon, formerly Scammon's Lagoon, and Magdalena Bay) means that the local fishermen lose their income. But in the new environment, shaped to a large degree by ecotourism, they become boat drivers and custodians (and are skilled at cutting free the occasional whales that still get entangled in fishing nets). There is only one fisherwoman at San Ignacio, Lupita, and she is a naturalist at the camp during the whale season.

Today there are about three hundred whales in this lagoon alone (about 10 per cent of which are estimated to be "friendly"; it is thought that these are whales that were here themselves as babies and so they have learnt that the humans here are "friendly" too). The most recent population estimate of "our" gray whales was about 19,000, with a high probability that it is close to the carrying capacity of the ecosystem of these animals. Our group constitutes one – the eastern – of two groups that exist in the North Pacific. One species, two populations. The other group – the western – has not been so lucky. It hovers on the brink of extinction with a population of around 150. They face threats from seismic oil exploration, entanglement in fishing gear in Japan and China, and ship traffic in their feeding and migration routes.

These migration routes might be changing. Though they once existed, there are no longer any gray whales in the Atlantic. Two recent exceptions: In 2010 a gray whale was sighted in the Atlantic Ocean, off the coast of Israel, then was seen off the coast of Spain before it disappeared. It is believed to have swum through a warm channel created by climate change.[2] In 2013 one was spotted in the southern Atlantic off the coast of Namibia. This was the first sighting of a gray whale in the southern hemisphere *ever*. Two of seven satellite-tagged western gray whales, instead of heading down Asia's Pacific shoreline to the South China Sea, travelled across the Bering Sea to North America. One made it all the way to Baja in 2011.

This is both marvellous and alarming. Gray whales may be about to move back into the Atlantic because we are opening a path for them through the Arctic. Climate scientists estimate that the passage will be ice-free year-round by 2030. It seems that there have been other similar migrations in the past. The whales appear to have moved into the Atlantic whenever it was warm enough for them to get through the Bering Strait. One migration took place 79,000 years ago, and then three others happened more recently, between about 10,000 and 5,000 years ago. This time is different. The climate change has been produced by humans, by greenhouse gases; the whales will have to contend with shipping lanes, oil drilling, and industrial fishing operations. But they will also likely have lots of good habitat to live in, more shallow shelves (as sea levels rise) where they can scoop up food. Gray whales are great explorers and they will go where there is food.[3] The ocean is changing and the species that can thrive there will change with it.

As we splash the whales and they splash us in San Ignacio Lagoon I wonder what they think, if they even conceive of us as humans, or if they comprehend us as part of a composite thing that we call a boat, but that they might understand as something else, perhaps another sea creature. I wonder what a whale would say if it could speak. They, like other creatures that live in the ocean, have a much more complex sense of space than us – gradations of light and shadow – and an acute and complex hearing range. They communicate in ways we do not understand. They seem to respond to the sound of the outboard motor. When whales approach the motor is turned to idling, a low thrumming. To me it seems undoubtedly the case that the whales who approach the boats are curious and fun loving. But when people say, and this is a truism, that they bring their babies to you, I am prone to wondering. Maybe they just bring their babies to the boat, most probably showing them that it is safe, that the boat has many sounds: a fairly complex sonic communicative system which includes a thrumming motor and screeching sounds – wows and oohs and ahs, and you beauty, and look look it's a baby – as well as tactile extensions that ripple the water, that touch and sometimes stroke.

Wittgenstein famously remarked that "if a lion could talk we could not understand him."[4] There is a paradox contained within this aphorism. For the lion would not use language as we know it, she would use a system of signs unfamiliar to us, and to which we do not have ready access. If she did talk she would not be a lion, but a human projection, as in *The Wizard of Oz*. Of course we have learnt to live with and communicate with some species whom we have domesticated and who have in their turn animalized us to some degree. Dogs and cats. And then of course there is the peculiarity of chickens.

In Pasolini's film *The Hawks and the Sparrows* birds talk. "I come from far away. My country is ideology. I live in the capital, the city of the future, on Karl Marx Street," announces the Hawk in this allegorical, caustically comic enactment of a debate between Marxism and the church. It is also a bitter representation of a devastated landscape following the Italian boom, and it is also a delightful homage to silent cinema. Between the loquacity of the hawk and the silence of cinema: poetry.

I imagine the whales may say to us "We come from far away" but I do not think they live in the country of ideology. And yet, like us, they do not live outside it. Between the visible and the invisible, loquacity and silence, the re-emergence of lost species is moving in ways it's hard to express. The way hope jumps and catches in your throat as you see a forty-ton whale rising up out of the water, slicing the air with precision and grace, and sinking down again into the deep. If poetry were at my fingertips I would tap out the words of an unknown language, but all I can do is try to negotiate the reefy shores where inexpressible awe hits the sponginess of sentimentality and cheesiness of anthropomorphism.

Back home Elvis jumps onto the bed, uttering a few guttural laconicities. I reply in human talk, a mix of English words and phatic noises. I believe he has a pretty large English vocabulary. My knowledge of "cat talk," on the other hand, is very basic. Sometimes I think he simply pretends or refuses to understand what I am saying. *Quién sabe?* Who knows?

Chickens, well, chickens are a more difficult proposition when considering this question of the talking lion. They are less loquacious and bombastically intellectual than the crow but they do seem to communicate through sound, which resonates in some way that I feel a part of. Not invariably and not all the time. They do not understand reprimands. I do not understand why suddenly, out of the blue, Sabrina has started pecking my leg quite viciously whenever I venture into the yard. She has also taken to bullying and pecking the other two, so perhaps she considers me another chicken. Yet there is what I take to be a kind of communication when I go out before bed to make sure the door to their inner house is locked. I speak and let them know it's me and not a predator approaching and they coo and chirrup very softly, the three of them forming a song line. It is a sound that moves into my chest, calming the spluttering old heart.

On a blue lagoon with gray whales, on the bed with Elvis, cooped up with the chickens: this is where species meet and where, between poetry and loquacity, wildness migrates, moving in and out of bodies.

NOTES

1 Hamilton-Paterson, *Seven Tenths*, 279.
2 Amy Wilson, "Whales Behaving Weirdly: Gray Whales Have Wandered into the Atlantic for the First Time in Nearly 300 Years. How Did They Get There?" *Orange County Register*, 8 February 2014, updated 10 February 2014, http://www.ocregister.com/articles/whales-600918-gray-whale.html.
3 Carl Zimmer, "Whales on the Wrong Side of the World," *National Geographic*, March 2015, accessed 10 May 2015, http://phenomena.nationalgeographic.com/2015/03/10/whales-on-the-wrong-side-of-the-world/.
4 Wittgenstein, *Philosophical Investigations*, 223.

CHAPTER 8

Time Gets Strange: Texan Hard-Luck Stories

JOEY RUSSO

> There are parts of Texas where a fly lives ten thousand
> years and a man can't die soon enough. Time gets
> strange there from too much sky, too many miles from
> crack to crease in the flat surface of the land.
>
> Katherine Dunn, *Geek Love*

TRACING HARD LUCK

Morning coffee at Hidden Lake RV Resort in Beaumont, TX, is a delicate ritual. It is both the display of a specialized storytelling form and a daily re-establishing of boundaries. What can and cannot be admitted into the space is anyone's guess, yet once settled upon in an improvisatory moment, these boundaries are then retroactively configured as the well-established rules. After the tension breaks around a story that might be drifting toward the unsayable, and hoarse laughter spreads around the circle of these middle-aged Texan women, the ordinary settles down again on its comfortable haunches, the field rests, and the next teller readies herself for the trial by story. Some have failed and experienced a sort of unspoken banishment from the daily arrangement of camp chairs outside Miss Laura's trailer.

It is three weeks before they finally ask me what I am doing there among them, these women who have perfected the telling of hard-luck stories, the method of the pregnant pause, the clucking of the tongue, the damning usage of "bless your heart," the limits of how far one may delve into the implications of another teller's story without stirring discomfort, or the stylistic flair of "expressive lying"[1] – in short, the catalogue of modes of talk that comprise the ordinary here. When I tell them that I am an ethnographer researching queer life in Southeast Texas, legendarily hostile region to the queer, the non-white, one of the least educated metropolitan statistical areas in the country and the holder of one of the highest murder rates in the state, they become silent. They stare down into their coffees, nervously fingering the sequined collars of their Malteses and Yorkies. The smoke of their Dorals or Capris hangs in the stifling morning humidity, the swamp air. I brace myself for I don't know what – feel that I perhaps betrayed the terms of an unspoken contract, that I will be characterized afterward as an aberrant hiccup in the seamlessness of this daily meeting. Bless his heart – he didn't tell good stories. But how I have misjudged them, the nuance and seamlessness of their craft. The awkward silence, in some miracle of shared atmosphere, shifts into a dramatic double beat – and the talk turns exuberantly toward tragicomedies of queer characters, sprinkled with dark laughter in the remembrance of odd childhood friends: beautiful brilliant brothers lost to Yankee cities or AIDS, old schoolmarms in slacks with rough hands, fey antiques dealers who wore monocles, ebullient choir leaders like Roderick Ferguson's sissies at the picnic, a pantheon of southern queers wrapped in the pall of loneliness that rurality brings. There is a shift in the object of the hard-luck stories. Instead of cataloguing the revelations of their own ailments or reposing in silences around the gravity of the hurricane that destroyed the entire town, the women's stories of the queer character, both accursed and sacred in its traversal of this place, take form.

The stories told to me during my eight or so months in the RV Resort broadened my thinking. I realized that if I wanted to talk about the scenes of life in which I encountered queer people in Southeast Texas, then I had to first grapple with the idea that there might be a regional atmosphere[2] that coloured the feel of these stories. I had to pay attention to the stories being told to me by everyone (queer or not), had to take seriously why they were all about suffering in some form, why they were about much more than the lives of humans, and had to recognize the manifold effects these stories have on those participating in them. This participation went far beyond simply sharing or recounting an experience of sadness. I had to think seriously about why the place I was conducting ethnographic fieldwork was held up as iconic – "Old Texas," a backwards, regressive, dangerous ideological zone – and how this reputation travelled not only outside of the region, but within it, amongst its inhabitants. This reputation was a badge of honour for some, talked about as a way of life that persists despite the perceived nefarious impingements of "liberalism." For others, it was a mark of shame, a leftover bigotry and backwardness that was luckily disappearing. I felt that in order to get at the feeling of this "monolithic" structure that was Southeast Texas, I had to consider these apparently incommensurable positions as co-constitutive relations that were grappling together with the idea of residual culture.

If, as Raymond Williams suggests, folklore is the study of residual culture, of those fading vestiges of past dominant ways, then the entire region of Southeast Texas is in this sense a folkloric object. It is a place that exemplifies a disappearing way, even for those who have never been and simply see it on the periphery as some shadowed place of backwardness, unencumbered by a grappling with modernity. The reality is of course much more pressing – to dismiss the way of a place as disappearing is to reduce multiplicity into the flatness of caricature. With closer scrutiny, one might find that the very elements that are identified as disappearing are in fact thriving across many parts of the United States. This is how I believe we came to a political impasse in the American presidential election of 2016, for instance. When a section of the public is addressed, perhaps unaware before that they numbered amongst this particular contingent, and the manner of that address takes as its defining principle the idea that they are "being left behind," then the onus on the addressor is not necessarily to appeal to something like rationalism. Rather, the obligation is to stir the fervour of this now activated, angry public that has become aware of the notion that they are seen as members of a residual culture and who see a viable discourse before them that focuses upon their being re-centred as emergent, to use Williams's language. As Lauren Berlant has reminded us of politics: "It is a scene where structural antagonisms – genuinely conflicting interests – are described in rhetoric that intensifies fantasy."[3] Their feelings must be addressed, for it is feelings that drive the fantastical discourse of their re-centring and, ultimately, their revenge.

To trace hard luck is to follow the tension that is created when new stories come from an "old" place. It is to hear this great impasse that this region finds itself at with the "outside" and to hear the strategies and stories that are generated which make sense of this profound impingement. The demands of an ethnography in such a region are foremost to make vivid the lives and stories that are in fact not receding into archaism. One of the great canards of conceptions of modernity in the United States has been the misuse of dichotomies – predominantly the idea that there are those who are "moving forward" and those who are being "left behind" or "moving backward" as discussed above; that some great monolithic ideological wave carries certain publics forward on its crest, leaving others to drown in its wake. The metaphor of the wave is apt if a bit clumsy, as these notions are often expressed through biological terms (evolution, atavism,

reversion), sometimes using rural/urban or south/north to represent backward/
forward motion.

TIME GETS STRANGE

The metaphorical wave of progress allows for the valorization of a particular political sensibility, while another way of thinking (usually a reactionary or conservative ideology of some kind) is relegated to region or place and a temporal
assignation, such as "southern backwardness"[4] in contrast to a notion of society
progressing. It abandons those unfortunates who have not conformed to the
machinations of this progress. They are going backwards or perhaps stuck, as it
were, in some previous epoch. I hope to show that the feeling of these temporally
arrested places, in the sense that Raymond Williams discusses in his theory of
structures of feeling, constitutes an "imagined elsewhere" while simultaneously
being grounded in the very real material conditions of the inhabitants' lives
in a place like Southeast Texas. These stories operate as adapted versions of a
traditional form celebrated in American folklore: that of the hard-luck story. The
hard-luck form is a genre of story told through a specific mode of framing that I
identify within the regional form of Texan storytelling.[5] The contemporary scene
of life in Southeast Texas that I encountered during my fieldwork was full of stories whose details necessitated the incorporation of previously taboo elements.
This is not to say that a standard of moralism has dissolved. Instead, storytellers
cope with the "way things are now," as they like to say, shifting their repertoires to
include frank sexual matters, drug abuse, queerness, the failings and embarrass-
ments of the body. These changes cope with the intensities of late modernity and
address previously unspeakable matters and shifts in language. They retain the
basic elements of the classic East/Southeast Texan story documented by collect-
ors and folklorists of the region, which almost always includes non-human animals and the looming shadow of industry as integral components:[6] men stealing
cattle and living to be plagued by the deed, justice coming to a cruel man in the
form of a mule's swift kick which brains him, feral hogs terrorizing towns, gargan-
tuan alligators pulled from swamps, hounds climbing trees, busybodies getting
their comeuppance in a dirty trough, the simple wisdom of an old man forced to
endure the highhandedness of a preacher's sermon, or a fed-up wife armed with
a pot of boiling water. Their repertoire of feeling expands, giving form to a shared
mode of experience that explores darkness and excess. There might not be a one-
line moral or a bit to chuckle about at the end. You might just be left there in the
discomfort of the story's bad place.

The hard-luck story is a regional form of what Richard Bauman called verbal
art. This verbal art animates the forms of desolation that always loom, and it

doubles as a show of proficiency, or competence as Bauman has it: "performance as a mode of spoken verbal communication consists in the assumption of responsibility to an audience for a display of communicative competence."[7] So, tellers of hard-luck stories do not only relate details – they are also locating themselves as adept witnesses who can in some sense perform the feeling of the region in insightful, disturbing, meaningful ways. They can embody the discomfort of a narrative form that is out of place or time. To address this uncomfortable marriage of Williams's notions of residual and emergent, it is helpful to recognize that the hard-luck story here circulates as a form that is at once a remnant of residual culture and an encounter with the severe industrial modernity of Southeast Texas. This severity is composed of a yearning for that which is lost and an acknowledgment of how "things are now" – different and harder than they were before in more complex and inextricable ways. People say their kids have "no link to the past," ravaged by drugs, enticed by the Internet, waiting to be killed off by cancers, twiddling their thumbs in the thickness of this oblivion. These pronouncements sit in the uncomfortable space between residual and emergent – they are the grappling of ebb and flow. This is the core of the hard-luck story – a relationship of entanglement[8] composed through a relation that is not seamless but abraded – it rubs the wrong way. Southeast Texas is a mixed ecosystem of Big Thicket piney woods razed of their longleaf pines and infested with pine beetles, Gulf Coast beaches always reeling from the last hurricane, and swamps and baygall filled with gators and the campfire tales of the lost "dog people" of the Neches River bottom.[9] It is the tense blend of Cajun-Louisiana and Anglo-Texan cultures, of vivid Black American and Creole histories[10] and rigidly anti-black, white-supremacist histories. It is the meeting place of debauchery and conservatism, of the queer body and its assailants – often occurring in the same subjectivities, in the same stories. It is the crossroads of deep fundamentalisms and profound sins. There is something extra in its regionality – what one Texas travel website cheekily calls a *lagniappe*,[11] from the Louisiana French term (adopted from Quechua) for a bonus thrown into a transaction by a merchant.

What does it mean to think about structures of feeling residing in a region's story forms? Stories become singular in their telling and exemplify or embody, for their participants, instantly recognizable craftsmanship and a moment of "things throwing themselves together."[12] It is as if the accounting of events performs some necessary accrual around the ladies in the RV park that throws them back into life – like a timeout huddle before plunging back into the game. One of Bauman's great contributions to the ethnographic analysis of stories was considering storytelling as verbal art; this brought the notion of aesthetics into the commonplace setting of the everyday interactional field, as well as redefined the boundaries of how certain forms become shared aesthetic events or, as he put it, "the esthetic dimension of social and cultural life in human communities as manifested through the use of language."[13] To think about a structure of feeling in a region's story forms (rather than as exemplified in a social movement or captured in a literary passage) requires the concession that entire structures of feeling can emerge from that which is not "emergent" in the sense that Williams describes. Ben Highmore's revisiting of Williams begins the work of shifting from the locating of structures of feeling in literary forms to a wider field: "The joining together of a socially phenomenological interest in the world of things, accompanied by an attention to historically specific moods and atmospheres, is, I think, a way of mobilising the critical potential of 'structures of feelings' towards important mundane cultural phenomena."[14] If we are to take seriously the idea that structures of feeling are not universal or shared, then we must look closely at those regions that lie outside the purview of a cultural critic such as Williams whose dichotomous method finds that the feeling of an age happens definitively, as it were, somewhere and not somewhere else. The entire basis of the structure of feeling is that its function is not in the maintenance of a supposed status quo, but in its disruption. As Williams puts it, "The effective formations of most actual art relate to already manifest social relations, dominant or residual, and it is primarily to emergent formations that the structure of feeling, *as solution*, relates."[15] The implication is that such emergent structures, not "most actual art," must take place under the constraint of some intensity in which they are recognized eventually as having been definitive. This intensity is traditionally recognized as located within movements that fall on the side of the urban, the left, and the radical. Williams's examples of structures of feeling set a precedent not only for where precisely the recognition of emergent forms can take place, but also for the explicit positionality to which the power of designation is assigned. That place is the left, and it is within the forms of critique common to the left that such engagements remain.

This is not to say that such engagements are unfounded, merely that they presuppose where the centre of culture lies and what must be done in order to wrench the definition of an epoch away from a dominant mode. The presupposition is that only some distortion within the dominant mode, some "modification or disturbance in older forms" can comprise a definitive structure of feeling. Its movement is defined by a break. In order to understand the feeling of a place operating outside of the strictures of definitive breaks of this order requires the aforementioned shift – in which structures of feeling can be located as viable forms that *do not* break definitively from other, precipitated forms, but that work within them, that might reside over longer periods of time rather than the temporary incandescence in the break of a movement. This shift in what structures feeling might best be recognized in the context of place – of those places outside of the purview of "change" as it is broadly understood – where the feeling subject's relationship to place, in this case the stagnation and gnarled quality of place, affects her sensorium profoundly. Given that the location of structures of feeling operates within this logic of change despite Williams's desire to describe the social present as an active process of perpetual unfolding, there must be examples for which emergent structures of feeling are, in essence, absent. Such a concept, in which the entire composition of place is based upon the notion of tyrannically stubborn and unchanging stagnancy, is exemplified in the profound mythos of the American South and, for our purposes here, Southeast Texas – a region that is, even according to many of its own inhabitants, superlative in these qualities.

SEEPAGE

Joyelle McSweeney's necropastoral, that mode "in which the fact of mankind's depredations cannot be separated from an experience of 'nature' which is poisoned, mutated, aberrant, spectacular, full of ill effects and affects,"[16] finds one of its nodes in the machinations of capital, the churning out of bodies made sick and unfit for service in the refineries in Southeast Texas. McSweeney outlines the processes of the necropastoral, chief among them for this study being seepage – a mode in which the subjectivity and body of the Southeast Texan find themselves engaged so profoundly that it has come to constitute a commonplace, even exhausted, form of hard-luck story. This is to say that seepage is both symbolic and literal, understood as both the process by which materials flow out of something and into something else and the noun that signifies these seeped or seeping materials. Seepage is action and object.

In the necropastoral machine of Southeast Texas, one is unlikely to avoid cancer. The disease is so commonplace here (considerably higher than the national average)[17] that its presence has become wrapped in the regional tradition. How cancer inevitably appeared in one's family is a familiar type of hard-luck story, starting with the mid-twentieth-century mesothelioma/asbestosis/Port Neches rubber plant stories that began official investigations into the links between the petrochemical plants and illness[18] and resulted in many lawsuits against oil and construction companies in the later twentieth century. These lawsuits did little to permanently alter the labour conditions in which workers became ill, having been exposed through industrial boilers, turbines, pumps, and pipe insulation. Husbands brought home asbestos-seeped coveralls, which their wives and children then laundered, thereby exposing the entire family in some cases. Southeast Texas became the cancer belt of Texas.

The style of the cancer hard-luck story tends toward the notion of inevitability: cancer is the defining event that waits somewhere along the path of every life, biding its time. Cancer has seeped into the air, water, food, bodies succumbing to the disease in ways that exceed the linked causal chains of industrial consequence. It is no longer only the providence of the poor, although the poor continue to die of it in higher numbers. It is now a mode, and so its experiential qualities are shared, they circulate as stories and repeat as repertoires – they fill medical waiting rooms with well-rehearsed tales of sickness, comparing ailments and side effects and severities. How a tumour was discovered, the ominous or apathetic way in which the doctor diagnosed, the intensities of chemo and radiation treatments, the remoteness of one's living situation and proximity to treatment facilities, the impossible cost of care and the wiliness of insurance companies, what the body does now that it has been besieged, the history of sickness in one's family, the fear of death and pain. The utility of seepage is twofold. It constitutes the yielding of both place and narrative to sickness. Cancer seeps into bodies as it seeps into stories. It is dealt with as what assails the body and the place into a situation of hard luck.

When I was told stories of cancer by the old-timers at the Mamie McFaddin-Ward Cancer Center in Beaumont – some of whom were there as patients and some as volunteers, sitting together in the waiting room doing puzzles around a table – they almost always made sure to preface the telling with a statement that situated the present as having succumbed to seepage. One man, a patient and a retired botanist who came to sit in the lobby of the centre most days regardless of whether or not he was being seen by his oncologist, told me about the days before "it got into the air." He had assisted an expert tree specialist brought over from Germany during the height of the pine beetle scourge in the mid-twentieth century and remembered days before the air and the forests were sick. A good friend of his who had suffered from chronic respiratory issues had been told by a doctor, off the record, that if he wanted his lung problems to go away he had to move up above one of the farm-to-market roads north of Jasper County somewhere. This road was evidently the boundary at which air became breathable again, outside the long shadow of the refineries that circle the Southeast Texan perimeter. The man's friend had taken the doctor's advice, and "sure enough, his breathing got better and he didn't have any trouble afterward." Another story that came up on multiple occasions at the centre had to do with a media spectacle that spoke to the intolerable shock of sickness emerging in the community. Hearing it, one could almost sense a kind of pride in its tragedy, a detailing of the ways in which the community itself reared back against the powers that asked them to fall in line, to take a number and wait their turn. The gist of the story was this: a man from Vidor murdered a Beaumont lawyer whose firm refused to represent him in an asbestos poisoning case. The Vidor man, elderly and perhaps suffering from some form of senility or dementia as well as mesothelioma, returned to the law office after being refused representation and murdered one of the attorneys with a shotgun. As it turned out, the murdered man was not the attorney who had refused him service, but his partner at the firm. So the murder was treated as a case of mistaken identity and all the more tragic for being so. The murdered lawyer story leaves the teller and their audience in a place of confoundedness; what to do with the information that many people are sick and the functionality of dealing with this event, the necropastoral event, are left open.

In his essay "On Confoundedness," Brian Blanchfield considers the sensation of time getting strange, which I understand to be expressed through hard-luck stories as dwelling within the perpetuity of the confounding event: "In confoundedness, the bottom has been obscured or has fallen out altogether. Clarification may yet be an antidote to confusion, the confused person understands, but the promise of bewilderment's finitude, the basic assurance that 'this too shall pass,' has dropped from confoundedness. So it is a form of suffering."[19] The primary sensibility of the hard-luck story is thus a shared reeling, a feeling that the orientations of those who have witnessed its telling have been left askew. This is the manner by which stories from a "residual culture" become emergent. They do so by performing an act of "presencing" the world that they describe, leaving us in the "now" of how things are. The very idea of the present within ethnographic analysis is fraught. Post–*Writing Culture*, debates have in some form carried on since the 1980s around the notion of the "ethnographic present" as either an unfortunate manifestation of postmodern "reflexivity" in ethnographic writing or a necessary method for dealing with the presence of the ethnographer in the field. For my part, the choice to write ethnographic scenes using a variety of tenses reflects a grappling with the complex framing of temporality by my interlocutors. The hard-luck stories use the now to signal a "shared time"[20] that does not reflect temporal coordinates, but the evocation of a shared feeling. It is the strange texture of this "now" that perhaps also seduces the ethnographer into what some criticize as the travesty of the ethnographic present. Since it is an experiential type of reflection, the feeling that originally arrested the attention of the ethnographer in whatever moment they are portraying seems agential. It seems capable of promoting itself. It wants to be happening "now" again. The supposed temporal dishonesty of the ethnographic present is ironically constituted by a desire to portray the moment of the present in the most capacious sense of the word – as a now that formally calls forth the past and hopelessly signals toward the future, while reeling in the strange time of the present.

NOTES

1 Bauman, *Story, Performance, and Event.*
2 Powell, *Critical Regionalism.*
3 Berlant, "Trump, or Political Emotions."
4 Herring, *Another Country.*
5 Bauman, "Verbal Art as Performance."
6 Brett, *There Ain't No Such Animal.*
7 Bauman, *Story, Performance, and Event,* 11.
8 Ogden, *Swamplife.*
9 Pittman, *Stories of I.C. Eason.*
10 Chambers, "Goodbye God."
11 "Beaumont," Tour Texas, https://www.tourtexas.com/destinations/beaumont.
12 Stewart, "Weak Theory."
13 Bauman, "Verbal Art as Performance," 290.
14 Highmore, "Formations of Feelings," 144.
15 Williams, "Structures of Feeling," 134.
16 McSweeney, "What Is the Necropastoral?"
17 "Age-Adjusted Invasive Cancer Incidence Rates in Texas," Cancer Incidence File, February 2018, Texas Cancer Registry, http://www.cancer-rates.info/tx/.
18 Harry Hurt III, "The Cancer Belt," *Texas Monthly,* May 1981, http://www.texasmonthly.com/articles/the-cancer-belt/.
19 Blanchfield, *Proxies,* 72.
20 Hastrup, "The Ethnographic Present."

Figure 9.1 Yoshiko Yamaguchi, Eames House, Pacific Palisades, 24 July 1951.

CHAPTER 9

The Future Is Hybrid:
Isamu Noguchi and the
Mid-Century Modern

YOKE-SUM WONG

PLAYING JAPANESE

Sometime on 24 July 1951,[1] Charles Eames took a picture.

Yoshiko Yamaguchi kneels in her kimono, the view of her gently interrupted by the shimmering reflections in the glass. She cuts a forlorn figure, beautifully serene as she gazes outside the glass walls of Charles and Ray Eames's iconic Pacific Palisades home, Case Study House #8. Behind her, early versions of the akari light sculptures designed by her husband-to-be, the celebrated sculptor Isamu Noguchi. Known for their choreographed dinner parties, the Eameses took great care with the staging details. The sparse arrangement of the room, a hybrid modernism of meditative minimalism, was attributed to Noguchi, who stripped the house entirely for the event[2] and had often said, "All that you require to start a home are a room, a tatami, and Akari."[3]

The occasion was a traditional Japanese tea ceremony and dinner hosted by the Eameses with Charlie Chaplin and Isamu Noguchi as honoured guests. The Eameses were admirers of Japanese aesthetics, at times organizing tea ceremonies with and for friends and acquaintances. This gathering was particularly elaborate.[4] The others present were Christian and Henrietta Lederbom, Betty Harford, Iris Tree and the screenwriter

Ivan Moffat, her son, and the actor Ford Rainey. In her memoirs, Yoshiko Yamaguchi, who was born in northern China and more comfortable in a cheongsam and high heels, remembered preparing a sukiyaki meal that Chaplin had requested.[5] Shizuye (Sosei) Matsumoto,[6] who supervised the tea ceremony, referred to Yamaguchi as her student. During the sake rounds, Chaplin stood up, announced he would present a special act, and went on to perform a *Nō* dance that Yamaguchi praised as "wonderfully done." Charlie Chaplin admired Japan and studied kabuki, *Kyōgen*, and *Nō* theatre to shape and perfect his own art. Yamaguchi and he would remain lifelong friends, with the latter considering the former a great inspiration. Both, perhaps, were united by their shared status of being blacklisted by the House Un-American Activities Committee (HUAC). Chaplin would leave for Switzerland, and his 1952 movie *Limelight*, often highly praised and acknowledged by critics as his most personal work, would open to a limited and cautious reception in a McCarthyite America.

Whatever myriad ways Cold War orientalism expressed itself in the wider American public after 1945, the everyday assemblages of the exotic east were an Asia Pacific jumble of Hollywood imaginaries, music, dinner party trends, and interior decor.[7] Yoshiko Yamaguchi was herself in America to film King Vidor's *Japanese War Bride*, the story of a Korean War veteran who returns to California with his Japanese wife only to encounter bigotry from family and friends. A *Life* magazine award for the best-decorated Levittown home purportedly went to a house with a chinoiserie Sino-revival theme.[8] Even in Nashville, Tennessee, Hank Williams's wife Audrey had decorated their home at 2510 Franklin Road with an oriental flair, using "shiny black lacquer and lots of dragons."[9] Amid the suburban Far East interior kitsch, the iconic coffee table that would define our contemporary affection for the mid-century modern North American design would be Isamu Noguchi's free-form glass-top table balanced on two biomorphic shapes in sinuous hardwood. Conceiving it in 1939 as the Goodyear[10] table for A. Conger Goodyear's newly built International Style house in Old Westbury, NY, Noguchi would eventually redesign the table.[11] The more minimalist variant of the Goodyear table served as illustration for Herman Miller design director George Nelson's "How to Make a Table" in 1944. In 1947, Herman Miller became the official manufacturer of Noguchi's redesigned coffee table.

The photographs of the dinner and tea ceremony would be sent to the Eameses' friend in Kyoto, Soko Sen. In a letter dated 26 October 1951, Charles Eames wrote:

> Any feeling that I may have about the relationship of this beautiful
> ancient ceremony to the architecture which houses it, can only be
> based on an intuitive feeling for I have no extensive knowledge of

either one. If our house was as sympathetic to the ceremony as it seemed, I believe it was because it had to some degree, the elements that seem necessary in any architecture that is to form a background for such an idea. The most important thing that it (the house) has in common with the Japanese tea house, is the fact that it uses extremely humble materials in a natural and uncontrived way. The bare and unadorned I-beams and open webbed steel joists serve very much as the stripped wood structural members of the tea house.

Charles, who was sometimes photographed domestically in his kimono or a yukata, would go on to express his discomfort with the intrusion of Westernized tables and chairs into such a setting and explained his view of architecture as "creating a space through which the body moves in relation to a very few and carefully selected objects." "The environment of the idea," he asserts, "must be humble, sensitive and unobtrusive." In the photographs, the tea ceremony and food are prepared and served on individual little tables befitting the event. The famous LTR (low table rod base) side table was made in 1950, of plywood and plastic laminate or wood veneer on U-shaped metal rods and cross braces. From an angle, the metal rods formed a starburst pattern, indicative of design in the atomic age, an age enamoured with the harnessing of the minuscule for power. The tea ceremony would do much to enhance the cultural versatility and popularity of the LTR table.

TUMBLEWEED

The tumbleweed is perhaps one of the most resourceful and resilient plants in nature, a diaspore that, once it matures and dries, detaches itself from its root and tumbles away, aided by the winds. During the tumbling, the propagules escape and scatter, or when it comes to rest in wet conditions, the tumbleweed releases the seeds and germination is made possible. Wikipedia goes on to state that the death of the plant's structure is important and functional – for it is in death that the seeds are released and reproduction occurs. Another generation of the species then reinvigorates the landscape.

There is a well-known photograph of Charles and Ray Eames in their house. Seated as if in earnest conversation, both are surrounded by their assemblage of objects in the room Isamu Noguchi had once cleared out for the tea ceremony in 1951. Charles Eames confessed that after the tea ceremony, the house stayed empty and they quite enjoyed the open space, but then over time, all of the stuff crept back, "bit by bit." The house was an "attractive collection of ready-mades, like a collage," built for such ludic arrangements with its informal interiors and

Figure 9.2 Interior of Eames House, Case Study #8, Pacific Palisades.

versatile furniture – objects and furnishings that could be moved about.[12] "The whole thing is a kind of game of found objects," acknowledged Charles. For Ray Eames, floors and ceilings were a canvas to play with, and the house was more akin to an artistic playground – it was like a Joseph Cornell box.[13] Home is where the art is.[14]

A keen eye cannot help but notice the delicate tumbleweed hanging from the ceiling of the double-storey, seventeen-foot-high living room, in the top right corner of the photograph. It is just not any tumbleweed, claims their grandson, Eames Demetrios. In 1941, in a badly spelled handwritten note simply dated "Tuesday," Charles Eames proposed to Ray Kaiser, his fellow student at the Cranbrook Academy of Art in Michigan. He was thirty-four and broke, but it was the beginning of one of the most dynamic and influential relationships in Amer-

Figure 9.3 Tumbleweed.

ican design history. Married in June 1941, and with little money, the couple took their road-trip honeymoon and headed out to California in search of the design solutions that revolved around their moulded-plywood chair production. Some-where in the southwest, Charles and Ray came upon the tumbleweed that would become very much part of their lives and would inform their design sensibilities. The tumbleweed and two abstract expressionist paintings by Hans Hofmann[15] would come to rest, along with a natural horn or a *cor solo*, hanging above the living room in their own ethereal landscape beside Noguchi's akari lanterns.[16]

Tumbleweeds more than featured in the Herman Miller showroom instal-lations and in the Eames silhouette photographs. They were prominent in the Eameses' studio and often formed part of the interior bric-a-brac alongside other disparate objects. They were objects to think and design with. But for Eames Demetrios, as he recalled, the tumbleweed in his grandparents' house had been a childhood fascination; it was "hypnotic," "spinning in the light." Over the years, the tumbleweed would become more brittle and diminished as bits and pieces fall away. Quoting his mother, the artist and graphic designer Lucia Eames, Charles's daughter from his first marriage to Catherine Woermann, he said, "When it's finally just a piece of string attached to the tiniest bare nub, it will be our responsibility – our generation's – to go out into the desert and find just the right tumbleweed and hang it from this ceiling."

I have often wondered how Ray Eames really felt when Arlene Francis introduced her on television as the "very able woman" behind the successful man on the NBC show *Home* (1956).[17] One swears that Charles turned away to wince or grimace in embarrassment. In New York to launch the Eames lounge chair, Charles Eames takes centre stage before Ray is brought in as Mrs Eames who "helped" her husband design the chair. Ray laughs, grins infectiously, and graciously obliges, standing there supportively while Arlene Francis addresses her questions mostly to Mr Eames, who keeps using the pronoun "we." When asked to talk about the house, Charles is quick to respond, "Ray and I worked on it. We designed it together, of course."

The house that Charles and Ray built is the Pacific Palisades home, better known as Case Study House #8, part of the Case Study series co-founded with Eero Saarinen to inspire a new generation of postwar house building. They moved in on Christmas Eve in 1949.[18] One of two separate buildings (the other is the studio), the house was designed and built for a "married couple both occupied professionally with mechanical experiment and graphic presentations."[19] A house, for the Eameses and Saarinen, had to be adapted to the living pattern of the inhabitants – it had to be the "center of productive activity," an environment of rest and renewal but also collaborative activity. The house should not be too demanding, maintenance-wise, and must serve as a background for work, its natural environments and landscape offering support amidst the daily stress of work and complications.

The site of the house was magical. The beauty of the rectangular box house was what you could do inside, what you could fill it with – its verticality and horizontal planes enabling the interplay of different shapes and forms. An *Architectural Forum* feature described it as "Life in a Chinese Kite," praising its light and airy design, marvelling at the "standard industrial practice assembled in a spacious wonderland."[20] Pat Kirkham called it "reminiscent of traditional Japanese architecture in its emphasis on lightness, elegance, minimalism, and rectilinear geometric form."[21] The Eameses deployed postwar everyday industrial materials to show how customized housing design could benefit from affordable, mass-produced, machine-made components.[22] The walls, made up of transparent, opaque, and Mondrian-inspired coloured panels, provided privacy, shelter, and light. They also became a canvas for nature's brushstrokes with the shadows of the eucalyptus trees that grew among the wildflowers in the meadow sloping toward the ocean. Ray remarked, "There were so many things we didn't expect when the house was designed ... the movement of the shadows of the trees against the translucent screens creates a wonderful play of light."[23] It was playing house, literally, for Charles and Ray – their needs in living and working fulfilled in a minimalist structure that was not built to be finished, but as a house and home, in constant process, and open to change.

Charles and Ray Eames, happily married in the summer of 1941, were not the only ones headed west that year. In July 1941, Isamu Noguchi left New York and headed for California in "an attempt to find new roots in the West."[24] He was not alone – his companions were Arshile Gorky and his fiancée, twenty-year-old Agnes Magruder, also affectionately known as Mougouch[25] ("little mighty one" in Armenian), and the muralist Urban Neininger. When the Parks Department twice rejected his Ala Moana playground designs, Isamu Noguchi purchased a used Ford station wagon, loaded it up with his tools and belongings, and persuaded Gorky and Magruder to leave for California with him. According to Masayo Duus's biography, Noguchi thought Gorky was stuck in an artistic rut, and a friend, the mosaic artist Jeanne Reynal, had arranged for a Gorky retrospective at the San Francisco Museum of Modern Art in August the same year.[26] There are conflicting accounts as to who accompanied Noguchi on that trip other than Gorky and Magruder, but if we were to collate all the accounts, there would have been at least six people stuffed in the old station wagon along with the sculpture equipment and personal belongings.[27] It is most likely that the only other traveller was Urban Neininger, who was a close friend and lover of Jeanne Reynal.

The road trip across the continent was a test of competing temperaments. It was hardly smooth, considering the length of the trip, with four people crammed into a packed station wagon. For Arshile Gorky, the trip reminded him of his Armenian childhood, and he proclaimed the greater beauty of the Caucasus at every point, to the irritation of his companions, even as they drove through the southwest on Route 66. Noguchi and Gorky even had differing opinions over whether the clouds were shaped like a "peasant woman in the sky" or were "abstract."[28] However, both men, recalled Agnes Magruder in her interview with Hayden Herrera, were in agreement that the Grand Canyon was "too big," "that it looked like a picture postcard," and that it needed to be made more interesting.[29] By the time they reached California, a rather miserable Gorky complained to his sister in a letter that he had "never made such a mistake in all [his] life" and that his friends only wanted him along on the trip in order to help defray the travelling costs.[30] Gorky's retrospective was at least a critical success, but Isamu Noguchi's journey west to search out new roots would find him eventually grappling with the Eastern roots within himself. Pearl Harbor changed everything.[31]

In an unpublished essay written in 1942, "I Became a Nisei," Isamu Noguchi wrote:

> To be hybrid anticipates the future. This is America, the nation of nationalities. The racial and cultural intermix is the antithesis of all the tenet [sic] of the Axis Powers. For us to fall into the Fascist line of race

bigotry is to defeat our unique personality and strength ... Because of my peculiar background I felt this war very keenly and wished to serve the cause of democracy [in] the best way that seemed open to me ... I felt sympathy for the plight of the American-born Japanese, the Nisei ... A haunting sense of unreality, of not belonging which has always bothered me seek for an answer among the Nisei.[32]

Out west, the Eameses and Isamu Noguchi could not have had more different experiences. In early 1942, while the Eameses were working on their bent plywood technique by developing a moulded-plywood leg splint for the US Navy, Isamu Noguchi was rallying on behalf of the Japanese Americans. Noguchi organized and acted as representative for the Nisei Writers and Artists for Democracy and was desperately trying to convince Roosevelt's government of Nisei patriotism to prevent the relocation of Japanese Americans from the West Coast. For Noguchi, who was of Japanese and American Irish descent, hybridity encompassed the burden and gift of being neither fully Japanese nor American. Aesthetic cosmopolitanism had once enabled him to move seamlessly between and across worlds. Nonetheless, on 19 February 1942, Roosevelt's Executive Order 9066, which authorized the internment of Japanese aliens and Japanese Americans from the West Coast, forced Noguchi to confront his Japanese heritage.[33]

Isamu Noguchi's time as director of landscape and park planning[34] in the Poston relocation camp in Arizona was voluntary. As an East Coast Nisei, Noguchi could return to New York, and he did so with the intention of publicizing the plight of West Coast Japanese Americans. Back in New York, he became disappointed by his radical leftist friends who did not oppose the relocation. Whatever idealisms he held for the Nisei cause, Noguchi felt strongly enough to enter Poston on 12 May 1942 with a vision of camp life as creative community building, an extension of a kind of artistic workshop, perhaps in the spirit of Bauhaus except under more surveillance. He believed he could inspire the Nisei to work toward a farm and craft settlement that would preserve Japanese tradition and culture. He was also initially inspired by a line from John Collier's speech to the Poston internees, "though democracy perish outside, here would be kept its seeds."[35] It wasn't long before the difficulties set in, and the awareness that Poston was no more than glorified imprisonment.

Eye burning dust, and the temperature seemed to stand at 120° for three solid months. Our food at 37 cents a day was no better than what inexperienced cooks could make it. And most of us became sick.[36]

The new arrivals keep coming in ... They are fingerprinted, declare their loyalty, enlist in the War Relocation Work Corps, are examined by a doctor and are introduced to their new home, 20 × 25 feet of tar paper shack, in which they must live for the duration five to a room.[37]

"Here time has stoped [sic]," Isamu wrote to Man Ray on 30 May 1942, "nothing is of any consequence."[38] The resources promised by the authorities were difficult to come by, even to fulfil the most basic of Noguchi's architectural visions of parks and recreational facilities in Poston.

> We have moments of elation only to be defeated by the poverty of our actual condition; the lack of water and equipment for farming, of tools and materials, our barrack surroundings. Sixteen dollars a month seems hardly an incentive to some. Others cool their ardour waiting in offices. We plan a city and look for nails.[39]

Perhaps more problematic was the eventual recognition that the Japanese American community was not a culturally unified one. Isamu Noguchi soon found he had little in common with the Japanese Americans at Poston who were mostly from farming or entrepreneurial communities, though there was a "feeling of mutuality, of identity, with those interned."[40] Noguchi's Japanese-ness became more realized when his voluntary status became one of internment itself, and while getting in was easy, getting out of Poston was not. Despite an amendment to Executive Order 9066 on 31 July allowing children of mixed marriages to petition for release, it was not until 11 November 1942 that Noguchi was finally allowed to leave.[41]

MY ARIZONA

In 1943, and back in his New York studio at 33 MacDougal Alley, Isamu Noguchi sculpted *My Arizona*, a hand-formed piece using an "unusual bonded (composite) magnesite mineral, its terra cotta/buff color representing the western clays and the spirit of a painted desert."[42] Measuring 18¼ inches by 18¼, it was Noguchi's memoir of Arizona, a sculptural cartography that evoked his experiences of Poston, the surrounding landscape, and the sinking of the USS *Arizona* in Pearl Harbor. The abstract starkness of the sculpture appears partitioned into four landforms with a dormant volcanic butte-like concave sphere, a pyramidal structure, a breast-like curve with a hook that recalls cacti vegetation, and an upside-down conical shape with fluorescent pink Plexiglas above it reflecting the skies, the light, and the heat – and perhaps offering shade from the intense temperatures that Noguchi and his fellow internees had endured.[43] The piece is hung on a wall as seen in a cluttered studio picture taken by André Kertész. Objects and variations of biomorphic sculptural assemblages are on display with *Miss*

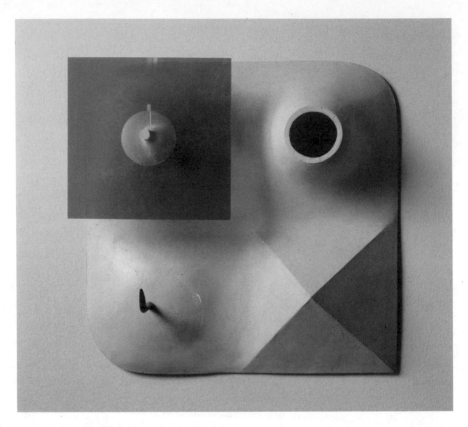

Figure 9.4 *My Arizona.*

Expanding Universe (1932), a streamlined aluminum sculpture of a female figure with arms and legs outstretched and hung from above.[44] Hung at eye level, *My Arizona* becomes an aerial view, soaring above the landscape and beyond the internment camp, perhaps imagined by Noguchi in those Poston days when he was petitioning for release. The Arizona desert had always presented a magnificent abstraction – vast, sublime, and forbidding spaces punctuated by mesas, buttes and plateaus, with dramatic skies, day or night. *My Arizona* resonates with confinement, self-containment, and embodied estrangement in an alienating landscape, echoing loss and poignancy. "Maybe it's the weather that makes everything so unreal," as Noguchi once wrote to Man Ray from Poston.[45] In his memoirs, Noguchi recalled, "The desert was magnificent ... the fantastic heat, the cool nights, and the miraculous time before dawn. I became leader of forays into the desert to find ironwood roots for sculpting."[46] His time in Poston, though brief in comparison to that of the West Coast internees, remained with him, perhaps with some guilt, etched in his artistic process.[47]

In 1977, Isamu Noguchi approached Gary Zeller, a materials expert and sculpture professor, to help preserve the deteriorating surface of *My Arizona*.[48] Together, they formulated a pigmented lacquer that was painted over the original surface. Noguchi then requested a silicon mould to cast three more versions of the piece, one in fibreglass, the other two in hydrostone – all in the colour, white to distinguish them from the slightly tan original. As the story goes, Isamu Noguchi then presented the original and one of the hydrostone copies to Gary Zeller as a token of gratitude, telling him that they would bring him good fortune one day. Noguchi took the mould and the other two versions with him. The fibreglass reconstruction is now the only officially recognized version and is located at the Noguchi Museum in Long Island, New York – the rest have vanished.

It was in Arizona that Isamu Noguchi's art became racialized, and the discourse that abstract art promoted as universal became one of double consciousness for Noguchi, who began to embrace a racial hybridity in his aesthetic language. It was in Arizona that Isamu Noguchi became a Nisei.

TURNING JAPANESE

"I was what you might call a dyed in the wool Manchurian girl," Yoshiko Yamaguchi recalls.[49] Born in the Liaoning Province in Manchuria on 12 February 1920, Yoshiko Yamaguchi never visited her Japanese homeland until she was eighteen. Moving effortlessly between languages, Japanese and Mandarin, Yamaguchi Yoshiko became the famed Chinese actress and singer Li Xianglan, also known as Ri Kōran by the Japanese, in the process "turning [herself] more or less into a woman of indecipherable nationality." She was also Pan Shuhua, the adopted daughter of a close Chinese friend. Caught up in the political turbulence of the Second World War and the Chinese Civil War, torn between her Japanese nationality and her attachment to China, Li Xianglan escaped execution, left China, and was repatriated in American-occupied Japan. Li Xianglan became Yamaguchi Yoshiko again.[50] In Tokyo, she continued performing, singing Chinese songs and arias from *La Boheme* and *Madama Butterfly*, appearing in Western musicals like *My Old Kentucky Home* (*Kentakki homu*) and Tolstoy's *Resurrection*, "changing [her role] from a cheerful Yankee girl to that of a tragic heroine."[51] As the Japanese film industry recovered, so did Yoshiko's cinematic career, and she began to work with directors like Akira Kurosawa. Eventually America – Hollywood and Broadway – called, and Yoshiko arrived in Los Angeles in April 1950 only to adopt another stage name, becoming Shirley Yamaguchi. Before she left, she told Japanese reporters that she wanted to meet Mrs Pearl Buck and Bing Crosby, and that she was "taking along kimonos for the stage," though her normal attire would be Chinese dresses.

Figure 9.5   Isamu Noguchi and Yoshiko Yamaguchi, Kita Kamakura (circa 1952).

In her memoirs, Yoshiko Yamaguchi does not remember when or where exactly she met Isamu Noguchi. Isamu, on the other hand, might have heard her best-selling Chinese song "Ye lai Xiang" (Evening fragrance) playing on the radio throughout Japan when he was there in the summer of 1950.[52] Several biographies affirm they first met at the opening of the Kimono Exhibition on 13 November 1950 at the Brooklyn Museum, an event organized by Pearl Buck to raise money for the Welcome House, an orphanage for Eurasian children fathered by American soldiers. Introduced by mutual friends, Ayako Ishigaki and her artist husband Eitarō Ishigaki,[53] Yoshiko and Isamu were drawn to each other by their mutual experiences of hybridity and displacement. By the third date, Isamu Noguchi had proposed to Yoshiko, and despite nearly a year of separation caused by work and travel, they were married on 5 December 1951 at the Meiji Shrine in Tokyo. To the Japanese and American press, the marriage between the famous movie star and the renowned avant-garde sculptor and son of a great Japanese poet was a media event, but it was also hailed as politically symbolic – a new chapter in relations between America and Japan.

Isamu Noguchi took to his renewed relationship with Japan with great enthusiasm, working with the famous Japanese architect Kenzo Tange on a design for a Peace Park in Hiroshima. Isamu desired to be more Japanese than the Japanese, seeking to restore the traditional aesthetic language that he admired. In early 1952, the couple settled in an idyllic location in Kita Kamakura, where the great Japanese potter Rosanjin Kitaoji lived and was their landlord. In a letter to his old friend Jeanne Reynal dated 2 November 1952, Isamu writes: "Just now we are sitting in our little garden, where we have spread mats and cusions [sic] to enjoy the autumn sun. Yoshiko-san is pealing [sic] a persimmon which grows plentifully in the garden. Before us the rice has now been cut and stacked high on poles. We wish you were both here as it is the kind of place where lovers belong."[54]

Kita Kamakura was a rustic "world of dreams," with its pastoral setting among the rice fields, the cherry blossoms, and the "thicket of bamboo."[55] Isamu constructed his studio beside the house and created an idealized world, carefully adhering to Japanese spatial rituals: "In Japan there is always the Tokonoma, the space for a scroll, a statuette, a vase, a sprig of nature. A beautiful convention ... an indulgence of space if you will where there is no space to spare, yet one always has the impression that it gives far more than it takes away."[56] Yoshiko, who was Manchurian born and had newly embraced America, had to learn to be Japanese again. When she returned from a day's filming, she had to change into Japanese attire with clogs that hurt her feet. She had once bought a pair of pink slippers to wear but Isamu threw them out, as they insulted his aesthetic purism. The marriage was tempestuous. Yoshiko could not play the demure Japanese wife for long and the couple argued constantly. Ironically, despite her ignorance of various Japanese customs, Yoshiko realized how truly Japanese she was. Isamu Noguchi's affiliation with Japan was that of a lost son attempting to rediscover a nostalgic past yet refusing to comprehend the basic customs and norms which "lubricated social life in Japan." Yoshiko told Masayo Duus in an interview in 1994:

> [Isamu] believed he was different from ordinary Americans and
> that he could understand Oriental feelings. But in the end he was
> an American. He always yearned for Japan, where he found half his

roots. But I think it was a Japan connected to his childhood experience, a time when his roots were not accepted. It was a Japan that was dead and gone. He was looking for a Japan that was no longer a reality. He was obsessed with things, and he yearned for things, that Japanese people did not really care about. Then he tried to approach Japan by logical reasoning. I thought he did that because he was an American.

Once embraced as a returning Japanese son with American roots, in post-Occupation Japan Isamu was treated as an American outsider, and his design for the Hiroshima Cenotaph, the result of Kenzo Tange's invitation, was rejected. An excoriating article appeared in *Tokyo Shinbun* chiding the arrogance of the outsider: "In Isamu Noguchi's blood there is mixed hay, which is from overseas."[57] For Isamu, nonetheless, the year at Kita Kamakura was one of the most magical of his life.

Although they were married for four years, Isamu Noguchi and Yoshiko Yamaguchi spent no more than a year together. They maintained homes in America and Japan, but their separation was also due to visa problems. If their temperaments were incompatible, the increasing pressures on their marriage and their eventual divorce in 1955 were aided by Joseph McCarthy's America, which placed Yoshiko under suspicion of being a Communist spy due to her complex past.[58] One of the most delicate pieces of unglazed Karatsu stoneware made by Isamu during his time at Kita Kamakura was a figure of Yoshiko, entitled *Yoshiko-san* (1952), measuring no more than 6 inches by 6. Despite its abstractness, it is a remarkable likeness of Yoshiko Yamaguchi in a kimono, except the piece feels almost brittle as the various parts appear barely to hang together, cracking and crumbling without – if not within. Another striking piece, measuring 14 inches and made of the same stoneware, *Marriage* (1952) depicts two figures wrapped in a blanket, but as loving as the piece appears, there is a hint of suffocation in the cracks in the stoneware. There are two heads featured, but only one pair of legs emerges from the bottom.[59] Yoshiko Yamaguchi recalled decades later, "it was hard for me to become a work of Isamu."[60]

LUNAR DREAMS

In his paean to Japanese aesthetics, the renowned author Junichiro Tanizaki writes of the elegant poetics of sunlight when filtered through shoji paper. "Seen at dusk," Tanizaki writes, "as one gazes out upon the countryside from the window of a train, the lonely light of a bulb under an old-fashioned shade, shining dimly from behind the white paper shoji of a thatch-roofed farmhouse, can seem positively elegant." For Tanizaki, the Japanese room delights in the "soft fragile beauty of the feeble light"[61] and depends on the interplay of shadows throughout the day. It is likely that Isamu Noguchi would have agreed with such a philosophy, assuming he had read Tanizaki's *In Praise of Shadows*, published in 1933.

"It has always been said that to start a home all that is needed is a room, a tatami and AKARI."[62] The akari light sculptures, some hanging, some standing delicately on three wiry legs, in various shapes and configurations, are some of the most iconic pieces in the Vitra collection. Akari lamps were handcrafted with shoji paper and bamboo, and they recall the essence of cherry blossoms, their lightness, collapsibility, and portability, according to Noguchi, adapting the traditional arts to modern-day uses.[63] During his trip to Japan in 1950, Isamu Noguchi visited Gifu City, famed for their paper lanterns, where he was inspired to make hundreds of unique akari lamps, deliberately asymmetrical – some irregular and deformed to dissuade copies, some without the bamboo that gave them shape so the lamps would cast light out of the crinkled mulberry paper.[64]

> The name akari which I coined, means in Japanese light as illumination. It also suggests lightness as opposed to weight. The ideograph combines that of the sun and moon. The ideal of akari exemplified with lightness (as essence) and light (for awareness). The quality is poetic, ephemeral, and tentative. Looking more fragile than they are *akari* seem to float, casting their light as in passing. They do not encumber our space as mass or as a possession; if they hardly exist in use, when not in use they fold away in an envelope. They perch light as a feather, some pinned to the wall, others clipped to a cord, and all may be moved with the thought.[65]

It was not the first lamp that Noguchi had designed. In 1943, he lamented that he had failed to patent the few three-legged cylindrical lamps he had designed for his sister and friends, which resulted in imitations all over the place.[66]

Akari, according to Isamu Noguchi, was the "logical convergence of [his] long interest in light sculptures, lunars and [his] being in in Japan."[67] Noguchi's interest in light sculptures can be traced to his *Musical and Luminous Weather Vane* (1933) and the development of embedded lighting in his sculptures. He eventually created a series of self-illuminated objects and panels he called *Lunars*. The atomic age and its frightening apocalyptic potential preoccupied Noguchi, who conceived of a time when humans would be reduced to living in caves. The illuminated object would be the "source of delight in itself – like fires it attracts and protects us from the beasts of the night."[68] The *Lunars* were more than just self-contained objects – they emerged out of the experience of physical confinement. They enfolded Noguchi's experience at Poston internment camp where he could have sat outside during cool desert nights, meditating by moonlight, longing for other interstellar worlds: "The memory of Arizona ... was like that of the moon, a moonscape of the mind ... not given the actual space of freedom, one makes its equivalent ... an illusion ... an illusion within the confines of a room or a box ... where the imagination may roam to the further limits of possibilities, the moon and beyond."[69]

MID-CENTURY MODERN

It is difficult not to find the Noguchi coffee table for Herman Miller in any well-appointed mid-century home interior or in design catalogues and popular decorating magazines such as *House Beautiful* and *Better Homes and Gardens*. Often nestled among the Eames lounge, the Saarinen chairs, or the Nelson bench would be the unmistakable glass-topped table with its sensuous biomorphic legs. The coffee table's provenance, however, emerged out of more unpleasant circumstances. It was during his internment period that Isamu Noguchi discovered that the British furniture designer T.H. Robsjohn-Gibbings had adapted the design for the A. Conger Goodyear table and advertised it as his own. When Noguchi secured release from Poston, he raised his concerns to Robsjohn-Gibbings, who responded by saying anybody could make a three-legged table. Noguchi redesigned the table but reduced the biomorphic legs to "rudiments" – deploying a technical process similar to the one used in his sculpture *Kouros* (pink Georgia marble, 1944–45), which had a construction technique of eight separate interlocking pieces that could be dismantled in two minutes.[70]

Kouros, despite being the term for Greek sculptures of male youth, was according to Isamu Noguchi "the effigy of man."[71] The sculpture was a "representation of mankind," and according to Amy Lyford,[72] it "reconsiders the degree to which the image of a stable, universalizing man could be relevant in a world where migration, dislocation, relocation, hybridity, and exile had become models for twentieth-century man's existence."[73] The sculpture's "relocatable" technique also spoke to human transience and the idea of "universal humanity as a construction" as well as framing this construction as "an empty one." *Kouros*, recalling Greek poetics, also emerged out of the fear of the destructive force of the atomic bomb, but also the dehumanizing Japanese American internment experience.[74] That the coffee table that recalls the same interlocking biomorphic articulations of *Kouros* is so celebrated in mid-century modern interiors is ironic, for in its very presence in more affluent white suburban homes is the connection to the shameful history of racial exclusion.

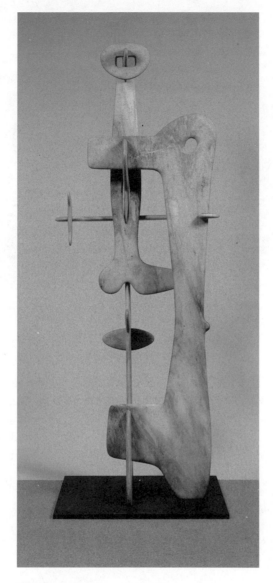

Figure 9.6 *Kouros*, 1944–45.

In its July 1961 issue, *Playboy* magazine assembled the six most influential designers for their lifestyle spread, and the photographer, Marvin Koner (1921–1983), took one of the most iconic design photographs of our time.[75] This was an image where "a Design Within Reach catalog was somewhere gurgling in a molded-plywood cocoon, waiting to be hatched."[76] George Nelson, Edward Wormley,

Figure 9.7   Noguchi coffee table, design circa 1944, manufactured 1947 by Herman Miller.

Eero Saarinen, Harry Bertoia, Charles Eames, and Jens Risom pose confidently with their designs, from the walnut serving cart to the womb chair, celebrating metal, textiles, and bent plywood. From the curvilinear to geometric minimalism and the mixture of industrial materials, the zeitgeist of the mid-century modern would converge in this overwhelming image of patriarchal whiteness. Buried in the contemporary discourses of the mid-century modern aesthetic with its sleek and sophisticated lines are the layers of gendered and racial ellipses. How odd to exclude Florence Knoll, whose influence in the commercial and public design worlds in 1950s America would have been inescapable. But more glaring here is the omission of Ray Eames – and of course, Isamu Noguchi.

NOTES

1 Office of Charles and Ray Eames, Charles Eames, photographer. California, 1951. I am grateful to the Eames Office photo archivist, David Hertsgaard, for his help in identifying the photographer here.
2 Paul Goldberger, "An Assemblage of Objects," *Lakeland Ledger*, 15 April 1978, 2B, https://news.google.com/newspapers?nid=1346&dat=19780415&id=pG9NAAAAIBAJ&sjid=BPsDAAAAIBAJ&pg=4692,3943584&hl=en.

3 A commonly quoted phrase (see, for example, "History of Akari," Noguchi Museum, http://shop.noguchi.org/history.html) but in the original catalogue, Isamu Noguchi uses the word "pad," not "tatami." One wonders if the word was edited or translated for an English audience. See Noguchi, "The Meaning of Akari," in *Space of Akari and Stone*, 95.

4 Kirkham, "'At Home' with the Eameses," 120–1.

5 Yamaguchi with Sakuya, *Fragrant Orchid*, 267–9.

6 Charles Eames refers to her as Susi Matsumoto. Eames correspondence to Soko Sen, Kyoto City, Japan, 26 October 1951, in Eames and Eames, *An Eames Anthology*, 92–3.

7 For more on how Asia held the imagination of a post–Second World War America, see Christina Klein's excellent *Cold War Orientalism*. Also within the world of art, see the chapter "The World in a Single Sculpture" in Dore Ashton's critical biography *Noguchi East and West*, 157–74.

8 Hales, "Levittown."

9 Jordan, *Jim Reeves*, 238–9.

10 Designed for A. Conger Goodyear's (1877–1964) house (built 1938). Images of the house by Ezra Stoller are available on Wikimedia Commons (too small for print reproduction), including at least three images of the original table photographed through the glass wall. A. Conger Goodyear was a member of the Goodyear family and an important art collector. He played an influential role in the history of modern art in America, being the founder and first president of the Museum of Modern Art in New York. He also served on the board of directors at what is now the Albright Knox Gallery in Buffalo, established the (then controversial) Room of Contemporary Art, and was then removed from the board after having purchased Picasso's *La Toilette* (1906) for the gallery.

11 Noguchi, *A Sculptor's World*, 26.

12 John Winter, "Eames House," in Ince and Johnson, *World of Charles and Ray Eames*, 89.

13 Jonathan Glancey, "How Ray and Charles Eames Changed the Way We Lived," *Telegraph*, 3 August 2012, http://www.telegraph.co.uk/culture/film/9447618/How-Ray-and-Charles-Eames-changed-the-way-we-live.html.

14 With apologies to the *New York Times* for the phrase, taken from the title of a review of *Wittgenstein's Mistress* by Amy Hempel. Amy Hempel, "Home Is Where the Art Is," *New York Times*, 22 May 1988, http://www.nytimes.com/1988/05/22/books/home-is-where-the-art-is.html. See also Demetrios, *Beautiful Details*.

15 Who taught Ray Eames.

16 Early photographs of the newly completed Case Study House #8 show the Hofmann paintings on the wall. See "Case Study House for 1949," *Arts & Architecture* 66 (December 1949), 26–39.

17 "Eames Lounge Chair Debut in 1956 on NBC," YouTube video, posted by "omidimo," 18 April 2011, https://www.youtube.com/watch?v=z_X6RsN-HFw. Also see transcript of "*Home* Show, NBC, hosted by Arlene Francis, Guests: Charles and Ray Eames, 1956," in Eames and Eames, *Eames Anthology*, 143–4.

18 Ince and Johnson, *World of Charles and Ray Eames*, 62.

19 Eames and Saarinen, "Case Study Houses 8 and 9."

20 "Life in a Chinese Kite: Standard Industrial Products Assembled in a Spacious Wonderland," *Architectural Forum*, September 1950, 90.

21 Kirkham, *Charles and Ray Eames*, 115.

22 Such materials also had origins in military technology. See Colomina, *Domesticity at War*.

23 Goldberger, "Assemblage of Objects."

24 Noguchi, *A Sculptor's World*, 25.

25 Paul Levy, "Mougouch Fielding: Painter Who Became Muse to Arshile Gorky," *The Independent*, 4 August 2013, http://www.independent.co.uk/news/obituaries/mougouch-fielding-painter-who-became-muse-to-arshile-gorky-8745437.html.

26 Duus, *Life of Isamu Noguchi*, 161.

27 I have tried to make sense of the different accounts of the trip through several biographies and sources. See Noguchi's brief memoir entry in *A Sculptor's World*, 24–5. As well, I have looked at several artist biographies. See Ashton, *Noguchi East and West*, 64–70; Duus, *Life of Isamu Noguchi*, 160–2. See also Herrera, *Listening to Stone*, 166–71; Spender, *From a High Place*, 218–22.

28 Noguchi, *A Sculptor's World*, 25.

29 Herrera, *Listening to Stone*, 171.

30 Spender, *From a High Place*, 222.

31 Japan attacked Pearl Harbor on 7 December 1941.

32 Written in Poston for the October 1942 issue of *Reader's Digest* but never published. See Lyford, *Isamu Noguchi's Modernism*, appendix B. Downloadable copy made available by the Noguchi Museum – see Noguchi, "I Became a Nisei."

33 Also see transcripts of the oral history interview with Isamu Noguchi, 7 November–26 December 1973. Archives of American Art, Smithsonian Institution.

34 Lyford, *Isamu Noguchi's Modernism*, 123.

35 John Collier was head of the Office of Indian Affairs and chief administrator of the Colorado River Relocation Center. Duus, *Life of Isamu Noguchi*, 168; Noguchi, *A Sculptor's World*, 25.

36 Noguchi, "I Became a Nisei," in Lyford, *Isamu Noguchi's Modernism*, 216.

37 Ibid., 217.

38 Isamu Noguchi, Arizona letter to Man Ray, 30 May 1942, Naomi Savage papers on Man Ray, 1913–2005, Archives of American Art, Smithsonian Institution.

39 Ibid.

40 Noguchi, *A Sculptor's World*, 25.

41 Lyford, *Isamu Noguchi's Modernism*, 127–8.

42 "Rare Original Noguchi Sculpture 'My Arizona' Depicts Poignancy of Japanese Detention Camps in World War II," *Business Wire*, 10 May 2004, http://www.businesswire.com/news/home/20040510006119/en/Rare-Original-Noguchi-Sculpture-Arizona-Depicts-Poignancy.

43 Figure 9.4 here has a deeper magenta Plexiglas, which was replaced sometime in the 1990s. I am very grateful to Janine Biunno, archivist at the Noguchi Foundation, for clarifying the history of the sculpture and its versions. The officially recognized sculpture of *My Arizona* (fibreglass) is the 1977 reconstruction.

44 *Miss Expanding Universe* (1932) measures 13.9 × 88.6 × 15.2 cm (40⅞ × 34⅞ × 9 in.) and emerged out of Isamu Noguchi's exchanges with Buckminster Fuller. Fuller was inspired by the astronomer Edwin Hubble's discoveries of the expanding universe and went on to speculate on his own space-time model of an "expanding sphere." Inspired by Fuller, Noguchi made the sculpture for the dancer Ruth Page (who bequeathed it to the Art Institute of Chicago) who in turn created a dance entitled *Expanding Universe*. Noguchi was also in search of a universal abstract human form, which he explored via dance, and of course later on in organic sculptural forms such as *Kouros* (1945). See Krausse and Lichtenstein, *Your Private Sky*, 169–70.

45 Noguchi, Arizona letter to Man Ray, 30 May 1942.

46 Noguchi, *A Sculptor's World*, 25.

47 I am grateful to the Isamu Noguchi Foundation for sharing their exhibition panel notes with me. See "Self-Interned, 1942: Noguchi in Poston War Relocation Camp" (18 January 2017–28 January 2018). The section on deserts and gateways shows particularly the significance of his time in Poston and how it has influenced his artistic process.

48 See auction information in "The Owners of Noguchi Sculpture 'My Arizona' Test the Artist's Prophecy in an October Auction at Rago – Iconic Works Held Privately since 1978," Rago Arts and Auction Center press release, October 2013, http://www.blouinartinfo.com/sites/default/files/iconic_noguchi_sculptures_in_private_hands_for_35_years_auction_at_rago_in_october.pdf.

49 Yamaguchi, 2.

50 The proper Japanese address is the surname before personal name. I use this address here deliberately to ascribe her 'return' to Japanese identity.

51 Yamaguchi with Sakuya, *Fragrant Orchid*, 259.

52 Duus, *Life of Isamu Noguchi*, 208. Isamu Noguchi arrived that year at Tokyo on 2 May 1950, feted as a great avant-garde Japanese American artist.

53 Deported by McCarthy in 1951 as both were affiliated with Communist activity.

54 Duus, *Life of Isamu Noguchi*, 259; Herrera, *Listening to Stone*, 294.

55 Ashton, *Noguchi East and West*, 132.

56 Herrera, *Listening to Stone*, 295. See images of the farmhouse and studio (among others) in "Isamu Noguchi: Projects in Japan," *Arts and Architecture*, October 1952, 24–6.

57 Herrera, *Listening to Stone*, 309.

58 Yoshiko Yamaguchi (1920–2014) also cited their childlessness as one of the reasons for the marriage's failure. She eventually remarried a Japanese diplomat, gave up her career as an actor and singer, and returned to Japan, where she became first a successful television host and then a politician. As a member of the Japanese Diet, she was one of the earliest politicians to recognize Japanese brutality during the Second World War and advocated for reparations on behalf of Korean comfort women. She also served as vice-president of the Asian Women's Fund, which was set up in 1994 as "atonement" money, to compensate the comfort women in South Korea, the Philippines, Taiwan, the Netherlands, and Indonesia. A website with Chinese, Japanese, and English sources chronicles her life and features her time as a politician. See "1948–2014 d.," *The History of Yamaguchi Yoshiko* (blog), http://yoshikoyamaguchi.blogspot.ca/p/1970-2014.html.

59 These pieces (among 120 works) were exhibited at the new Museum of Modern Art in Kamakura. The exhibition was put together with the help of Yoshiko Yamaguchi. Herrera, *Listening to Stone*, 304–5.

60 Ibid., 301. Yoshiko Yamaguchi's posthumous *Fragrant Orchid* (2015) is the most recently translated autobiography, which may have cobbled together a number of other sources including several Chinese and Japanese autobiographies. Ian Buruma's 2008 novel *The China Lover* (Penguin) is fictional but based on Yoshiko Yamaguchi. He paints her in a mysterious light, never quite getting to who she really is, likely with the intent of showing that she inhabited many worlds. In that respect, it may be a more honest depiction.

61 Tanizaki, *In Praise of Shadows*.

62 Herrera, *Listening to Stone*, 300.

63 Noguchi, "Japanese Akari Lamps."

64 Duus, *Life of Isamu Noguchi*, 251.

65 Noguchi, *A Sculptor's World*, 33.

66 See transcripts of the oral history interview with Noguchi, Archives of American Art, Smithsonian Institution. He talks more about the materials (aluminum) of the earlier lamp for Knoll.

67 Ibid.

68 Noguchi, *A Sculptor's World*, 27.

69 Schauer, "Isamu Noguchi."

70 "I'm leery of welding or pasting. It implies taking an unfair advantage of nature. In *Kouros* there are no adhesives of any kind – only the stones holding themselves together." Noguchi, "Interview with Isamu Noguchi," 133. See also feature on sculpture in *Arts and Architecture*, February 1947, 20–1.

71 Noguchi, "Interview with Isamu Noguchi," 133.

72 Lyford, *Isamu Noguchi's Modernism*, 154–7.

73 Lyford, "Noguchi, Sculptural Abstraction."

74 In 1945, Noguchi was trying to avoid internment again, this time to Manzanar, California. Lyford, *Isamu Noguchi's Modernism*, 145–6. For a remarkable account of Manzanar, one of the biggest internment camps, through the photographs of Dorothea Lange and oral testimony, see Gordon and Okihiro, *Impounded*.

75 John Anderson, "Designs for Living," 46–7.

76 Rosecrans Baldwin, "The Digital Ramble/Furniture Design," *T Magazine, New York Times*, 23 April 2009, http://tmagazine.blogs.nytimes.com/author/rosecrans-baldwin/page/2/?_r=0. The photograph by Marvin Koner, courtesy of *Playboy* magazine, is also reproduced in the article.

Coloniality and the Carbonscape: Reflections on White Settlement and Sociogeny from inside a Cookie Factory

MARK JACKSON

CHAPTER 10

GUIDE QUOTES (AFTER SYLVIA WYNTER)

Coloniality ... refers to long-standing patterns of power that emerged as a result of colonialism, but that define culture, labour, intersubjective relations, and knowledge production well beyond the strict limits of colonial administrations. Thus, coloniality survives colonialism. It is maintained alive in books, in the criteria of academic performance, in cultural patterns, in common sense, in the self-image of peoples, in aspirations of self, and so many other aspects of our modern experience. In a way, as modern subjects we [breathe] coloniality all the time and every day.

Nelson Maldonado-Torres, "On the Coloniality of Being"

The transformation of subjective experience is, in the case of humans, culturally and thereby socio-situationally determined, with these determinations in turn, serving to activate their physicalist correlates. In consequence, if the mind is what the brain does, what the brain does is itself culturally determined through the mediation of the socialized sense of self, as well as of the "social" situation in which this self is placed.

Sylvia Wynter, "Towards the Sociogenic Principle"

The biggest barrier to energy change is not technical but the cultural and political structures of feeling that have been produced through regimes of energy consumption.

Matthew T. Huber, *Lifeblood*

Our friends the R.N.W.M. police came west and saved the Indians from drinking that bad whiskey ever since then they look after the Indians.

Joe Little Chief's "winter count" describing the duration termed "1874"

Signs don't come from the mind. Rather, it is the other way around. What we call mind, or self, is a product of semiosis.

Eduardo Kohn, *How Forests Think*

It is primarily to emergent formations (though often in the form of modification or disturbance in older forms) that the structure of feeling, as solution, relates. Yet this specific solution is never mere flux. It is a structured formation which, because it is at the very edge of semantic availability, has many of the characteristics of a pre-formation, until specific articulations – new semantic figures – are discovered in material practice.

Raymond Williams, "Structures of Feeling"

More effective at setting each twig aquiver in the passing of waves than a pebble dropped into a pool of water, Spiralism defines life at the level of relations (colours, odours, sounds, signs, words) and historical connections (positionings in space and time).

Frankétienne, *Ready to Burst*

FUMES/FUMING

Late one summer afternoon, a car full of strangers appeared in our yard. We watched from the kitchen window as it spun and lurched about on the grass between the house and the barn. Seemingly enjoying itself, it was doing doughnuts, joy-riding. Our dogs barked maniacally at the intruder. Without a muffler, the car coughed and roared a cloud of exhaust as it marked up the grass. It was a four-door Ford Fairmont sedan, dark blue, mud speckled, and heavily dust-bound by the gravel roads that surrounded our farm. Inside were six or seven "Indians."[1] Seemingly more annoyed than afraid, my mother sent me out to see what was going on. I must have been fourteen or fifteen.

They were drunk. Out-of-their-skulls drunk. Drunker than I expected, then, that anyone could be and still be able to drive. Laughing and hollering out the open windows, the Indians spun about in their car, seemingly oblivious to where they were or what they were doing. I flagged them down by waving my arms, wary of an unpredictable lurch or spin. I remember the fear-tinged incongruity of trying to convince a joy-riding car filled with strangers – Indians, no less – to come to a halt on what passed for our lawn, of all places. Mum watched anxiously, somewhat alarmed, from the kitchen window. Only once in our thirty-two years on the farm did a dirty, dilapidated car of drunks come barrelling into our yard. Coyotes, stray cats and dogs, moose, deer, cougar several times, loose cows, lost travellers, mistaken addresses, Jehovah's Witnesses, yes, sometimes frequently. Indians, no. I eventually managed to get the car to cease and desist, probably in much less time than it felt.

The car came to a stop all akimbo. Its doors had flung open; some had popped open as it spun around. The trunk, too, had sprung up; our lawn, an old pasture, was less than flat. The Indians fell about, staggering, shouting and laughing at me and each other. I probably looked wounded in that all-at-once sheepish, indignant, and scared but trying to be manly way teenage boys do. They offered me their empty or near-empty vodka and whisky bottles. (When I was a little older, I learnt that a liquor bottle of this size and shape was called a "mickey." Inexpensive, a mickey holds enough to get you drunk but is insufficient, alone, to kill you. The bottle's slim, concave profile allows it to fit easily into an inside pocket. A mickey rests comfortably in the hand. When upended, the liquor resonates as it does in the westerns; the micky's cheap screw top lacks, however, that fleshy, squeaky-echo pop authenticity of a cork.)

A young, chubby woman in the front seat looked ill. The rest of the occupants were male, young as well, except for a barely conscious grey-haired, nearly toothless old man in the litter-strewn back seat.

Not much sense was made. There wasn't much sense to make. They were drunk, and lost, and even if they were lost, it didn't really matter because they were drunk and seemingly happy. They weren't aggressive. I recall not being much afraid. More amused, and worried for them, particularly the woman and the old man in the back seat. Head slung forward, a tooth or two poking out of his otherwise gummy wet mouth, a thin, grey, almost absent moustache; he drooled, groaning for whisky. He was nearly unconscious. I asked the others if he was okay. Between a language I didn't understand, likely Cree, and moans for more whisky, the others, laughing, said to find him a beer; there was no more whisky. I found a couple of bottles of beer in a torn cardboard case in the trunk. He didn't want a beer, but I opened it for him anyway. Situations, especially unfamiliar ones, often occasion their own ends.

They were simply drunk. "Harmless Indians who need a bit of help" is something like what I said when I went back inside. Mum snorted. After some discussion, we got together water and cookies. I remember I carried the water and a cookie packet outside on a tray with short Ikea glasses. The Indians stank of exhaust, cigarettes, and booze. We stood around, them laughing at the tray and glasses, fumbling with the cookies as they ate, lighting more cigarettes, me feeling awkward, amused, and worried, refusing the "smokes" they offered.

Once they had rested and gathered their bearings amidst the nonsensical conversations that their drunkenness had with my (naivety and) sobriety, they wanted to be on their way. The Indians said that they lived on Hobbema, a reserve perhaps an hour's drive some way south of us. (Curious how one lives "on" a reserve, or "on" a farm, or "on" land, and "in" a town or city, or "in" the country; rarely, if ever, bundled "with.") "Hobbema" was how I knew the reserve, although it was, in fact, made up of four separate but adjacent reserves: Ermineskin Indian Reserve No. 138, Samson Indian Reserve No. 137, Louis Bull Indian Reserve No. 439, and Montana Indian Reserve No. 139.

The reserves were just east of what is, today, the Queen Elizabeth II Highway. Then it was simply the No. 2. The "QE II" also runs parallel to a north-south rail line. In 1876 under Treaty 6, when they and many more began to be signed into the Dominion of the Crown, the four reserves – IR137, IR138, IR139, and IR439 – were inaugurated alongside the rail line and the highway. The names for those who were moved onto IR137, IR138, IR139, and IR149 were also re-written with Treaty 6. Prior to the implementation of the reservations under the treaty, collective names reflected specific place relations. Nesaskwayak ("the north treeline") became Ermineskin IR138. Nipisihkopahk ("willow meadows") became Samson IR137. Kispahtinaw ("the end of the hill") became Louis Bull IR439. And Akamihk ("across the river") became Montana IR139.

The terms of Treaty 6, still a binding legal document, include, amongst many others, the following stipulation:

> The Plain and Wood Cree Tribes of Indians, and all other the Indians inhabiting the district hereinafter described and defined, do hereby cede, release, surrender and yield up to the Government of the Dominion of Canada, for Her Majesty the Queen and Her successors forever, all their rights, titles and privileges, whatsoever, to the lands included within the following limits, that is to say ...[2]

The treaty text goes on to describe the "embracing ... area of 121,000 square miles, be the same more or less. To have and to hold the same to Her Majesty the Queen and Her successors forever."[3] The clasp of the queen, elsewhere in the document described as "bountiful and benevolent," also includes the stipulation that "no intoxicating liquor shall be allowed to be introduced or sold, and all laws now in force, or hereafter to be enacted, to preserve Her Indian subjects inhabiting the reserves or living elsewhere within Her North-west Territories from the evil influence of the use of intoxicating liquors, shall be strictly enforced." Each family under Treaty 6 was further entitled to a small parcel of land, which it could sell back to the Crown for twelve dollars. Agricultural implements and hunting and fishing gear were also variously promised.

Few, if any, of the agreements, other than buying back land in extinguishment of any future claim, were honoured by the Crown. Treaty land, when first allocated, included mineral rights. Everything within a bounded area and under one's feet to the centre of the earth belonged to the owner. If oil or minerals were found within that area, then the owners would profit from those – now – resources. Buying back treaty land extinguished mineral rights and placed sub-surface ownership under the Crown. All non-treaty and non-reserve land excluded sub-surface ownership. The crown could do as it liked to access or sell anything found beneath surface soils.

Of the eighty-six Cree and Stony representatives who were signatories to the treaty in 1876, all signed next to their transcribed and typeset English names with a handwritten "x." In eleven subsequent "Adhesions" to the treaty between 1876 and 1954, dozens of further signatories also signed with an "x," save for three in a Rocky Mountain House signing on 24 May 1944: J. Yellow-Eyes, L. Bear Child, and Ꭰ<ᒉ''ᐣ.[4] Each of their hands can easily be discerned as distinct. Collectively, the reservations 137, 138, 139, and 439 under Treaty 6 became Hobbema. Hobbema was named after Meindert Hobbema, a seventeenth-century Dutch Golden Age landscape painter. The name was bestowed in 1891 by the then president of the Canadian Pacific Railway (CPR), Sir William Cornelius Van Horne. Van Horne, an American from Illinois, and a Montreal resident while president of the CPR, was an admirer of Hobbema's paintings. He needed a name for the new flag station on the just-built rail line between the colonial towns that emerged around Fort Edmonton and Fort Calgary.

When the Ford Fairmont careened into our yard, Hobbema was known to me as simply a place of poverty, violence, high suicide rates, and alcohol abuse. The gangs that continue to trouble the reservation today might have been emerging at that time along with the rise of rap and hip-hop culture and its easily translated urban sensibilities, which capture and communicate alienation, disempowerment, solidarity, and marginalization. Hobbema, or Maskwacis[5] as the area has become known, is midway between the small towns of Wetaskiwin and Ponoka. Wetaskiwin is Cree for "the hills where peace was made" but is better known for its cheap car sales jingle ("Cars cost less in Wet-ask-i-win" – sing it) and the co-op, a large United Farmers' Association (UFA) "agro-supply" and farm fuel outlet. We often bought government-subsidized purple diesel for the tractor at the UFA. Subsidized fuel was purple because dye was added to prevent its use off the farm; if you were stopped by the Royal Canadian Mounted Police (RCMP), and your vehicle's fuel tank tested positive (i.e., the fuel was purple), you would be fined and would lose your access to subsidized fuel. Ponoka is Blackfoot for "elk" but was better known as the location of a large livestock auction and, more infamously, one of the province's main mental asylums, the Alberta Hospital. The Alberta Hospital became notorious as a site where routine eugenics procedures, which influenced German national socialist policies in the early

1930s, continued into the 1970s. Socially vulnerable and marginalized people, including poor people, the mentally disabled, unmarried women, Ukrainians, and Aboriginal and Metis populations, were targeted, usually for forced sterilization.

Hobbema's reserves lay, then, beside a rail line and a highway, and between an agricultural hub and the asylum. We had driven through Hobbema a few times, but always on the way to somewhere else, usually buying or selling goats and cows or other farm stock and supplies. Reserves were never destinations unless for, rarely, a rodeo, horse races, or, even more rarely, a pow-wow; such events, and those in them, were simply spectacles for our awkward, sometimes curious, gaze.

Before they left our yard, the "Indians" wanted to say thank you. Welcome to stay until they sobered up, and certainly in no condition to drive, they nevertheless said they were fine and needed to be leaving. Since I had shown them care, they had something they wanted to do to say thank you before they left.

They said they felt something special in me and they wanted to bless me. Except for the old man who was too drunk to stand, they stood in a close circle around me. I was in the middle amidst their alcoholic breath, feeling profoundly awkward, part of me doubting their sincerity and their ritual, but doing it to humour them. The other part of me was curious and quite excited: I had never been blessed by "real Indians." As children, we played either cowboys and Indians or Romans and Gauls. My brother stood watching by the elderberry tree. In a markedly more serious and sober tone, they sang a short prayer, again probably in Cree, and asked in English (I guess so that I could understand) for my blessing from "the Creator." Afterwards, laughing again, they said I was a good guy. "Hey, buddy," they said, "you're a good guy. Thanks, man." Who knows if it was genuine or not. I felt then, and feel now, that it was, and that their blessings very much were.

I thanked them too for their kindnesses. They didn't have to share, or do, what they did, however genuine, or addled, or both. We shook hands all around, slapped each other's backs awkwardly, smiled; they piled a little soberer, but still quite drunk, into their car and disappeared up our long gravel drive. Perplexed, pleased with myself (I was blessed, after all), anxious for them, and more than a little guilty at letting them drive off simply because it was easier, I returned to the house to clean the glasses.

They came with me into the kitchen. Dried remnants on the rims of the glasses and amidst my clothes, their otherwise departed bodies had become car exhaust, cigarette smoke, alcohol, and resonant blessings. They clung, lingering, as traces from strange worlds do. I wondered whether anything had changed in me because of their song, whether I was indeed "a good guy," or better, different. Much of me continues to believe my projection of myself through my imaginaries of them. That's how colonialism endures. That's how it works.

Figure 10.1 Carl Blomquist with son Jack. 1895.

CALMAR WITH A C

The yard where they spun doughnuts was, for most of my life, home. It lay – I have not been back since my family left in 2005 – between a Scandinavian-inspired renovated farmhouse and a similarly inspired horse barn. Both designed by my Scottish architect father, the buildings, and several others, lay on our farm, which was located three and a half miles south of the small town of Calmar, on Alberta's Highway 795. Calmar, with a C, was then and is still quite rural, a farming, then oil-and-gas, now also exurb commuter town whose name was bestowed in 1899 by the first postmaster, Carl Blomquist (see figure 10.1). Blomquist named Calmar after his hometown in Sweden, Kalmar, with a K.

Our farm, a quarter section (160 acres), was set off 795 by a long gravel drive. The house and barn, invisible from the road, were sheltered behind a poplar wood. We enhanced its shield with numerous shelterbelts of laurel and golden willow. As children, we planted the trees in soil once cleared of trees by settlers not long before our arrival in the summer of 1974. Jack, the small child pictured with Blomquist in front of his sod hut in figure 10.1, might well have been alive to watch us plant trees where he previously had helped to clear them. A small creek, Conjuring Creek, filled with numerous beaver, which we either killed or had killed because they felled swathes of the wood that flanked the creek, ran through the centre of the farm. It divided what we termed our "front" and "back" fields. My brother and I played in and explored the creek's woods throughout the year. When it froze over in the winter, we learned to skate and play hockey on the ponds created by the beaver. In winter, trappers worked lines in the same ponds up and down the creek. With axes, they chopped holes in the ice for their traps. If a trapped beaver hadn't drowned by the time the trap was checked, the occasional crack of a rifle shot echoed through the wood. I too shot at my first undomestic-ated animal – a beaver – there. Once, in a remarkable shot, which was mostly luck, I shot one at a distance between the eyes. It died instantly. As its corpse floated toward me on the bank, I could see a small, perfect hole in its forehead issue forth a soft, insistent stream of blood. Later, when I was older, thirteen or fourteen, it was also in the creek, alone with a gun in my hands, watching a small beaver circle a pond looking for its absent mate or mother, that I vowed never again to hunt simply because I could.

Blomquist and his family – from Sweden by way of Minnesota, then North Dakota – arrived eighty years before we did to what was known colonially as the North-West Territories, later Alberta, the name bestowed in 1905 in honour of the fourth daughter of Queen Victoria and wife of the fourth governor general of Canada. Blomquist was driven there by unemployment, promises re-neged, and drought. First by steamship, then train, and finally animal wagon, he arrived with several other Swedish families to the area known as Conjuring Creek in 1895. The creek was a renamed trail that connected the Nêhiyaw (Cree) and Îyârhe Nakoda (Stoney) of Hmi-Hmoo (Woodpecker Lake) and Metewew-sakahikan (Wizard Lake) with Amiskwaciy (Edmonton), Wabamun (this is easy to say for English speakers, so colonial governors didn't change it), and Mask-wacis (Hobbema). The creek was called "Conjuring" because it meandered from its source, Wizard Lake, north to the Saskatchewan River. A long, narrow lake, also known as Lizard Lake (Osikiyas Sakahikan) in Cree, and Imnesto Imne (Nakoda for "narrow lake"), Wizard Lake was named after a translation from the Cree name, Metewew-sakahikan. On its shores shamans (*Medewiwin*) conducted "shaking tent" (*Jiisakiiwin*) ceremonies.[6]

Our Scandinavian-inspired farmhouse emerged, however, simply because my father enjoyed the feel of a modern Scandinavian aesthetic. Ours was a Carl Lars-son/William Morris Arts and Crafts meets semi-hippy back-to-the-land vision; at least, that was the intent and spirit when we arrived. We knew nothing of *Mede-wiwin*, nor the origins of the name for the creek that wound its way through our property, nor the fact that soon after Blomquist arrived in 1895, thereafter sum-moning other Swedish families from Minnesota and the Dakotas to the rich and fertile land, the area would become known, until 1899 when it changed its name to Calmar, as "Swedish Settlement."[7]

Blomquist did not arrive in what became Calmar via the train, which later linked the region with other agricultural and resource way stations. The train, when it did arrive, brought communities of people from the numerous hearts of Europe, disgorging them across the North-West Territories in pulses, whose towns, like Calmar, puddled their diaspora: Thorsby, Warburg, Breton, Buford, Telfordville, New Norway, Millet, Kavanagh. In one such pulse, Calmar became largely Ukrainian, and but for the name, the Swedish influence quickly disappeared. When the Canadian Pacific Railroad (CPR) attempted to rename the early settlement's newly built siding and station Calverley after a small West Yorkshire village, the town's residents refused, rallying behind Calmar. Much, later, I learned Ukrainian dancing as a young boy at the local school; it is what everyone did.

"South East Quarter of Section 12, Township 49, Range 27, West of the 4th Meridian" was our farm's formal property description. We called it Lauriston Farm. Lauriston was the name of a thirteenth-century castle and estate that overlooked my mother's home village in Aberdeenshire on the east coast of Scotland. Lauriston was also near the herring port of Stonehaven where my father lived as a child. When the Highland cows arrived some fifteen years into our lives on Lauriston, it was felt, by us, that they fit in well. Others, the more industrial amongst our farming friends and neighbours, felt differently; smaller of frame, slower to yield, and long-horned, the Highland cows, though lovely to look at, were uneconomic. When my parents sold the farm in 2005 and moved to another farm hundreds of miles away in northern British Columbia, they took the name with them.

Not far from our Lauriston, on an unremarkable small rise just south of the town of Devon, through which we drove every day on the way to school, the Late Devonian period – or, to be more precise, the Frasnian – burst into 1947. Leduc No. 1, as the well came to be known, went deeper than previous attempts to find crude. On 13 February, one thousand six hundred and twenty-three metres and seven centimetres below the surface, the bore well broke into a puddle of fossilized life. It was a Thursday. Several million years of photosynthetic energy, stored mainly in Palaeozoic stromatoporoids (sclerosponges) and their ancient symbiotic ecologies,[8] had been dormant, but brewing, for 382.7 million years. When tapped, the puddle and its possibilities burst up to the surface with a rumble that is said to have shook the ground. The fifty-foot geyser, a mix of combustible gases and light and medium crude, was set alight by a burning sack, an honour given the youngest member of the drilling crew. From this rushing, ancient, energy-laden stratigraphy, by way of southern England, the town of Devon got its name.

When the Devonian blew, re-ignited, into our Holocene, time and space shrank. The vast stratigraphy of the Leduc Field rapidly changed the surrounding landscape and economy. The land around us, once used for agriculture and subsistence in processes Carl Blomquist would have recognized and built, transformed into one of the world's largest export regions for hydrocarbons: crude oil, natural gases, coal, and bitumen. Blomquist would have faced two- and three-day horse-drawn journeys to the larger towns of Leduc and Edmonton nearby. Our return carpool journeys to our urban private school in Edmonton, Tempo (both a term for rate of motion and an acronym for the motto *Tota Edocenda Maxime Parentum Officium* – "all teaching is pre-eminently the duty of parents"), where we learned geography, Latin, calculus, stoichiometry, history, and handwriting (before I flunked out, aged thirteen), took a total of two hours.

It was on Tempo's fields that we played football for most of the sixty-eight-day *Amoco-Dome Brazeau River* 13-12-48-12-W5M blowout. On 17 October 1982, two hundred million cubic feet per day of poisonous hydrogen sulphide erupted, uncontrolled, from Devonian reservoirs underneath the lodgepole pine forests of Drayton Valley, some 130 kilometres away. Only when the sour gas stench became too much, our eyes and noses burning, stomachs nauseous, were we forced inside. Before the oil ran out and hydrocarbon exploration shifted to fracking methane, the rhythmic suck of bobbing white-faced oil derricks was a common sight on our drive to and from school, past Devon, and through (though never stopping at) Stony Plain 135 Indian Reserve (Enoch Cree Nation).

We settled south of Calmar, along Conjuring Creek, during the oil crisis of the early 1970s. Although my father had a good job as an architect and planner designing the local university hospital, my parents also harboured back-to-the-land plans: wood stoves, self-sufficiency, goats, and carob. Such sentimentality was largely foreign to the other settlers around us. (We never used "settler" to refer to ourselves; others, prior to us, were settlers, yes. We were different, we thought: educated, urban, and superior. Our trying hard not to be superior only made us, and our self-conscious class differences, stand out even more.) Our family responded in our settlement practices with concern regarding the ecological risks industrialization and consumption wrought. We were suspicious of the oil exploration and seismic crews who, from time to time, lumbered uninvited and unimpeded across our fields, front and back, pressing inaudible sonic waves into the ground in slow, measured divination. Skeptical as we were of the powers that seismic premonition brought, our comfortable lives, of course, were as much dependent on these hydrocarbons, their possibilities and their promises, as were the resistant, mildly political, contradictory sentiments to which we learned to give voice. We wished, silently, for oil to be found under our land. Finding oil or gas meant not insubstantial fees paid to us by the oil company every year for access to the well. With an access fee, one could renovate the kitchen, build a new shed, buy a motorcycle or, in good times, a new truck. Many around us did just that with their yearly payments. Neither oil nor gas was ever found under that Lauriston Farm.

It was not until I left that I began to understand better what arrival meant. Not their arrival in our yard, but *our* arrival. Not that I had any choice about my own arrival, either in Conjuring Creek when I was three, or earlier, in Calgary's no longer extant General Hospital, in a city that emerged after an eponymous walled fort. Built in 1874 and 1875, the years immediately before Treaty 6, on a flat flood plain at the junction of the Elbow and the Bow rivers, Fort Calgary, as photographs show, was a rectangular palisade of felled trees. With a large gate, flanked on either side and in each of the camp's corners with look-out towers, it was just like in the storybooks. Fort Calgary was not dissimilar to the Roman forts pictured in the Asterix and Obelix comic stories we loved as children, and from which my brother and I first learned about an idea of "History." Fort Calgary's wooden palisades were disappointingly, however, not sharpened as in storybook Gaul.

The Elbow River, on the banks of which Fort Calgary was built, was so named because the Tsuu T'ina (Sarcee), Nehiyawak (Cree), Îyârhe Nakodabi (Stony-Nakoda), and Siksika (Blackfoot) referred to the flat expanse and meeting place for various plains and foothills peoples, as, respectively, Kootsisáw' (elbow), Otos-kwunee (elbow), Wincheesh-pah (elbow), Moh-kíns-tsis (elbow). The land-river interface is shaped like an elbow. Simple. Calgary is an estate on the northwest coast of the Isle of Mull, the other side of Scotland, whence my parents emigrated when they settled in western Canada in the late 1960s. Itself anglicized, Mull's Calgary is said to derive from combining the sounds of the Gaelic words *caladh* and *garaidh* (the haven by the dyke).[9] Simple. In 1876, Lt-Col. James Farquharson Macleod of the Royal North-West Mounted Police (RNWMP) named the fort at the prairie edge of the foothills after his family's ancestral estate on Mull. Macleod, who in 1874 also named Fort Macleod, south of Calgary, after himself, is reported to have said, in an equally plausible story of the Scottish estate's origins, that *calgary* means "clear flowing water."

In 1874–75, Fort Calgary was known, briefly, as Fort Brisebois, after the area's first RNWMP commander, Éphrem A. Brisebois, who was appointed by Macleod to rid the area of illegal whisky traders. Brisebois was a worldly soldier who fought both in the American Civil War and as a volunteer with the Papal Zouaves against Garibaldi and Mazzini's Risorgimento efforts to unify Italy. He often clashed with his superior, Macleod, who, in 1876, changed the name to Fort Calgary after forcing Brisebois to resign from the police.[10]

But 1874, 1875, 1876, and 1877 are not how those who lived in the area prior to the arrival of Macleod and company would have referred to the years of Fort Calgary's building, or to the signing of treaties there and farther north. Time was narrated, instead, by a "winter count."[11] Each winter around the time of the solstice, an appointed keeper or amanuensis of the winter count – *ai sinakinax* is the

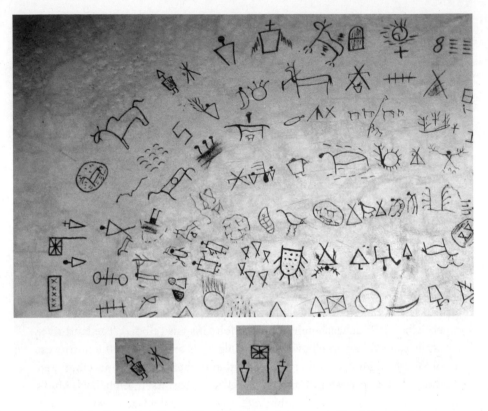

Figure 10.2 Three details of Piikani (Peigan) winter count, Head-Smashed-In Buffalo Jump.

Blackfoot term for "writers of history"[12] – would be entrusted with an oral story recounting the period since the last winter solstice. Those gathered would collectively narrate the period since the last winter count with an eventful happening: hunger or bounty, a hard winter, the death of someone important, a unique cosmological occurrence, etc. An "epitomizing event"[13] or circumstance became the reference, and was remembered mnemonically with a phrase. Sometimes the oral story of the winter count was also transcribed in pictographic form on a hide – usually, for Plains peoples, a bison hide.

One of the few remaining pictographic winter counts in southwestern Canada is a Northern Piikani (Peigan, or in Siksika Aapátohsipikáni) hide preserved at Head-Smashed-In Buffalo Jump. The hide narrates, in a series of simple pictographs of human, animal, mythical, and other cosmological figures, 114 years of events central to its keepers. Each different, the pictographs spiral from the centre of the hide outwards. The count begins its telling near the hide's centre with a circle of six tipis. Counting backwards from the last image drawn, an image that denotes the year the bison disappeared completely, approximately, in colonial terms, 1881, the centre approximately corresponds to, in colonial terms, the winter of 1767. Because different groups of people kept their own winter counts, there is no one standard for narrating and remembering duration or recounting history across Turtle Island.

In this Piikáni example, first contact and the arrival of white settlers is also variously recorded. The arrival of the Royal North-West Mounted Police in what became Fort Calgary is recorded on the hide with a pictograph denoting two adjacent figures (see figure 10.2). On the left, a simplified human figure stands. A shaded box above its feet symbolizes the scarlet Norfolk jacket worn by the Canadian dominion constabulary. (The red distinguished Canadian cavalry from blue-jacketed Americans.) An unshaded triangle with a neck connecting to the shaded square represents the iconic white cotton and cork pith helmet worn by the RNWM cavalry. To the right of the human figure is a tipi drawn of three intersecting lines. Above the leftmost pole, a tiny circle presumably indicates the moon or another cosmological figure.

Two later transcriptions of winter counts similar to that recorded with the Peigan hide are held in the archives of the Glenbow Museum. One, in the hand of the *ai sinakinax* Joe Little Chief, notes, alongside the date 1874, the description in the epigraph opening this chapter and the ostensible reason Fort Brise-bois/Calgary was founded as a colonial settlement: "Our friends the R.N.W.M. police came west and saved the Indians from drinking that bad whisky ever since then they look after the Indians."[14] Another winter count, in the hand of a contemporary *ai sinakinax* of Little Chief, Teddy Yellow-Fly, the son of a Black-foot woman and a Chinese father, notes that while "The Year Little Coyote was killed by Running Rabbit" corresponds to 1874, a simpler description corresponds to 1875: "The year the Royal N.W.M. police arrived."[15] Both Joe Little Chief and Teddy Yellow-Fly agree that 1877 relates to the year Treaty 7 was signed. No doubt 1877 became the wider sign of feeling bound to a colonial designation of historical time. Joe Little Chief recounts the significance of signing the treaty, that year's epitomizing event, with the following transcribed entry, which resembles a description of 1877 more than it does an epitomizing event narrated in a pre-colonial winter count.

> 1877 That was the big year that is the year we made peace with Her Majesty Queen Victoreia the bigest treaty ever paid to the Indains of North American the five tribes Blackfeets Bloods Peigan and Sarcee also the Stonys of that was a big day lot of Indains on horse back

riding back and forth singing war songs finely Crowfoot's brother told him you go and sign treaty the buffalo is gone now we have to live the white man way or we starve so do not forget our people and the future generations try and keep as much land as you can the future generation will make use of it.[16]

The Peigan hide winter count symbolises Little Chief's "big year" with three interrelated figures (see figure 10.2). Two inverted triangles, one on the right with a cross, and another on the left with a darkly shaded circle and neck, flank on either side a Union Jack flag and flagpole. The sign of the darkened circle and neck is used throughout the various winters narrated on the hide to represent Peigan ancestors. It is reasonable to assume that the triangles represent two peoples, one Christian and one "Indain," "reconciled" and bound under the British flag by the Crown treaty.[17]

When the RNWM police arrived in the region of Moh-kíns-tsis and began to erect the post that became Fort Calgary, they too were presented, by the Siksikaitsitapi (Blackfoot-speaking tribes, literally "Blackfoot-speaking real people"), with something that both constituted and signified a bond and responsibility.[18] But it was a very different and somewhat untranslatable – for the settlers – bundle of contractual relations.

Amongst the most sacred and important members of the social lives of the Siksikaitsitapi are *amopístaani*, or "medicine bundles." *Amopístaani* translates as "bound-together-by-wrapping-around"[19] and refers, typically, to two different types of bundles: *Niinaimsskaahkoyinnimaan*, the Thunder Medicine Pipe Bundle, and what is said to be the oldest amongst the Siksikaitsitapi, *Ksisskstakyomopistaan*, the Beaver Bundle (literally, "beaver-bundled-up").[20] *Amopístaani* are bundles of gathered materials and objects: animal and bird skins, feathers, tobacco and herbs, counting sticks, dried plants, pipes, stones, necklaces, amulets, etc. The materials, and what they speak, were gifted to their human holders – *liyaohkiimiiksi* (literally "the-ones-that-have-water"), specifically, people entrusted with their care – by the Beaver, non-human people with whom the holders, and their wider human relations, interacted. In the case of the Beaver Bundle, early *liyaohkiimiiksi* were entrusted by Beaver with the knowledge inhering in the relations of the bundle's contents. The bundle, given by the Beaver, its ancestors, and spirits, thus constitutes the manifest material connections to the ecologies within which the *liyaohkiimiiksi* and their peoples lived.

Bundles, then, are more than simply assembled representations of the relations they denote. They are, rather, literal ecologies of thought, the living relations themselves.[21] The bound-together-ness of the constituent parts of the bundle in leather, woven cloth, bone, wood, and the like inhere contractual relationships humans have with the ecologies that structure life and its possibility: plants, animals, elements, forces, and beings. In other words, the bundles *are* the living instantiation of the social structure of the relational lifeworld within which humans, as a particular form that emerges from a shared more-than-human culture, participate.[22] Bundles, in Siksikaitsitapi, are *niitaikso'kowammootsi'opi*: "how we know our relationships to be," or "how we are related to each other,"[23] wherein "each other" is the holistic interrelation of living, material immanence. In ceremonies that care for, and attend to, the bundles, stories of this immanent relation are narrated in the bundles' unpacking. As onto-poetic forms, the stories are gifted to their keepers' lineages by the living relations of the bundles themselves: the Beaver and its many supporting relations.

Government representatives who arrived to police what became Fort Calgary were entrusted to enrol others into social and economic bonds of responsibility and reciprocity. As such, they too were understandably recognized and welcomed by Siksikaitsitapi with *amopístaani*. For in the bundles lay the pre-textual stories, the constitutive relations, the forms of knowledge, and the ethical possibilities (they are one and the same) necessary, in Blackfeet eyes, to live within the relations of Moh-kíns-tsis. Such knowledge, immanent within the land, the places, and the relations the bundles embodied, would have been essential for living at this prairie edge of the foothills.

Colonial newcomers like Brisebois and Macleod, of course, had none of the means to recognize, let alone understand, the bundles and their living relations. Nor, more significantly, did they have the willingness to learn to listen to the gifted bundles' cosmo-political potential. That the Beaver and related ancestors had bestowed the knowledge enshrined within the bundles and their blessing would have been fanciful nonsense. Colonial officials took their rationales and legitimacy from other bondings, blessings, and their associated relics, as the first sentence of Treaty 7 makes plain:

> Made and concluded this twenty-second day of September, in the
> year of Our Lord, one thousand eight hundred and seventy-seven,
> between Her Most Gracious Majesty the Queen of Great Britain
> and Ireland, by Her Commissioners, the Honorable David Laird,
> Lieutenant-Governor and Indian Superintendent of the North-West
> Territories, and James Farquharson MacLeod, C.M.G., Commissioner
> of the North-West Mounted Police, of the one part, and the Black-
> feet, Blood, Piegan, Sarcee, Stony and other Indians, inhabitants of
> the Territory north of the United States Boundary Line, east of the

central range of the Rocky Mountains, and south and west of Treaties numbers six and four, by their Head Chiefs and Minor Chiefs or Councillors, chosen as hereinafter mentioned, of the other part.

Brisebois, likely amongst the first to be gifted a Beaver bundle by "the other part," was a Catholic mercenary, and though he and a Métis woman later married, a choice which, to Macleod, made him a maverick, sensing in a Beaver Bundle what he felt towards his own reliquaries, tabernacles, and treaties would have been unthinkable. For settlers, Beaver were not ancestral, nor did they share knowledge; they were either expendable wealth or ecological pests upon whose management the settlers' presence depended.

Brisebois and the RNWMP set in train a series of structural relations of coloniality in which property bequeathed mineral wealth, which in turn evolved into industrial extraction, which in turn threatened ecologies. The Beaver, ignored and exploited by an original colonial presence, came later to embody, to those re-colonizing and re-settling an industrialized land with the purported aim of thinking differently, a threat to the ecological relations and knowledge originally gifted.

KALMAR WITH A K

I heard, again, of Kalmar with a K in 2008–09 when I was in China, on a short ethnographic excursion to Yiwu, in Zheijiang Province. Yiwu is an important node in the world's small commodities market and one of China's self-described "economic miracles." I was there, ostensibly, to study the urban imaginaries made possible by the accelerated condensing spirals of spaces and times we sometimes call neoliberal globalization. Yiwu's Futian Market, a wholesale pavilion 5.5 million square metres in size and encompassing some 75,000 booths devoted to showcasing "made in China" commodities to buyers from around the world, resembled, to me, nineteenth-century arcade spaces, if also grossly inflated by what a carbonscape affords. Indeed, the urban plan of the city itself, with its neighbourhood sectors devoted to the production and sale of socks, or Christmas ornaments (approximately 70 per cent of the world's supply of which originates there), or automobile accessories, or cheap jewellery, or fake flowers ... anything, really, you can think of, manifests this consumptive imaginary par excellence. At the south entrance to the Futian Market, a large mosaic of the fabled Silk Road and its traders exemplified these contemporary neo-East and neo-West imaginaries into which Yiwu was keen to write itself. The city's slogan above the mosaic proclaimed: "A Sea of Commodities, A Paradise for Shoppers. New Market, New Yiwu, New Horizon, New Progress."

Yiwu had become so successful, in such a short period, that it sought to locate satellites outside itself. One of the planned European centres for the Futian commodity-scape was to be, in miniature, in Kalmar, southeastern Sweden. The rationale for this peripheralization of buying centres from the Yiwu metropole was to enable buyers to travel to the "made in China" phenomenon, but to do so closer to home. Given my own connections with Kalmar, not visiting southern Sweden was not an option.

When time allowed a year or so later, I stood, in early September 2010, amidst an abandoned cookie factory cum exhibition market near the edge of the Baltic Sea. I was in the quiet city of Kalmar to research, as I discovered, why its proposed wholesale exhibition hall, which sought to connect European buyers with one of the world's largest small commodities markets in the eastern manufacturing district of Zhejiang Province, had failed. On the northern outskirts of Kalmar, the exhibition market was to have been set up inside the unoccupied remains of one of the town's many abandoned factories. The factory sites, many quite large, were cut into forest clearings along now vacant roads. Square sided, the boarded-up buildings were surrounded with tumbledown security fencing. They were abandoned forts where little stirred. On several occasions, I visited the empty industrial stretch on which the proposed market was to be located during the week or so I spent in Kalmar, yet I never met another human soul.

When complete, those who would fill the retail market – Chinese traders, entrepreneurs, and investors – were to be housed in a specially built settlement just down the road. Their Sino-Scandi homes were to be arranged as a gated community, sheltered from the road by a large wall. The planned, brightly coloured, square-sided box homes, with steep pitched roofs, curving clay tiles instead of tin, and lions guarding their entrances, were never built. Midway through the cookie factory's extensive conversion, national and geo-financial events intervened. In 2009, the project to build the exhibition site in the image of Yiwu was finally abandoned and the workers sent home.

Its remains were strewn about me. The speed with which the site was closed by the Swedish authorities was reflected in the site's rubble. Bales of unused workers' gloves. Downed tools. A rice cooker. Clothes. Chalk graffiti – lotus flowers, a monkey's face, numerous (unreadable to me) *hànzì*. Building plans lay on the floor; I took them home with me. The set of keys and spare coins that lay forgotten on a pile of neatly folded clothes, however, I left. Unused mortar had solidified in plastic pails tied to the bamboo ladders that leaned against semi-finished interior walls. Half-pinned plastic flapped above. Dripping water echoed as it puddled in now empty rooms. Outside, under the grey Baltic clouds, a chill wind stirred the pine trees circling the site. Its *sus*[24] was both melancholic whisper and blessed indifference to the peeling posters whose images of jewellery, dolls,

Figure 10.3 "Feel China, Enjoy Life!" Kalmar, Sweden.

tennis rackets, and electric handsaws endorsed the words "Feel China, Enjoy Life!" (see figure 10.3).

The site's workers, imported from China to build the market, had been discovered by Swedish authorities to be working for Chinese rates of pay, without due attention to safety standards and in contravention of numerous labour regulations. The project was also later discovered to be a front for moving private capital out of China. Swedish intermediaries had enticed Chinese foreign investors with the false promise of Swedish passports. Chinese investors looking to hide money saw Kalmar as an out-of-the-way frontier opportunity for expanding their economic influence and private means. Based on a business model that worked extremely well in China, it was thought that Yiwu should work as well in Northern Europe too.

Everything to build the market except the workers – they flew from Wenzhou – had been imported on container ships to Kalmar's Baltic port: bricks, steel, mortar, twig brushes, gloves. It was cheaper to ship everything necessary from China than to build it using regionally sourced Scandinavian materials. The irony was that Kalmar's economy had been decimated by the very forces of globalization that were invited back to revitalize it. Production of tractors, mobile phones, and cookies had all been outsourced to China years earlier. Kalmar's economy declined. The empty buildings were now being converted into wholesale "hypermarts" where European buyers could cut deals with traders without travelling all the way to China to source cheap, made-in-China commodities; Europe was being provincialized by China, but through variants of its own horizons. Small colonies, protected as special economic zones and financed by the Chinese economic boom, were set up in places like Kalmar (other similar initiatives emerged in Dubai, Parma, Budapest, and Amsterdam) where export market platforms brought China to the West, but on Chinese terms.

As I stood in the empty factory, the ghosts of its workers and their memories traced home on half-finished walls: footprints marked themselves in concrete dust; nearby gloves clutched with hollow hands. Outside, the posters implored me to feel China, enjoy life.

Something meanwhile was happening deep in the ocean on the other side of the Atlantic. Oil was billowing out, uncontrolled, from the sea floor. Deepwater Horizon was targeting the Macondo Prospect, a mid-Miocene hydrocarbon-bearing turbidite formation approximately five times deeper than the Leduc Formation. The Macondo Prospect was named in 1998 after the fictional ill-fated plantation town at the centre of Gabriel García Márquez's novel *One Hundred Years of Solitude*, which, in the story, is destroyed by a hurricane. In April 2010, a hurricane damaged the Deepwater drilling platform above the Macondo Prospect, thus setting off a chain of events that led to an explosion and the well's collapse to the bottom of the sea where oil billowed out not far from its drowned ruins for over 150 days.

A week after my visit to Kalmar, I attended an academic conference on the nearby small island of Hven in the Øresund Strait. Hven is famous for being the site where Tycho Brahe, the Danish astronomer, located his sixteenth-century planetary observatories, Uraniborg and Stjerneborg. It was on Hven that Brahe, possibly with his assistant Johannes Kepler, began the astronomical measurements for what became the empirical foundations for defining planetary motion, Kepler's verification of the Copernican thesis, and Isaac Newton's theory of gravity. Every night, Brahe would stare up into sixteenth-century heavens at ancient, yet-unseen starlight. We, the conference goers who had gathered to discuss island geographies a mile or so from the ruins of Brahe's observatories, stared at another kind of telescope, a screen, on which live events were pictured from far away at the bottom of the Gulf of Mexico. Willing the well to be capped lest the disaster continue, a disaster that made our watching possible, we gazed at the images sent by a remotely piloted submersible: rushing, roiling, swirling plumes of darkly stored sunlight. Variously coloured in the robot's machinic gaze, the ancient plumes, before unseen, sunlight now in a different form, swelled out, insistent, uncontrollable, a wound in the form of a perfect hole.

CODA

On 18 January 2017, the East Wind pulled into Europe. After an eighteen-day journey across east and central Asia, the thirty-four-carriage train, which departed from Yiwu on 2 January, arrived first in Moscow. It then moved on to Europe's largest inland port, Duisburg, Germany, where it split, sending cargo to Milan, Madrid, and the UK. The locomotive's final stop was Barking in East London, where it was greeted with dancing dragons, red flags, Union Jacks, and dignitaries heralding a new era of Sino-Anglo trade relations. In Barking, it turned around to head back, laden with goods for China's growing consumer markets: timber, meat, wine, beer, olive oil, cheese, fashionable clothing and accessories, industrial parts, electronics, and optics.

The train was the first of what is now a weekly service, and was established under China's One Belt, One Road policy, which seeks to reconstruct the ancient trade of the fabled Silk Road between China, Europe, and Africa. The engine itself, ceremonially launched at the Yiwu Railway Freight Station in Jinhua on 18 November 2014, enshrines Mao's dictum: "The east wind will prevail over the west wind." Indeed, the East Wind is an attempt to respond to the failure of previous trade efforts like those enshrined in the ruins of Kalmar's cookie factory. Emporia in Kalmar, Schiphol, Parma, and elsewhere never attracted much European trade interest. In a business sense, it was easier to for buyers and wholesalers to travel by air to China. China, nevertheless, has persisted, and despite the need to change trains due to different rail gauges between east and west, the eighteen-day train service is faster than a thirty-day sea voyage and cheaper than air freight. Crucially, it is argued, the train allows small and medium manufacturers and distributors access to urban markets in Europe at a fraction of sea- and air-based shipping costs. In its inaugural trip, the East Wind brought to Europe approximately £4 million (US$4.9 million) worth of socks, cloth, household goods, knock-off bags, and cheap commodities for the tourist markets in Spain, Italy, and the UK. London's Camden, Barcelona's Barri Gotic, Venice's St Mark's, and Rome's Via Sannio depend on Yiwu's ability to manufacture cheaply "baubles, bangles, and beads," or in this case key rings, phone covers, fridge magnets, and souvenirs – multicoloured plastic Gaudi lizards or John Bull terriers via Zhejiang Province – and the possibilities afforded by hundreds of millions of years of stored sunlight.

One hundred and four years prior to Fort Calgary's founding, Captain James Cook warned in his diary entry for Saturday, 18 April 1778, against the easy assumption that "natives" engaged in trade would be enticed and satisfied by "trifles ... beads and such things."[25] Some two weeks earlier, on Tuesday, 31 March 1778, he had anchored his ships, *Resolution* and *Discovery*, in a cove on what would become known as Canada's west coast. The inlet was halfway up the west coast of Vancouver Island. When Cook's ships laid anchor in the cove, they unknowingly did so near Yuk^wat, the spring and summer settlement of the Muwachat. In Nuu-chah-nulth, the language spoken by the Muwachat, Yuk^wat means "place of wind,"[26] exposed as the settlement is to the ocean's winter storms and summer breezes. As soon as they had anchored, Cook and his parties were met by, as he wrote, "a mild inoffensive people [who] shewed great readiness to part with anything they had ... but were more desirous of iron than anything else, the use of which they very well knew."[27] The Spanish naval ship *Santiago*, captained by Juan Pérez, had anchored and traded in the inlet some four years earlier. After confusing the Nuu-chah-nulth direction "to come around" with the cove's proper name, Cook named the inlet Nutka; today the sound is still known as Nootka Sound.

Cook and his ships remained anchored in Nootka Sound for nearly a month, sailing out on the Sunday, 26 April 1778. In that time he came to distinguish between "Our Friends the Indians" and "Strangers"; "our friends" were the people who lived in Yuk^wat. "Strangers" were visitors from other settlements. In his diary entry of 18 April, he notes the familiarity that comes with presence when the first "Strangers" arrive: "On the 18th a party of Strangers in Six or eight canoes came into the Cove where they remained looking at us for some time." He noted their eagerness to trade and their particular interest in metals.

> Our articles of trafick consisted for the most part in trifles, and yet
> we were put to our shifts to find these trifles, for beads and such
> things of which I had yet some left, were in little esteem. Nothing
> would go down with them but metal and brass was now become their
> favourate, So that before we left the place, hardly a bit of brass was
> left in the ship, except what was in the necessary instruments. Whole
> Suits of cloaths were stripped of every button, Bureaus &c of their
> furniture and Copper kettle, Tin canasters, Candle sticks, &c all went
> to wreck.[28]

Ship men latter boasted of giving such "lovely trinkets" away in trade for sea otter pelts, which they then sold some months later in China for vast profits, enabling them "to supply themselves with necessities [like] silk gowns, fans, tea and other articles." Coal would be discovered and mined on Vancouver Island, not far from Nootka, in 1835, in what would be called Fort Rupert by the Hudson's Bay Company. Fort Rupert was built on the site of Kwagu'ł, a Kwakwaka'wakw village. In Kwak'wala, the Wakashan language spoken in the area, Kwagu'ł means "smoke-around-the-world."

ACKNOWLEDGMENTS

I would like to thank Chris Andersen and James L. Dempsey for their historical advice, and the Nuffield Foundation for a small grant that enabled travel to China and Sweden.

NOTES

1 I use the term "Indians" in scare quotes to indicate, quite self-consciously, the term I would have used at the time, and the term the people in the car would have used then, as many continue to use it today, to describe themselves, at least to me, a white settler. I also aim to indicate, rhetorically, the problematic of its continued and contested legitimacy. My use elsewhere in the chapter of "Indian" should be read with this authorial reflexivity in mind.

2 Government of Canada, "Copy of Treaty No. 6."

3 Ibid.

4 There is only one faintly legible signature written in Maskwacis Cree syllabics inscribed on Treaty 6. The name is not transliterated into the Latin alphabet, unlike those simply marked with an X. It is copied here in the knowledge that, due to it being very difficult to read, I may have copied it incorrectly.

5 Since 1 January 2014, when it changed its name, Hobbema has come to be known by its ancestral Cree designation, Maskwacis (bear hills).

6 Fromhold, "Wizard Lake."

7 Tom Dirsa, "How Did Calmar Come to Be?," *The Pipestone Flyer*, 7 December 2012, http://www.pipestoneflyer.ca/community/301135791.html.

8 Moore, "Devonian Reefs in Canada," 367.

9 Ayto and Crofton, *Brewer's Britain and Ireland*, 82.

10 *Dictionary of Canadian Biography*, vol. 11 (1881–1890), s.v. "Ephrém A. Brisebois."

11 My thanks to the sociologist Professor Chris Andersen and the historian Dr James L. Dempsey for their help in learning more about winter counts.

12 Tovias, "The Right to Possess Memory," 100.

13 Fogelson as cited in Nabokov, *A Forest of Time*, 35n18.

14 Joe Little Chief, "1830–1911, Joe Little Chief's Blackfoot Stories, no. 18: From 1830 the Year Crowfoot Was Born," M-4394-23, Glenbow Archives, http://www.empire.amdigital.co.uk/Documents/Details/Joe%20Little%20Chiefs%20Blackfoot%20stories%20no18.

15 Teddy Yellow Fly, Fonds glen-2520 – Teddy Yellow Fly fonds, M-4423-p05, Glenbow Archives, https://albertaonrecord.ca/teddy-yellow-fly-fonds.

16 The entry is copied verbatim. Little Chief, "1830–1911."

17 Highlighting "reconciled" with scare quotes simply notes how colonization is often con-tractually bundled within rhetoric and practices of supposed kindness and agreed peace-making. Yet, such bundling is always under the terms and parameters prescribed by the colonizer. As part of their symbolic and material reproduction, therefore, such contracts constitute an epistemic and ontological violence. For detailed critiques of the politics of reconciliation and recognition see, for example, Coulthard, *Red Skin, White Masks*; Povinelli, *The Cunning of Recognition*; and L. Simpson, *As We Have Always Done*.

18 Bastien, *Blackfoot Ways of Knowing*, 9.

19 Heavy Head, "Feeding Sublimity," 126.

20 Bastien, *Blackfoot Ways of Knowing*, 11.

21 Lokensgard, *Blackfoot Religion*, 97.

22 The characterization of the bundles and their being gifted to human forms by beaver forms reflect an anthropological theory of multinatural perspectivalism, which, as Vivie-ros de Castro notes in *The Relative Native*, emerges from the widely held indigenous prin-ciple that both humans and animals participate in a fundamental culture, but differ in nature. Multinatural perspectivalism inverts the modern Eurocentric principle of culture differentiating from a shared nature.

23 Bastien, *Blackfoot Ways of Knowing*, 211.

24 *Sus* is the Swedish word for the whispering sound of wind blowing through pine leaves. The English term *susurration* hints at these Nordic roots. The Greek-inflected word *psi-thurism*, meaning the same, is perhaps similarly onomatopoeic, if also more awkward.

25 Cook, "Journal, 29 and 30 March, and 26 April 1778," in *The Journals of Captain James Cook*, 302.

26 Atleo (Umeek), *Principles of Tsawalk*, 43.

27 Cook, *The Journals of Captain James Cook*, 296.

28 Ibid., 302.

CHAPTER 11

In, around, and under
Moose Jaw, Saskatchewan

KAREN ENGLE

> For every spot on this alternate earth to which I
> was transported appeared wholly occupied by what
> once had been. Thus each sound and each moment
> came toward me as the double of itself.
>
> Walter Benjamin, *Berlin Childhood around 1900*

CARVING A GROOVE

Picture a black rubber wheel, no more than eight inches in diameter. On either side of this wheel, a simple black plastic handle, similar to the handles on old BMX bicycles, attaches to the end of a central bar. The wheel sits in the centre of this bar. End to end, the whole thing couldn't have been more than twelve inches in length.[1] It lived in the mystery room of my maternal grandparents' house at 1084 Redland Avenue in Moose Jaw, Saskatchewan. This room is located between the house and the carport. Extruding out from the dining room, it attaches to the house proper but sits outside of the primary structure. The room has two doors: one leads into the dining room and the other leads out to the carport. It is the architectural embodiment of Derrida's interior exteriority or exterior interiority: the structure of the trace that returns death to the subject, infuses alterity into presence, and illuminates difference as irreducible.[2] This room is a hinge between worlds. It was uninsulated and unforgiving in Saskatchewan winters, allowing the weather to come inside and providing an early lesson in the permeability of structure. Emptied out, the room measures 9.5' × 13' but so long as my grandparents lived there, I never saw it emptied out. This room collected all the things the rest of the house could not hold: things that weren't used regularly or at all, or that had been abandoned and forgotten. It was cold storage for familial junk. Items here hung in suspended animation for decades, until my parents were tasked with the job of delivering these objects into new networks of circulation or decay. In this room, the wheel lived and waited for our visits, when it would call me over for a temporary reprieve from its banishment, and the game could begin again.

The game: I would bend over to hold onto the handles and then run the wheel around the entire main floor.[3] Starting in the dining room, I only ever went in one direction: dining room → kitchen → back hall → front hall → living room → dining room. The wheel and I ran thousands of circuits over the years. We paid no mind to grownups visiting in the living room, or refilling their coffee cups in the kitchen. In part, the game was an exercise in speed and dexterity: how fast could I wheel while navigating the alternately darkened and light-filled rooms, the textural shifts from carpet to lino to carpet again and, occasionally, adult legs that got in the way. But the crux of the matter was repetition. One circuit accomplished nothing, but counting one hundred circuits, in segments of ten, indicated achievement and endurance. These were private victories. Privately, I counted off laps, set goals, and finished a project nobody else knew I was working on. Running the wheel provided one of my first lessons in the confusions between the world-building pleasures of ritual and the compulsions of the Protestant work ethic.[4]

These repetitions generated more than ritual pleasure, and satisfied more than a child's compulsive drive; they also created a pathway through 1084, the house my mother grew up in and that my grandparents lived with for as long as they could. Much like neural pathways are carved through repetitive firings, I carved a private trajectory for being-there, one that established a zone of familiarity through repetition that worked much like classical mnemonics.[5] 1084 designates a large two-storey green wooden and brick house on the corner of a North Hill street in south central Saskatchewan. It also encompasses the breadth and depth of nearly a century's maternal history. I don't recall the moment that wheel stopped calling or the year I forgot that old circuit of repetition, but at a certain point I became aware of a space left by its absence. This absence has a specific gravity to it, a weight I carry within me. But it is also a cord that extends from me all the way to Moose Jaw, attaching me to this place that is not mine but that nevertheless works on me.

The language of psychoanalysis haunts the margins here, like the waiting wheel. Any invocation of repetition, compulsion, of cords that bind (umbilical or otherwise), or a return to the maternal cannot but draw us back to Freud. I have indeed invited a certain Freud into this scene, not in order to Oedipalize my thinking, but in order to explore what happens to *feelings of structure* when they come into contact with fantasy, memory, and history.[6] As Joan Scott suggests, the "incommensurability" of history and psychoanalysis can provide a productive workspace, one that can "challenge history's conventional self-representation."[7] This essay is an attempt to think through some of the affective implications of *feelings of structure*, our inversion of Raymond Williams's now classic – and obstinately ambiguous – phrase "structures of feeling."[8] The "structure" in *feelings of structure* designates both the physical, built environment as well as less tangible structures of memory and history as they intersect in this place that is not mine, yet connects to me, innervating my nervous system and asking me to create new circuits of movement and knowledge. The point is not to write a history of Moose Jaw, or to write an auto-ethnographic account of 1084, but to try to communicate the affective experience of being in this place, both now and then, attending to the vibrations of memories as they intersect with histories since excavated and illuminated. Sara Ahmed describes affect as "what sticks, or what sustains or preserves the connection between ideas, values, and object" and as "the messiness of the experiential, the unfolding of bodies into worlds and the drama of contingency, how we are touched by what we are near."[9] 1084 is the thing that "sticks" here; it is my draw to this place and its surroundings, and the reason I returned to Moose Jaw in the summer of 2016.

GOING UNDER

In the mid-1980s, the Business Improvement District commissioned a study from the Main Street Project Office to investigate the veracity of long-standing legends of a network of tunnels running under the south end of downtown, from River Street down to Manitoba Street. Stories that posit the existence of underground tunnels snaking their way beneath the streets in order to connect buildings for the purposes of gambling, opium use, and bootlegging during Prohibition have circulated for decades.[10] The study began by looking for physical and archival evidence of the tunnels. Two investigations were conducted, one in 1986 and the second in 1987. Neither report provides a conclusive answer to the question of the tunnels' existence. The first investigation, for instance, finds evidence to support the claim that tunnels had indeed existed, but proceeds to qualify this assertion with the following statement: "Information retrieved from archival sources, physical evidence, and conversations held with long-time residents leads us to believe that a misconception surrounding the definition of 'tunnels' may have been instrumental in fostering many of the 'stories' and 'legends' of Moose Jaw's history. The common definition of 'tunnels' suggests a long, dark, narrow passage, perhaps underground. Yet tunnels, as described in archival excerpts, could have also referred to any undetectable means of access between one building and another."[11]

While the second report states "there were not even vague references to the tunnels in the archival sources," both reports conclude that more investigation is warranted.[12] Over the years, the local newspaper has published multiple stories of tunnel discovery, along with anecdotal accounts by long-time residents and disputing statements by local historians. I check and recheck the dates on these articles compulsively, wondering if my grandmother was reading them when they were new. The archive is like a connecting wire to the moment she held the paper in her hands at the kitchen table. We are reading together.

The "real" historic tunnels may refer to some combination of passageways between buildings, or coal chutes, or small hiding places for bootlegged liquor. What we know for certain is that the city approved construction of new tunnels as part of a more general push to attract tourism.[13] In 1997, the Tunnels of Little Chicago opened its doors to the public for the first time. For the next few years, tourists paid for a single tour that combined stories of Chinese immigration with a local history of bootlegging. After a new management company, the Tunnels of Moose Jaw, took over in 1999 and implemented its more ambitious business plan, two new tours were launched in 2000: Passage to Fortune and the Chicago Connection. Passage to Fortune takes visitors through the experiences of early Chinese immigrants in the city, while the Chicago Connection immerses visitors in the atmosphere of Al Capone's mythical presence in Moose Jaw during American prohibition.[14]

When we descend into the tunnels today, we are entering newly constructed simulations of tunnels that never existed precisely as we experience them today, except for the parts where we may possibly pass through something original. Ultimately, it is impossible to know where we are underground, where simulation ends and the real begins, where history blends into entertainment, and where the present and the past bleed into each other in the dark.[15]

SECRET PASSAGES

At 1084, some drawers concealed their real function. If you pulled out the bottom drawer of the vanity in the pink second-floor bathroom, you saw a gaping hole where the drawer's backing should have been. This hole was the mouth of a laundry chute that ran all the way down to the basement. There was a similar cupboard in the green and black main-floor bathroom that you could open to see things already falling through the house. This portal to the underworld provided an early lesson in mimesis: the drawer and the cupboard camouflaged their true natures as passageways to the beyond. I could open a drawer and see the darkness of the underworld seeping up to the second floor. My sister and I would play with these portals. One of us would deposit something in the magical drawer from up top, and the other would wait on the main floor to watch its freefall. Then we ran down to the basement to retrieve the object, switched positions, and initiated another repetition. This game is analogous to Freud's famous account of his grandson's repetitive fort-da game with a wooden reel.[16] Watching his grandson toss away and then retrieve the reel repeatedly, Freud interprets the action, in part, as the child's attempt to take revenge on the mother who leaves him against his wishes: by tossing the reel and then retrieving it, the child also gains mastery over the object. More compelling than this strictly Oedipal interpretation, however, is Freud's observation that this game is about "disappearance and return."[17] For me, the laundry chute game provided a similar lesson in disappearance and return. These falling objects were surrogates for my own descent to the underworld. I would never be able to fall through that chute and return to tell the tale, but I could repeat the experiment ad infinitum with a proxy in order to accumulate evidence of the inside. The lost and found objects taught me that things return from the underworld all the time.

Not once, in all those years of chasing objects down, did I think about the number of repetitions my grandmother made, carrying loads of laundry up those three flights of stairs over five decades.

ETERNAL RECURRENCE

Some people believe that Chinese immigrants originally built the tunnels in order to escape the threat of violence above ground, or to "bring illegal aliens into the country and [hide] them in the tunnels."[18] Any evidence that Chinese men built or used these tunnels is anecdotal and yet, even in sources that acknowledge the lack of evidence for these claims, they continue to be repeated.[19] For instance, John Larsen and Maurice Libby introduce the tunnels into their history of Moose Jaw with the story of their Chinese origin: "Stories abound of opium dens, and of large-scale communities of Chinese seeking to avoid taxes and immigration fees."[20] After clarifying that "there's little evidence to support either legend, but the stories persist," Larsen and Libby posit an explanation for the legends: "If some Chinese men did make use of the tunnels, they were most likely motivated by the simple desire to avoid public persecution, to remain out of sight, and to dispel fears that the Chinese population would adversely affect the local economy."[21] Other anecdotes are cited and re-cited. In the second report commissioned by the Moose Jaw Business Improvement District to investigate the legends of the tunnels, I read that "a woman who lived in the Elk Block in the 1940s remembers seeing people, mostly Chinese coming up out of a hole off the alley between River and Main when there was a fire in a boarding house in Manitoba."[22] That same year, the *Moose Jaw Times Herald* published an article citing the sole anecdotal eyewitness who almost always shows up as the source each time a story of Chinese origins appears. L.J. (Moon) Mullins recounts: "The Chinese started building the tunnels in 1908 to 1909 ... [and] used the tunnels to travel safely from one point to another."[23] Through speculation and repetition, a constellation of associations forms between the Chinese immigrant and the underground.

In a 1998 *Globe and Mail* article on the "rejuvenation of Moose Jaw" that featured, among other developments, reference to the history of the tunnels, reporter Maggie Siggins provides a brief snapshot of immigrant experience: "Many of these people were without the required legal documents, and were so terrified of government authority and the rampant racism of Moose Jaw's elite that they actually burrowed their way, by pick and shovel, into the city's underbelly. Whole families lived underground; babies were born there who didn't see the light of day for a year or more. Slave-wage jobs were performed at night – the city's laundry was done in these caves – until enough money was saved to pay the hated head tax levied on Chinese immigrants by the federal government."[24] Siggins does not provide dates for her version of Chinese Canadian history, although she does claim that the tunnels became used for Prohibition around 1916, so her account above must be presumed to reflect life pre-1916. Archival records render the claim of whole families living underground beyond dubious. As Alison Marshall's research indicates, very few Chinese families could afford to send women over to Canada, particularly once the head tax was raised to $500 in 1903: "As a result, by 1911, Prairie cities such as Winnipeg and Regina had only a handful of Chinese women."[25] By 1922, only two Chinese women lived in Moose Jaw, both of whom arrived that year.[26] Given these numbers, the image of entire families subsisting in the "underbelly," along with babies growing up in the dark like rabbits, appeals more to early twentieth-century racist figurations that referred to Chinese people as living in warrens and hovels, or moving in "herd-like numbers" on prairie-bound trains, than it does to any documented reality.[27] With respect to Siggins's assertion that many Chinese immigrants were in Moose Jaw illegally, research indicates quite the contrary: that a rigorous process for documenting and registering newcomers was firmly in place.[28]

It's like spirit possession, how the language of government officials and journalists from one hundred years earlier flows through the reporter's fingers in

1998, to be laid out in a national newspaper that resurrects while dismissing it the spectre of the "yellow peril."

LEMON CHICKEN

My grandmother always ordered Chinese food from the National on Main Street.[29] The sauce for the lemon chicken was thick and yellow, and the dish came with pale slivered almonds on top for decoration. Fried rice, chop suey, and egg rolls arrived in round aluminum takeout containers with perfectly circular cardboard tops. Those containers filled me with misgiving. For years, I watched characters on television shows eat Chinese takeout from little square boxes with folding tops. Those boxes were testament to the fact that I had never had the real thing; any food that showed up packaged in an aluminum circle was pure ersatz. As I grew up, I developed a taste for steamed dumplings over egg rolls, and ginger beef over chow mein. I believed that these new tastes were more authentic, particularly since they were consumed in a genuine Chinese restaurant in north Calgary.[30] My mother taught me that this food was Northern Szechuan, not Cantonese, which was all that fried stuff at the mall. But leftovers always came home with us in those same round aluminum containers. The disappointment I felt in their presence was tantamount to the interruption of a fantasy of authenticity. Those little circles followed me from province to province: there was no escaping the fact that my imagination of real Chinese food was always rooted in a tangled knot of simulation and prairie labour history. After all, the fortune cookie was invented in San Francisco, and an American named Frederick Weeks Wilcox invented those elusive white takeout boxes in Chicago.[31] At the end of the nineteenth century, Wilcox did a very American thing: he patented "what he called a 'paper pail,' which was a single piece of paper, creased into segments and folded into a (more or less) leakproof container secured with a dainty wire handle on top."[32] And that elegant box top that folded over and fit tongue in groove, like sleeping lovers, that had captivated my televisual attention for years was inspired by Japanese origami.[33]

VENTRILOQUISM

Walking along the High Street one day, I pass Joe's Locksmith. The window display pulls me up short. There's a large map of Canada in the window, with two red dresses and a collection of short typed statements. The first one I see hangs in mid-air suspended by string: *I was your next-door neighbor.* I retrace my steps and read: *My killer is out of jail* and *I was your age.* Along the bottom, cut-out paper vamps proceed from one end of the window to the other, like they're engaged in a national trek from west to east. Framing the top, one long, straight line of declarative statements: *I babysat your kids; I was an artist; I loved to square dance.* More of those messages hang suspended in mid-air, more still are scattered along the bottom of the window. Several pins have been stuck into the map. Those pins traverse the nation. As I read the display description, I learn that Joe the locksmith has designed this window in order to commemorate and "give voice" to some of the missing and murdered Indigenous women in this country. The Facebook page associated with this window, the Display Project, explains:

> Maryanne Pearce's dissertation of "An Awkward Silence" includes a database of all the missing and murdered Canadian women and girls since the 1940s. There [were] over 80 pages in the database, and I went through the pages and highlighted all the names that were identified as First Nations, Metis, Inuit and Aboriginal. Then I Googled every name, figured out where they were either from, last seen or were found and put them into those respective provinces. Then I put a pin on the map of Canada to denote where they fit in. A lot of the places I had never heard of before, so I had to do a lot of searching in order to find where to put the pins.
>
> As I Googled each name, I learned something about each of the girls, and I wanted to give them one last voice. These girls and women had dreams. They had courage. They were resilient and they were strong. A lot of them had defeated their demons and their lives were taken from them. For what I learned, I created "impact statements," something I feel they would have wanted to say if they had one last chance. Maybe not everything, but I wanted to leave an impact.
>
> It took me over 100 hours to complete this map. Then, on Sep 30th, I installed the map and the impact statements.[34]

Windows divide the interior from the exterior: "they inhabit a space neither inside nor outside, public nor private."[35] They are liminal zones, and as such, windows materialize the realm of the temporal bleed, of the convergence between here and there, now and then. Windows manifest in the tradition of nineteenth-century spiritualists: they bring us face to face with the lost other. As I walked back and forth across the length of this display, I saw myself moving through the picture. I saw the city's image reflected in the window's representation of hundreds of murders willfully committed to oblivion through national neglect and indifference. The photograph reproduced here redoubles the experience: it projects a timeline of death while it reflects the current moment of

Figure 11.1 Missing and murdered women window display, Moose Jaw, Saskatchewan, August 2016.

the photograph. The photographer's reflection and the passing minivan, the gas station in the background and the parked cars juxtapose a quiet present with innumerable violent pasts on a single surface, but in this zone, the "now" of the image is spectral. The traces of these dead women are somehow more present, more tangible, than the living.

This window presents an opening into a new conception of time and of history, one that embraces Christopher Witmore's notion of "percolating time," in which past and present fold in on each other, affect each other, and constitute each other. He writes: "percolating time results from the sorting of various pasts caught up within mixed sets of both simultaneous and successive relations ... we must recast material pasts as having action, as having a stake, as being co-present, co-creative and co-constitutive in contemporary landscape processes."[36] The window puts the current moment of the city, with its traffic and passersby, into the picture. It operates as an invitation to see the imbrication of self with other, and of history with future. Kathleen Stewart refers to such sites as "bloom spaces." These spaces call to us for reasons that are felt before they are understood, and they demand our attention in order to materialize. A bloom space operates as a "hinge between the actual and the potential [that] can pop up as an object out of place, the sense of an absent-presence, a road block, a sticking point."[37] This window on the High Street is a portal into an alternate national trajectory, one that recognizes the presence of Indigenous women, not simply as ghosts pinned to a map, but as actually existing "co-present, co-creative and co-constitutive" subjects.[38]

KATACHRESIS

Photographic portraits mark the starting point of each tour. For the Chicago Connection, a very recognizable Al Capone swings outside the building's entrance. Across the street, over the entrance to the Passage to Fortune tour, a red sign with another photographic portrait indicates the point of descent. This portrait depicts a Chinese man in non-Western dress who is not identifiable as anyone in particular. He is a sign for the experience of an entire group – a synecdoche – whereas the Capone portrait manages to signify both the historical individual and the feel of an era. Capone, who was likely never in Moose Jaw, invites us to follow in his footsteps. The unknown man across the street marks a portal to a time actually experienced by hundreds of men whose identities are nevertheless buried in memory or history. Photographic portraits have served multiple purposes over the years, from indicating bourgeois respectability to defining a class of criminality. In essence, the photographic portrait is "a sign whose purpose is both the description of an individual and the inscription of a social identity."[39] How do we read the individuality of the unknown man?

The portrait as starting point of the tour marks a division between the present and the past; it tells us that we are entering a world of ghosts.[40] But what if you're not a tourist? What if you're just walking up Main Street and you see this photograph hanging there in the middle of the modern world? Chinese-ness appears as archaic; it stands out as strange, not just as historical like Capone. The pairing of this nameless Chinese man with the notorious gangster, and the juxtaposition of these two tours, generates a katachresis.[41] The fact of the tunnels is their only point of connection, and yet the facts of the tunnels are far from established. In the early twentieth century, Edward Curtis made photographs of Native men and women in traditional dress. He removed any hint of modernity from these images so that viewers would know that Natives are anything but contemporary. On Main Street, the Chinese face appears like the residue of another time-space, altogether foreign.

Style matters here. Alison Marshall's research indicates that by the early twentieth century, many Chinese men in Canada were wearing modern Western suits and cutting their hair.[42] The man hanging above Main Street, however, appears to be sporting the traditional queue, or long braid. While one local newspaper

Figure 11.2 Al Capone marks the entrance to the Chicago Connection tour, August 2016.

Figure 11.3 Anonymous Chinese man marks the entrance to the Passage to Fortune tour, August 2016.

article maintains that the Passage to Fortune tour is set in the late 1800s, the guide addresses various political and social events spanning the twentieth and early twenty-first centuries during the course of the tour.[43] As we move through darkened spaces designed to reproduce harsh and uncivilized living conditions for early immigrants, we learn about everything from successive head taxes, to the Exclusion Act of 1923, to twenty-first-century federal reparations. Curiously, the physical spaces of the simulated tunnels do not keep step with the temporal arc of the tour's narrative. We are invited to lift heavy, antique irons and consider with revulsion the waste bucket one unlucky immigrant will be tasked with emptying from living quarters lacking modern plumbing. The closest we come to a more modern scene is the kitchen of an imaginary restaurant that one of the laundrymen eventually manages to open, but this is followed by a claustrophobic opium den constructed of rustic wooden bunks and dank, low light.[44] The built environment feels sinister and inhospitable; it seems to align with an earlier, non-specific but brutal time, a time that echoes the abstract temporality of the mysterious Chinese man outside.

This must be what the late 1800s was like for Chinese immigrants. And yet, the primary setting through which we move – Burrows and Sons Laundry – is at odds with a key aspect of late nineteenth-century laundries: Mr Burrows, the laundry owner, is white. Historical records, however, indicate that early on most laundries were Chinese owned and operated.[45] We know the colour of Mr Burrows's skin because he appears in animatronic form toward the end of the tour. At the far end of the living quarters, we hear a man's voice from the shadows. Our tour guide, a young woman playing the role of the racist and angry laundry manager, Mrs Dawson, leads us toward the voice and we see a figure standing in semi-darkness. He makes small, mechanized gestures and exchanges a few aggravated words with Mrs Dawson. She addresses him as Mr Burrows and explains that she is orienting the new group. He has no time to spend with us, so Mrs Dawson hurries us on to the next stop on the tour. It's a brief encounter, and yet this intrusion of the robotic throws me for a loop. Animatronic figures are relatively new versions of automata: mechanized figures designed to mimic life. One effect of an automaton is to blur the "boundaries between vital and inert, intelligent and rote."[46] In the case of Mr Burrows, the confusion does not lie in his approximation to flesh and bone. He is no Olympia to our Nathaniel; we are not meant to be fooled.[47] The confusion resides in his narrative disruption of the tour. Once the guide activates Mr Burrows, Mrs Dawson must then time her exchange with him perfectly, since his voice is actually a recording. It's like a perfectly executed soft shoe. Once he has finished the programmed gestures and the recording is complete, the figure returns again to an inanimate state. If Passage to Fortune is living history, then Mr Burrows shows us the nature of that history: a repetitive and closed loop whereby an absent ventriloquist speaks through an effigy that represents white fantasies of ownership and mastery. Time doesn't just bleed between a distinct past and a current present down here; it hemorrhages in all directions.

THATCHER'S TREES

Wilbert Ross Thatcher was the ninth premier of Saskatchewan, and he grew up in Moose Jaw. He was a Moose Jaw celebrity. His son Colin went to the same high school as my uncle. Our family circles intersected, if irregularly. My mother told me that during his tenure as premier, which concluded in 1971, W. Ross Thatcher planted trees along the highway between Moose Jaw and Regina as part of a beautification project for the prairies. I was nine years old when Colin, also a politician, was charged in the murder of his estranged wife, JoAnn. This was my first encounter with a real murder. People whispered about it in the living room of 1084; they repeated the stories they knew about Colin, the times they'd sat at dinner with him, or spoken with his father. They never spoke much about his mother. In 1989, a made-for-TV movie was released: *Love and Hate: The Story of Colin and JoAnn Thatcher*. Based on a book by Maggie Siggins, that same reporter who fantasized about immigrant life in the tunnels, the film opens with an expansive shot of the prairie landscape. We see a cloud of dust on the left-hand side of the screen, and then a truck emerges from the dust and kicks up more as it drives down a prairie road. There are no trees in sight. The women of Moose Jaw were steadfast, and they tightened their sphere of loyalty around the Thatcher family. The general consensus within my grandmother's circle was that Colin could never have done such a thing.

In August of 2016, my father revisited the site of his first ever haircut in Regina. The barber (whose father had cut my father's hair) told the story of how, during the Thatcher trial, he was the barber for Thatcher, his lawyer, the prosecutor, the police chief, and the judge. All those men had sat in the same chair my father was sitting in that day in August. That chair had collected and recorded them, the vibrations of their rage and guilt, their fear and determination. You can draw lines of attachment from that chair directly to the courtroom, the prison, the body of JoAnn Thatcher, and all the men who came before and after. You can draw a line of attachment from Colin Thatcher to my father. That chair is a spinal cord. Taking information in, relaying information out, it holds the specific gravity of each man in its memory.[48]

The vertebral column of trees linking Moose Jaw to Regina is another kind of relay site. It tracks the growth of crops, the trucks moving past, dust storms on the horizon. When Allan Blakeney took over as premier in 1971, he ordered the government to stop watering those trees. Driving the highway now, you can see that some have survived without the water. I look at them and see murder.

THE ORDER OF THINGS

Passage to Fortune begins at the end. We descend into the front entry of Burrows and Sons Laundry, a simulated shop front meant to transport us back in time. We are told that the cash area and drop-off area are the only parts of the laundry white customers would have seen. This tour, however, will take us behind the scenes. We are told that our tour follows the figure of Mah Lee, an immigrant who began work in a laundry and eventually saved up enough money to open his own herbalist shop and bring the rest of his family over to Canada.[49] We are taken into a reconstructed herbalist shop to see the success story for ourselves. The tour guide emphasizes that Mah Lee is a fictional character; his story has been assembled through research conducted by the Tunnel Corporation. He is not real, but he is representative. Then we are shepherded into a third room in order to watch a short video that provides context for the tour. We are told that the video is not a documentary, but helps to tell the story of Mah Lee through the memory of his great-granddaughter. The lights go out and a woman appears on the screen. Dressed in the white coat of a physician, she sits in a nice office and tells the story of her great-grandfather, Mah Lee, a first-generation immigrant who survived much hardship, but who managed to succeed with hard work and dedication. Her closing words are: "I'm proud to be a Canadian." We begin at the end, with happy assimilation.[50] Before we step "behind the scenes" of the laundry and into the inhospitable living conditions of these men, we learn that the story ends with economic success and national pride. The tour's title, Passage to Fortune, recapitulates this very Hegelian arc: history follows a path, always progressive, and the end is a good one. I wonder, not for the first time, about the surreal juxtaposition of buildings here: located right next door to the Tunnels of Moose Jaw stands my grandmother's favourite Chinese restaurant: the National.

ON FLATNESS

I grew up in Calgary and we had the mountains. It made us feel superior to Saskatchewan, a superiority that we expressed through the following joke: "In Saskatchewan, you can watch your dog run away for days." We laughed every time that joke got told. It spoke of a place flattened out and full of nothing, because to watch your dog run away for days presumes several factors:

1 Perfect visibility. You can see across the land for untold miles in any direction: that perfect visibility across time (you can see into the future through days of running) and space (somehow the prairie grasses are not an impediment to tracking your dog through the landscape);

2 Action is brought to the prairies; it does not exist otherwise: your dog is an imported presence whose movement sets off the landscape as an unchanging scene or picture;

3 Time is out of joint with the rest of the world and therefore modernity: you have time to watch your dog run for days, because there is nothing else to do.

EXCAVATION

The Tunnels of Moose Jaw website makes it clear that these guided tours are "a blend of history and entertainment."[51] They are, moreover, theatrical in nature. Tour guides are dressed in period-appropriate clothing and adopt the personas of various fictional characters, while tourists are hailed into their tours either as new immigrants (Passage to Fortune), or as bootleggers (the Chicago Connection). If you choose to be a bootlegger, your guide takes you across the street and up a set of stairs. You spend time in a saloon, in Capone's office, and in his bedroom, and then scamper to the basement to avoid detection, observe a gambling setup, and make your escape out the back door. If you choose to be an immigrant, the guide takes you up a block and then down a set of stairs, into the basement of a nearby building. Once under, you stay under. Chicago Connection tourists spend time both above and below ground, but Chinese immigrant tourists never see the light of day until the tour's end.

Before we penetrate behind the scenes of Mr Burrows's shop, our guide explains that she will be playing the role of Mrs Dawson, whose job is to instruct new arrivals on the specifics of their new jobs and accommodations. We are also told that Mrs Dawson will occasionally revert back to her tour guide persona in order to clarify or elucidate some piece of history. Passage to Fortune is not like one of those Civil War re-enactments or pilgrim villages in the US where you don't break character.[52] Mrs Dawson will yell at us, and then the tour guide will break in to tell us about various racist national policies. Somehow, we are supposed to be able to make the reciprocal shifts back and forth in time, know when to become ourselves and how to put this history in its proper place. Finally, we are reminded that during the period of history in question, immigrants faced pervasive racism, and that words like "coolie" were used to reinforce and perpetuate racist attitudes.[53] We are warned that we will hear this word used during the tour. After this précis, and the nationalist palliative video that follows, the performance begins in earnest.

"Line up against the wall, coolies!" It's Mrs Dawson, and she's clearly aggravated by us. But her job is to orient us to our new life and so, grudgingly, she does. This is now the second time the word "coolie" has been used: first in the "now" as a pedagogical example, and next in the virtual past as a performative iteration. While the second instance is designed to shock, and by implication to show us how far we've come, the repetition suggests something altogether different to me: resurrection. Barbara Kirshenblatt-Gimblett writes: "The tourist stands at the edge of an open grave, not with spade in hand to bury old traditions but with a pen to record them. The process of negating cultural practices reverses itself once it has succeeded in archaizing the 'errors'; indeed, through a process of archaizing, which is a mode of cultural production, the repudiated is transvalued as heritage."[54] The word "coolie" bleeds between past and present, showing the interpenetration of temporalities.[55] We as tourists are not merely standing at the mouth of the grave; we have willingly descended to the underworld in order to search out and reanimate the remains of history. I move through the tunnels wondering how we can be expected to keep "coolie" dead and buried, since both the guide and Mrs Dawson went to all the trouble of digging it out.

MEMORY LOOPS

There was a board game in my uncle's bedroom at 1084 that my sister and I used to play. It was called Careers and it projected your future onto two dimensions. The game board consisted of an exterior square circuit with several loops branching off and rejoining this exterior track. You played for a combination of fame, happiness, and money by secretly attaching different point values to each one and thereby arriving at your own unique success formula. With your formula in hand, you must then complete several loops and circuits on the board in order to accumulate the required Victory Points in each category. Whoever reaches their goal first is the winner. First developed by sociologist Dr James Cooke Brown in the fifties, the game was apparently "his homage to showing people that being successful in life can take many forms."[56] I was a creature of habit, however, and never varied my top-ranked category: fame. No matter whether money or happiness came next, I could never complete enough loops and circuits in time to win.

I drive or walk by 1084 every day. I change my angle of approach, from north to south, and east to west. More than anything, I'm hoping for a glimpse of my grandmother pulling into the carport or my grandfather, eyes closed, listening to the radio. I try to bring them closer through a ritualized looping of memories: the house is on the corner of Redland and Hall; my mother's bedroom was pink; my uncle's was blue; they both had walk-in closets; the bathrooms concealed portals to the underworld; sometimes we played Careers on my uncle's bedroom floor; the linoleum on the stairs down to the basement was speckled; there was a built-in L-shaped bench in the kitchen; and the dining room was always dark. I am no medium; the repetitions and invocations don't bring me any closer to the manifestations I seek.

ASCENDING

The final segment of Passage to Fortune is a room of photographs on display that have been retrieved from British Columbia and Alberta archives. The tour guide leaves us to reflect on the images by ourselves. They depict a variety of scenes and span the nineteenth and twentieth centuries. Not all of the images are captioned or dated, making it impossible to situate them in a linear historical narrative. Among the photographs on display, I see Chinese men working on the railway, immigrants outside of a house, a Head Tax Certificate, and "interior" shots that depict Chinese men inside of, presumably, their own homes. One image in particular catches my eye: two men are positioned at the side of a wooden clapboard building displaying two signs, both of which read LAUNDRY. One sign is white with black text, and the other is black with white text. One of the men sits astride a bicycle; the other stands next to him, a coat draped over his arm. They are both wearing cardigan sweaters with ties and dark trousers, and they stare directly into the camera. The caption simply states: "Chinese Laundry." The image is undated.[57] Behind the man on the bicycle, a shed-like structure attaches to the side of the house with an inky darkness at the centre. It appears to be a window without glass, but I know it's a portal into another world. The day looks cold. Snow covers the sole of one of the bicyclist's shoes and the roof of the shed. This structure echoes the uninsulated room jutting out the side of 1084: it's another interior-exteriority. The blackness at the centre of the image and the structural extrusion of the shed combine to show us how history cannot be framed up and contained neatly. Things bleed, disappear, get tacked on, get built up, lose their voice, and fall out of sight. Constellations develop from connecting lines in the darkness. Darkness gives them form.

I don't know where or when the photograph was taken; it is impossible to place the image into a specific context and so I can only invent my own associations.[58] I think of Chinese men on the prairies forming their own homosocial networks as a means of survival.[59] I think of immigrant-owned businesses and how a haircut can be read either as a sign of Chinese nationalism or as a marker of conformity to "Western" style. I think of all the things that stick in my memory: a barber's chair; a murder of trees; a set of portraits; takeout dishes full of real Chinese food; a network of tunnels and laundry chutes; spectral windows; and a wheel that lives in a room that attaches to 1084 from the outside.

As I prepare to leave the tour and ascend back up to street level, I note that none of these photographs depict Chinese men underground.

POWER LINES

Late in life, my grandmother developed her own practice of repetition. She walked. Whether her walking began with the loss of her car – and therefore her accustomed mobility – or whether she was responding more generally to the home invasion by an unforgiving dementia, Gram was compelled to leave the house every day in order to lay down new circuits of anxiety or boredom or de-

Figure 11.4 Power lines, August 2016.

sire. Neighbours report seeing her striding down the streets, carving out routes that could never compensate for the synaptic pathways that were shutting down or overgrown. She was always a woman with purpose. As the circumference of her life narrowed, she adapted by carving smaller and smaller circuits, until she forgot the need to repeat altogether.

ACKNOWLEDGMENTS

As always, Patrick Fowlow read every word, multiple times, without complaint. Thanks to Jane Ku, Yoke-Sum Wong, Miriam Wright, and Jonathan Wynn for directing me to helpful research sources. I'm also grateful to my parents, Don and Nola Engle, for taking me on what Dad has named our "roots" tour through Regina and Moose Jaw in the summer of 2016.

NOTES

1 This object in question was an abdominal exercise wheel.
2 Derrida writes: "The outside bears with the inside a relationship that is, as usual, anything but simple exteriority. The meaning of the outside was always present within the inside, imprisoned outside the outside, and vice versa." Derrida, *Of Grammatology*, 35.

3　I don't recall how the game began, or who found the wheel first, but it seems to me that I played it longer than anybody else. As the youngest member of the whole family, this makes sense: simple, circular repetition appealed to me far longer than it did to teenage cousins or an older sister already practising adulthood in the living room.

4　See Durkheim, *Elementary Forms of Religious Life*; Weber, *Protestant Ethic and the Spirit of Capitalism*.

5　See Yates, *Art of Memory*.

6　De Certeau is crucial here. In *The Writing of History*, de Certeau posits the productive encounter between history and psychoanalysis so long as the historian resists the simplistic superimposition of Freudian concept onto historical event: "Recourse to the death of the father, to Oedipus or to transference, can be used for anything and everything. Since these Freudian 'concepts' are supposed to explain all human endeavour, we have little difficulty driving them into the most obscure regions of history. Unfortunately, they are nothing other than decorative tools if their only goal amounts to a designation or discreet obfuscation of what the historian does not understand" (288–9). If the historian can resist this easy sleight of hand then new openings on the scene of writing are sensed. As Joan Scott elucidates, "For Certeau the seductive dance of Freudian analysis necessarily distorts even as it sheds new light on the territory of the historian." Scott, "Incommensurability of Psychoanalysis and History," 68.

7　Scott, "Incommensurability of Psychoanalysis and History," 65.

8　Ben Highmore's recent discussion of Williams's term is relevant here. Arguing that the term is necessarily vague, Highmore asserts that "structures of feeling are ... what get remaindered when ... specialists get their hands on culture and divide it up into distinct realms of 'psychology,' 'sociology,' 'economy,' 'history.'" Highmore, "Formations of Feelings," 149. This essay takes seriously Highmore's position that "the phrase itself is designed to refuse or delay the sort of precipitation that results from analysis" (ibid., 156). What kinds of cultural history become possible when feelings of structure, and structures of feeling, are taken seriously?

9　Ahmed, "Happy Objects," 29, 30.

10　The Moose Jaw Public Library Archive contains newspaper articles covering a period of forty years chronicling the various stories, and attempts to debunk these same stories, by residents, journalists, and local historians.

11　Lydia Lewycky, "Main Street Project, Moose Jaw, Saskatchewan," news release, April 1986, Moose Jaw Public Library Archives.

12　Joyce Playford and Lois Baillie, "Report on the Tunnels for the Business Improvement District," 1987, Moose Jaw Public Library Archives.

13　See Ervin Buckmaster, "Tunnel Lore Focus of Rejuvenation," *Regina Leader-Post*, 12 May 1995; Ron Walter, "Some Tunnels Look 'Scary,'" *Moose Jaw Times Herald*, 17 August 1999; Ron Walter, "Tunnels Plan Unveiled," *Moose Jaw Times Herald*, 11 January 2000.

14　Most scholars dismiss the stories of Capone visiting Moose Jaw as pure fiction.

15　Hillel Schwartz's discussion of reenactment and repetition is relevant here. As he remarks, our "predicament ... [is] our habit of relying upon reenactment and repetition to establish the truth of events and the authenticity of people." Schwartz, *Culture of the Copy*, 290. He is referring here to the use of *Roots* as a historical documentary in American schools. See particularly the chapter "Once More, with Feeling."

16 See Freud, "Beyond the Pleasure Principle," in *On Metapsychology*, 284–5.

17 Ibid., 284.

18 See Larsen and Libby, *Moose Jaw*, 30–1; Playford and Baillie, "Report," 1987.

19 The Chinese origin story is repeated in the following articles: Cheryl Mooder, "Al Capone: Where Are the Tunnels?," *Moose Jaw Times Herald*, 11 September 1987; "Mr. Gordon Hurlburt," 13 March 1986, Moose Jaw Public Library Archives; Philip Jensen, "Urban Legend," *Beaver*, June/July 2001; Maggie Siggins, "In the Tunnels of Moose Jaw," *Globe and Mail*, 30 July 1998; Ron Walter, "Using the Tunnels for Work, Not Pleasure: Lawrence Mullins Recalls His Days Running Messages under Moose Jaw," *Moose Jaw Times Herald*, 21 July 2002; "Local History Disneyfied to Sell Better: By Omission and Selective Viewpoint, Moose Jaw Offers G-Rated Version of Past," *Moose Jaw Times Herald*, 8 July 1997. The theory of Chinese immigrants building the tunnels is disputed by historian Paul Yee in Corey Atkinson, "Put Tour in Context: Historian," *Moose Jaw Times Herald*, 2000.

20 Larsen and Libby, *Moose Jaw*, 30.

21 Ibid.

22 Playford and Baillie, "Report," 3.

23 Mooder, "Al Capone."

24 Siggins, "In the Tunnels."

25 Marshall, *Cultivating Connections*, 111.

26 Ibid., 112.

27 Ibid., 111. Kay Anderson cites several instances from both the popular press and official government reports referring to Chinese dwellings as unhygienic and warren-like. The following quotation comes from the *Royal Commission on Chinese and Japanese Immigration* in 1902: "The degraded Asiatics ... live generally in wretched hovels, dark, ill-ventilated and unwholesome, and crowded together in such numbers." Anderson, *Vancouver's Chinatown*, 37. Anderson reproduces a cartoon from 1907 depicting the Chinese as living in warrens in "The Idea of Chinatown," 588.

28 Marshall, *Cultivating Connections*, 112.

29 For a history of Chinese restaurants in the prairies, see Cho, *Eating Chinese*.

30 Cho not only describes how "authenticity" was never on the menu in Chinese prairie restaurants but notes the persistence with which Chinese restaurants serve up a particular definition of Canadian-ness: "One of the most curious features of the small town Chinese restaurant is its matter-of-fact definition of Canadian food." Ibid., 53.

31 Thanks to Yoke-Sum Wong for pointing me to this history of the takeout box. For a brief version of this history, see Hilary Greenbaum and Dana Rubinstein, "The Chinese-Takeout Container Is Uniquely American," *New York Times*, 13 January 2012. For the history of the fortune cookie, listen to Mars, "A Sweet Surprise Awaits You."

32 Greenbaum and Rubinstein, "The Chinese-Takeout Container Is Uniquely American."

33 As a graduate student, I finally received the gift of the "paper pail" from a Brooklyn takeout. The food tasted no better, no worse, than the meals my prairie circles had served up.

34 "The Display Project," Facebook Community page, https://www.facebook.com/The-Display-Project-135772670162996/. The red dresses are in recognition of the REDress Project. Jaime Black, *The REDress Project*, http://www.theredressproject.org/. The vamps invoke the *Walking with Our Sisters* Project. See Christi Belcourt, *Walking with Our Sisters*, http://christibelcourt.com/walking-with-our-sisters/.

35 Colomina, *Privacy and Publicity*, 6.

36 Witmore, "Landscape, Time, Topology," 218–19. As an archeologist, Witmore uses the tools of his discipline to illustrate the argument. He is very clear, however, that the conception of time and history as complex and non-linear are equally crucial for all areas of research: "The motive is to suggest possible modes for enriching our syntheses of material pasts and understanding how these pasts have action for the contemporary world as it is lived in ways which undercut divides between presents and pasts, humans and things, humanities and sciences." Ibid., 197.

37 K. Stewart, "Worlding Refrains," 344.

38 As I write this, six young Indigenous girls between the ages of ten and fourteen have committed suicide in Northern Saskatchewan within the last month. See Andrea Hill, "Another Suicide in La Ronge Heightens Northern Sask. Crisis," *Saskatoon Star Phoenix*, 31 October 2016. Living conditions for Aboriginal communities across the country are horrific, and the United Nations declared in 2015 that Canada has a human rights crisis on its hands. See, for example, Coalition for the Human Rights of Indigenous Peoples (Amnesty International), "UN Human Rights Report Shows That Canada Is Failing Indigenous Peoples, " 23 July 2015, http://www.amnesty.ca/news/public-statements/joint-press-release/un-human-rights-report-shows-that-canada-is-failing.

39 Tagg, *Burden of Representation*, 37. The inversions and shattering effects of surrealist portraits are no different: the destabilization of identity as fixed may be the outcome, but the question of identity remains a core theme.

40 See also Johannes Fabian's discussion of visualism in anthropology as tantamount to a "denial of coevalness or temporalization." Fabian, *Time and the Other*, 106.

41 Witmore explains: "*Katachresis* is a juxtaposition of two seemingly disparate things, accounts or situations which can create aleatoric frictions, transactions and associations." Witmore, "Landscape," 218.

42 Photographs in her second book, *Cultivating Connections*, depict men and women in modern Western fashion. Her first book, *The Way of the Bachelor*, focuses primarily on western Manitoba and she acknowledges that certain differences existed between this region and the rest of the nation. For instance, 1911 seems to be a watershed date for men in Western Manitoba to cut off their queues. This date aligns with a statement written by the Chinese minister assigned to the United States, Wu Tingfang, asking "the Qing court to abolish the queue." Marshall, *Way of the Bachelor*, 71. She also indicates that "there is ample evidence that many Chinese immigrants in Canada cut off their queues at least a decade before 1911." Ibid., 194.

43 Florence Hwang, "Passage to Fortune Officially Opened," *Moose Jaw Times Herald*, 28 July 2000.

44 For a brief account of the role the British Empire played in the opium trade with China, see Chan, *Gold Mountain*.

45 It wasn't until governments passed restrictions and imposed licensing fees in the early twentieth century that the number of white owners increased. Marshall, *Way of the Bachelor*, 61–2. Larsen and Libby have similar data that is specific to Moose Jaw, although their data reflects a later period of time: "By the twenties, *Henderson's Directory* showed between fifteen and eighteen laundries operating in Moose Jaw – the only one not owned by Chinese was the large commercial Moose Jaw Steam Laundry" (45–6).

46 Riskin, *Genesis Redux*, 14.

47 Hoffmann's short story "The Sandman" features a young student, Nathaniel, who naively mistakes his professor's automaton – named Olympia – for a real woman and falls in love with her. Hoffmann, *The Tales of Hoffmann*. Freud made this story famous in his essay "The Uncanny," which uses Hoffmann's tale as a means to define the uncanny and its relation to the castration complex. Freud, "The Uncanny," in *Art and Literature*, 335–76.

48 Avery Gordon was the first person to show me that furniture could have memories, but Proust's description of Aunt Léonie's furniture calling to him after he donated it to the brothel should not be missed. Gordon, *Ghostly Matters*; Proust, *Remembrance of Things Past*, 1:622.

49 See Marshall's history on laundries in Marshall, *Way of the Bachelor*.

50 Given the recent survey results that indicate a significant majority of Canadians think immigrants should do more to fit in, I find the conclusion of this video particularly significant. From early critiques of so-called multiculturalism to the current moment, Canada still has much to face up to with respect to immigrant experience.

51 Tunnels of Moose Jaw, accessed 14 December 2017, www.tunnelsofmoosejaw.com.

52 See, for example, the chapter "Plimoth Plantation" in Kirshenblatt-Gimblett, *Destination Culture*, 189–202.

53 As Chan tells us, the word comes "from the Chinese word *kuli*, meaning 'bitter strength'" (*Gold Mountain*, 39). Originally, the term referred to the practice of selling men for cheap labour to Western nations, but also came to designate the men who performed such labour. The term is not exclusive to Chinese labour history.

54 Kirshenblatt-Gimblett, *Destination Culture*, 161.

55 As Witmore writes: "it is to say that pasts are thoroughly blended into the present; that pasts push back and have an impact within contemporary relations in a multiplicity of ways." Witmore, "Landscape," 195.

56 Todd Coopee, "Careers – Board Game Alley," Toy Tales, accessed 14 December 2017, https://toytales.ca/careers/.

57 This image can also be found on the Tunnels of Moose Jaw website: http://www.tunnelsofmoosejaw.com/gallery/historic-chinese-photographs/.

58 Derrida's seminal essay, "Signature Event Context," is also important here as a reminder that there is no simple original context to which this image could return. See *Margins of Philosophy*, 307–30.

59 See Marshall, *Way of the Bachelor*.

CHAPTER 12

Overwintering: On Robyn O'Neil's Apocalyptic Landscapes

LINDSEY A. FREEMAN

> I like how you make those men do bad things.
>
> Former Texas governor Ann Richards, whispered to
> Robyn O'Neil at an art opening

> Lives are by definition precarious:
> they can be expunged at will or by accident; their
> persistence is in no sense guaranteed.
>
> Judith Butler, *Precarious Life*

Robyn O'Neil produces epic works of art in the contemporary age with a mechanical pencil. Since 2002 she has created catastrophes on a miniature scale through a series of drawings of natural disasters and severe landscapes populated by a few majestically drawn animals and hundreds of small male figures dressed in identical black sweatsuits.[1] In contrast to the clumsy and awkward tiny human figures, the animals, at home in the natural world, are large and impressively beautiful. In the zoomed-in scene in figure 12.1, we see the middle panel of a triptych, almost entirely filled by an enormous bison, standing woolly and strong. The nose is so full of graphite that it appears wet. The animal dwarfs the mountains behind. The human figures are scarcely taller than its hoof.

Gazing on these landscapes can cause viewers to shrink down, to imagine themselves among the beautiful creatures,

Figure 12.1 Detail from *As Ye the sinister creep and feign, those once held become those now slain*, Robyn O'Neil, 2004.

swirling nature, and menacing middle-aged men. The size of the bison compared to the humans enhances the vertiginous effects of the drawings. The men are diminutive, most measuring from about the tip of the thumb to the first knuckle, or less; they seem even smaller compared to the expansive landscapes, which sometimes fill paper sheets five feet tall and fourteen feet wide. On the page the men appear to be fragments of a society in reverse on their way to extinction. The miniaturization of the human form in O'Neil's landscapes brings up anxieties around extinction and environmental uncertainty, and her use of repetition creates a feeling of the uncanny. The uncanniness is magnified by the men's miniaturization.

O'Neil's use of repetition also provides a critique of conformity and indifference that allows for a space to think about the contemporary age – an age where acts of mass violence and natural disasters are expected to occur at an increasing rate and where post-disaster living will be a more common experience for more people across the globe. If the narrative of the series is followed, it is impossible not to think in terms of biotic crisis, social death, and total extinction. O'Neil's works draw attention to the precariousness of modern existence, which as Judith Butler employs the term "characterizes every embodied and infinite human being, and non-human beings as well."[2] As we take in O'Neil's drawings we are given the space to imagine, and to grieve the loss of the world – as we know it – in its entirety. With this contemplation, we can employ what Henri Lefebvre calls a "tragic consciousness," which allows us to see our times clearly in order to think critically and to imagine otherwise.[3]

In the 1903 essay "Metropolis and Mental Life," German sociologist Georg Simmel demonstrates this kind of thinking when he writes: "The deepest problems of modern life flow from the attempt of the individual to maintain the independence and individuality of his existence against the sovereign powers of society, against the weight of the historical heritage and the external culture and technique of life."[4] Later in the essay Simmel argues that the defining struggles of humankind have moved from man versus nature to man versus man. In the twenty-first century, characterized by climate change caused by human beings, we now know that this is not the case; we know that the battles of man verses nature have only ramped up the battles of man verses man, both in the metropolis and in the countryside. Across O'Neil's oeuvre, we see our fears of what might happen if we fail to protect each other and are flung into the wild – tossed into a tense environment where structures of feeling become diffuse and unpredictable, and where feelings of structure are difficult to grasp.[5]

SNOW.

Everything that stands will be at odds with its neighbor, and everything that falls will perish without grace.[6]

O'Neil's landscapes are made from the raw material of dreams, the fluids of the unconscious, and the particular flavours of fear and delight that can only be inspired by the colder months of the year. Through her drawings, we are shown a wild place, a place at first dominated by snow. Variety comes in the shape of the drifts, the texture perceived on the mountaintops, and the thickness of the snowfall on the firs. Against this backdrop, dashes of forestry spice the snow-laden landscape like black pepper on cottage cheese; obsidian skies loom; jagged mountains threaten; and trees with branches held at the sharp, awkward angles of broken limbs bristle the bucolic scenes. The atmospheric and geographic conditions rendered in graphite make for a surreal environment of brutal indifference. Like the shot of ouzo swallowed by the beautiful husband in Anne Carson's

Figure 12.2 *Everything that stands will be at odds with its neighbor, and everything that falls will perish without grace*, Robyn O'Neil, 2003.

poem, O'Neil's drawings are a "slow hot snow" that burns from the inside.[7] It is not clear where the mercury hovers, but certainly the digits are small or negative.

We can imagine that the wind chill must cut through the fibres of the cotton workout gear the men wear, pushing through the muscle and the fat, going straight to the bones, and then remaining in the marrow like stubborn soldiers in the trench. The human figures in O'Neil's work are tiny, but tenacious, while winter is a strong, sturdy thing. The men put up a good fight, but they do not work well together, and in the end the weather wins. As we follow the series, we see the men perish, sometimes singularly, sometimes in groups, sometimes by natural disasters, sometimes by acts of violence. Death permeates the paper landscapes; broken, bowed, and bent bodies drawn in graphite look like calligraphy with a death wish.

A not-so-subtle commentary on conformity and indifference to community and the environment runs through the series. The corporality of the masculine figures in O'Neil's drawings lacks variety: the men are all rotund and middle-aged. They all appear to be white. Their repetition is claustrophobic, so that while looking at them we feel an intensification of the process of conformity, one of the maladies of the contemporary age.[8] We "feel constrained by uniformity, by universal sameness," as the anthropologist Marc Augé writes in *Non-places*,[9] although what we find in O'Neil's drawings are not the same kinds of conformity that Augé catalogues; there are no superhighways, airports, or non-descript hotel and travel centres in her imagined world. Either these things have never arrived or they have been eradicated. We do not know because it is impossible to tell exactly where or *when* her world is. The sweatsuits and sneakers suggest the twentieth or twenty-first century, but the landscapes stripped nearly bare of cultural markers could exist either in the future or in the past.

More striking than the lack of modern infrastructure and architecture in this ending-beginning world is the absence of women. This was a deliberate choice by the artist to show that the world, as she drew it, would not continue. It ends here with the men and their sweatsuits and the snow and the mountains and the floods. Diversity becomes a thing hungered for and the drawings work by sparking imaginations of other possibilities, other ways of living, other landscapes. When I first encountered the series, I couldn't help but wonder if there were women on the other side of the world somewhere. I thought they might reside in a place like the one described in Charlotte Perkins Gilman's *Herland,* or some other single-gendered world.[10] Alternatively, I imagined that they had been part of this world but had already been erased.

The works chill because they seem as if they could be the future. They are apocalyptic, and perhaps predictive. O'Neil is intentionally vague about the time period portrayed in her works. She has said: "If these drawings can be depictions of both a world that has just ended and a world just being born, that's what these are."[11] The temporal confusion of the works makes nostalgia impossible: hers is a world where longing and remembering cannot be located. Her landscapes are not bothered with regular temporal rhythms and to enter this world we must pause ours as well. To look at the artist's work the clock must be smashed, or if it is valuable, put in a drawer out of the way, and the calendar must be tossed out the window; this is no time to be concerned with the ritual x-ing out of days. What we see in the drawings could be the future to come, or a future that was narrowly avoided, or a past that we have started over from and then forgotten that hangs hazily in the back of our collective memories. The past, present, and future swirl in the flux of looking.

Under the influence of confused time, we enter into O'Neil's miniature world, which is a world frozen. As Susan Stewart argues about miniature worlds in general, "stillness emphasizes the activity that is outside [their] borders. And this effect is reciprocal, for once we attend to the miniature world the outside world stops and is lost to us."[12] As we are suspended in attention, moments of feeling and thinking about other worlds are made possible, but eventually, the attention to the miniature world gives way and we snap back to life in living scale. In imagining other worlds, in other spaces and other times, we inevitably circle back to re-imaging our own landscapes and time. In the process, the switches in scale and the experience of encountering people, places, and objects, both familiar and strange, have subtly subverted our memories and senses of reality, opening us up to experiences of the tiny uncanny.

Oh, how the heartless haunt us all.

In O'Neil's series global climate change has reared its head, and what we think of as the social world and all the feelings of structure that accompany it have eroded. One of the consequences of climate change is an increase in overwintering, the process where some living organisms wait out the winter season when weather conditions make normal activity, or even survival, difficult or damn near impossible. Overwintering can occur as a result of miscalculations caused by sudden changes to the weather or environment, or of following the dominant organisms in the group, which have misjudged weather patterns. The mix-up of the seasons makes living creatures, including humans, vulnerable to winter storms of snow, ice, and sleet, as well as the floods caused by thaws when spring temperatures arrive.

In O'Neil's smashed, snowglobe world of overwintering, fellows go about their strange business – hanging each other, striking each other with sticks, some falling on their knees, others watching without intervening. While the series progresses to a tragic end and the men are steadily killed off, there are brief breaks in the violence when they gather in clumps of solidarity. At times, sweet cross-legged circles form, hands are held, pairs take constitutionals small grouplets assemble into affectionate knots, and heart-shaped gatherings take form. In these moments, the men move more carefully, checking in with each other to see what's up, like night checks in on the crazy snowflake in Charles Simic's poem "Lunatic."[13] This momentary reprieve in the steady stream of brutality does not last. Still, given a shred of hope, I search the following scenes for evidence of individuals being kind, like how I rifle through a bowl of pistachio shells, hoping to find a remainder among the hollow husks that still houses something good inside. Coming up empty, the lack spawns a nightmare of a new anti-social anti-society of male maniacs and its opposite, an imagined futurity of something totally different – something that could only exist beyond these works on paper, something outside the white walls of the gallery on which they hang, something better than this world.

Midway through the series, O'Neil has drawn lines of men in loose diagonals. There are still so many of them. The end is coming, but it might take some time. The sweatsuited characters line up for makeshift skates and beautiful and complicated formations of skaters take to the ice. Meanwhile, a crater opens in the snow; the sky above the dark cavity is filled with what appears to be birds or bats or some other kind of black-winged creatures. The ersatz flock turns out to be mostly made of kites with a few birds of prey mixed in. O'Neil described the scene: "These birds do this incredible thing where they cartwheel in a free fall while having sex. So, they're connected physically, gripping talons, and they're falling FAST while this is happening. And sometimes, they're so in the moment that they don't separate in time and they fall to the ground while connected, dying on impact together."[14]

The men watch the avian spectacle, as we watch them watching. An uprooted tree that once filled the hole lies on the ground with its roots exposed; the up-turned arbour is almost obscene. There is a raw darkness below the tree. It is the underworld, a hint of what could come. In this drawing we can see a metaphor for how social attachment works, how "loss and vulnerability seem to follow from our being socially constituted bodies, attuned to others, at risk of losing those attachments, exposed to others, at risk of violence by virtue of that exposure," as Butler writes in *Precarious Life*.[15]

We, the Masses.

While we cannot know the exact time period in which the series takes place, or the precise geographical location, we do know that the inspiration for the characters comes from the Midwestern United States. The male figures in O'Neil's landscapes are loosely based on her father and his best friend Marty, regular guys from Omaha, Nebraska, who often did sporty things on the weekend in similar outfits to those worn by the men in her drawings. They are men who loved playing sports and watching others play sports on TV. The figures in the drawings take on other qualities too, absent from the artist's dad and his friends. They are darker, more violent. O'Neil describes the particular qualities of the figures as stemming "from a loss of individuality ... permeating that region and other places ... The fear of breaking out, and the desire to just be normal ... the horrors that exist when people en masse decide to just do as the others are doing."[16] The drawings are a commentary on the indifference to climate change, as well as indifference to fellow humans.

O'Neil realized after she had been drawing the men for some time that the sweatsuits were also influenced by the uniforms worn by the Heaven's Gate cult. The millenarian group became widely known after a mass suicide event in 1997. Leading up to the gruesome end, followers felt that the earth was being recycled, cleansed of people. Members of Heaven's Gate were waiting on an alien spacecraft following the Hale-Bopp Comet to pick them up. This was to be a return of sorts. The followers of Heaven's Gate believed that ancient astronauts visited Earth centuries ago, leaving behind the seeds that eventually led to modern human existence. The space travellers from the long-lost past would return on the heels of the Hale-Bopp Comet to collect the most spiritually enlightened of their progeny. When the comet passed and no spaceship surfaced, thirty-nine Heaven's Gate members took their own lives. They were found with diamond-shaped swaths of purple fabric covering their faces down to their knees; underneath they were dressed in black sweatsuits and black Nikes with white swooshes. Vodka, sedatives, and plastic bags were discovered at the scene.

There are echoes of cleansing in O'Neil's drawings too, but no sense that any of the men are chosen above others to survive. The characters in her landscapes are not waiting on ancient astronauts. If the men expect cosmic events or miraculous interventions to appear on the horizon, we've no indication of this in their behaviour. They take on nature and each other with such reckless abandon that their inevitable end is expected, but nevertheless tragic. The darkness in O'Neil's works can come as a surprise. If you glance quickly from across the room, you might only see gorgeous landscapes, or exercises in miniature figurative drawing and displays of artistic techniques. They are those things too, but more importantly O'Neil takes on the emergent (or pre-emergent) unpleasant undercurrents of contemporary life and draws them on the surface.[17]

FLOODS.

Masses and masses rove a darkened pool; never is there laughter on this ship of fools.

As the series progresses, a diluvian scene develops. Water rushes in. A thaw! The men take to rafts. Splaying and sitting in knots, they float on sutured, logged structures as snow gently falls. The men are mercurial; sometimes they push each other off into the water. Nature is unpredictable – there is the unexpected slap of waves – the swells coming in from the top, along the flanks, and every which way. Like in many of O'Neil's renderings things are turned around. The landscape becomes liquid, sublime, and unruly. No structures can be felt, as uncontained nature overwhelms. The snow-blanketed vistas, the jangly mountain peaks, give way to the heaving waters that nip and lick at the minute men. The world explodes and "everything inanimate and animate are indistinguishable."[18]

The scene is an artistic rhyme to Kai Erikson's 1972 sociological study of the aftermath of the Buffalo Creek disaster in West Virginia, *Everything in Its Path*. Buffalo Creek was devastated when a dam operated by the Pittston Coal Company burst, releasing 132 million gallons of coal slurry. Great waves of black water containing waste from coal processing washed over the hollows below. One hundred and twenty-five people were killed. More than four thousand were

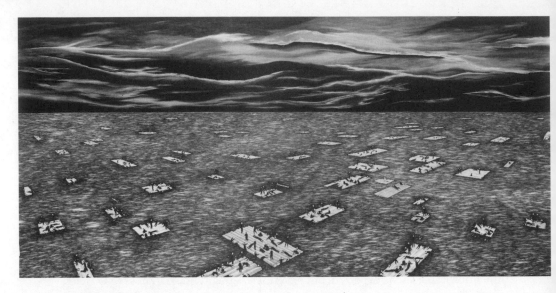

Figure 12.3 *Masses and masses rove a darkened pool; never is there laughter on this ship of fools*, Robyn O'Neil, 2007.

left homeless. Survivors remembered how the water was transformed into something terrible, simultaneously solid and liquid. They remembered a black mountain three storeys high and on the run, giving chase to the community, snapping telephone poles and lapping up houses as easily as a kitten laps milk.[19] In legal papers, Pittston Coal called the accident an "Act of God." Everyone knows now the disaster was caused by human error and that the suffering of the community was compounded by the indifference of Pittston Coal.

Before the catastrophe, the folks of Buffalo Creek, West Virginia, had come to count on a certain measure of calm and certitude in their lives despite the inherent precariousness of living and working in a mining community. Although many in the area worked dangerous jobs and could expect industrial accidents from time to time, the bursting of the dam and its hellish unleash was beyond all expectations. Desperation and vulnerability flooded the community. One of the most devastating remarks uttered by a survivor – "Everybody was close. Everybody knowed everybody. But now everybody is alone" – rips out the stuffing of the cozily sewn community. Erikson shows how a new overwhelming feeling of anxiety and dread destroyed the "quiet set of understandings" that had shaped the communal structure.

A similar loss of community and faith in institutions can be found in the aftermath of Hurricane Katrina and its devastation of New Orleans and surrounding areas in Louisiana and Mississippi in 2005. It is not surprising that after the disaster, Erikson's *Everything in Its Path* was reissued. The Federal Emergency Management Agency of the United States government (FEMA) even uses an excerpt from the book in training documents to educate its agents about the raw emotional and fractured social landscapes that can remain in the months and years after a terrible disaster, after nothing is the same.[20] In times of post-disaster, it is unmistakably clear, as Lauren Berlant writes, that precarity carries with it an affective structure that is unevenly distributed throughout society. While precariousness is a condition of all life, as Butler reminds us, it is "not simply an existential truth – each of us could be subject to deprivation, injury, debilitation or death by virtue of events or processes outside of our control."[21] It is important to remember that some feel this more than others and more regularly. Folks living on the margins, both economically and socially, experience the precarity of modern life more often and more acutely.

The fact that all life is precarious is a quality of what Butler calls "the social bond, the various relations that establish our interdependency."[22] We see this social bond not only between people, but also across landscapes, time, and space; we might be most attuned to social bonds when they are threatened, weak, or broken. Interdependency comes into view at these moments. In these times of undoing, communal failures are revealed. As Butler argues: "no one person suffers a lack of shelter without a social failure to organize shelter in a way that is accessible to each and every person."[23] In O'Neil's landscapes, we can peer into a world where the sense of community has disappeared. There are no shelters whatsoever in O'Neil's landscapes – no Woolfian room of one's own, no den, no inglenook, no place for what Proust called the "poetry of hibernation."[24] There is no nourishment to be found either, not even hoosh, a polar stew most often made of penguin meat, melted snow, and old biscuits that explorers in harsh arctic landscapes have historically feasted upon.[25] There is none of what the Danes call *hygge*, the ethos of coziness and sense of camaraderie experienced in the face of harsh winters. Here there is no reprieve from the elements and no protection from the others who are largely malevolent.

Whatever these men feel, they feel it out in the open. Two particularly devastating scenes show a lone miniature middle-aged man cowering under a curved tree on a cadaver-white hill and then lying face down. All by himself, he seems at least safe for the moment, but hopeless and friendless. The drawings are called *Forgetting 1* (2008) and *Towards the Tranquil* (2008).

We are not o.k., we can not live like this anymore.

Catastrophes create moments of suspension, wrinkles in time, rips in the humdrum commute, work, breakfast, lunch, dinner, sleep, alarm clock, shower, get dressed, do it all again trajectories of our lives. O'Neil is no stranger to these tears in the everyday. The artist was raised in Nebraska and in Texas, a swath of America that is sometimes called Tornado Alley. When O'Neil was five years old, Hurricane Alicia devastated Houston, ripping the roof off her home, leaving an impact on the young artist. And, in September 2008, Hurricane Ike pounded Houston and Galveston, causing damage to her home. She spent years as a volunteer weather watcher. She logged the high and low temperatures each day, measured rainfall with a special type of gauge, and reported any unusual weather activity. She threatens to become a tornado chaser.

In her work as an artist, O'Neil's pencil drawings deliver a register of feeling that rides on the breakdown of community and the wild unpredictability of nature. Her art brings to the surface deep psychological and sociological fears of violence, ecological disaster, and social erosion. Her drawings also convey the anxiety that even the most regular, everyday person among us will behave with indifferent cruelty in times when regular society is broken down or interrupted. In her works, hugging turns to pushing and there's no telling what one man might do to the other. Kindness and menace seem equally possible. This is the uneasiness that is often felt during the liminal times of disasters and their aftermaths.

In *Paradise in Hell,* Rebecca Solnit argues for another kind of liminal post-disaster space, one where people come together in temporary utopias. She writes that disasters rupture our everyday ways of being and allow for new social ties to form, simultaneously releasing us from our old social bonds, hierarchies, and set positions. She goes on to say, "in many disasters ... strangers become friends and collaborators, goods are shared freely, people improvise new roles for themselves."[26] Solnit insists that the news media focuses on the extreme cases, highlighting the injured, the killed, and the abused. Through these kinds of reports, locations of post-disaster are transformed into hellish Superdomes: arenas of theft, rape, murder, and human waste.

Solnit offers a sunnier view of humans caught up in disaster and human nature writ large. She argues that when disasters strike, it is often the everyday folks (not the police, government officials, or the super wealthy) who respond with kindness and communal zeal. She draws on the work of the disaster sociologist Charles Fritz who argued that in moments of crisis people actually respond by helping each other rather than fleeing or fighting for limited resources. Fritz believed we should think of human reactions to trying times as "tend and befriend" instead of fight or flight. He wrote provocatively that everyday life is always already a disaster and that a catastrophe – earthquake, flood, poisonous gas leak, wild animal attack – liberates us from this condition.[27] Inspired by Fritz, Solnit writes: "[Disasters] are a crack in the walls that ordinarily hem us in, and what floods in can be enormously destructive – or creative. Hierarchies and

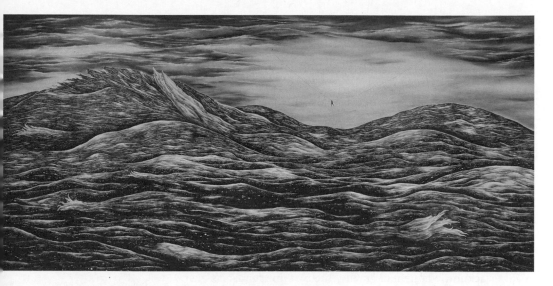

Figure 12.4 *These final hours embrace at last; this is our ending, this is our past,*
Robyn O'Neil, 2007.

institutions are inadequate to these circumstances; they are often what fails in
such crises. Civil society is what succeeds, not only in an emotional demonstra-
tion of altruism and mutual aid but also in a practical mustering of creativity and
resources to meet the challenges. Only this dispersed force of countless people
making countless decisions is adequate to a major crisis."[28] Solnit argues that
in disasters most people are survivors and not victims. Maybe this is because
most disasters end. Fritz and Solnit focus on the temporary periods between disaster and recovery when short-term utopias can crop up. In the best scenarios,
Solnit notes, positive changes carry over to more normal times.

In O'Neil's landscape drawings there is no after, only continuous unease and
uncertainty. The scenes she creates have more in common with what Walter Benjamin writes about in "Theses on the Philosophy of History," where "the 'state
of emergency' in which we live is not the exception but the rule."[29] The disaster-
emergency keeps going because the men keep doing what the other men are
doing. Not one among them is able "to blast open the continuum of history."[30]
Not one among them is able to turn the tides in the steady flow of destruction,
and so what could have been simply the slow death of exaggerated ordinariness
goes on instead in fast-forward mode.[31]

The absence of history hovers over the series. How long have the sweatpanted
men been destroying themselves, each other, and the environment? As we think
back to the lone man sitting by a tree with his legs outstretched in the first case,
and then folded over in a hopeless shape that resembles the child's pose in yoga

in the second, it is impossible to know the duration of this disaster or series of disasters, but it feels like forever.

These final hours embrace at last; this is our ending, this is our past.

Finally, we reach the last man. The hungry sea swells below a solitary figure hanging on a rope connected to who knows what. The rope's ends disappear into the clouds. The task of getting to the other side seems impossible. This is not the great funambulist Philippe Petit balanced delicately on a wire between the old Twin Towers, moving deftly from one structure to its double over the busy streets of New York City. Nor is it the great tightrope walker Charles Blondin who tempted the falls of Niagara on so many occasions, once even stopping midway to cook and eat an omelette. No, this is an awkward-bodied everyman about to slip into the sea, like a Dear John letter slips into a post box with only a muffled acknowledgment of gravity. The first line reads: It's over.

HELL.

The episodes do not crystallize but build to an end. In the last work before O'Neil's five-year hiatus beginning in 2012, the men are briefly resurrected in a composition called *Hell*. O'Neil thought she was done with the sweatpant guys, as she calls them. She had finally killed them off. But she wasn't done. She brought them back to populate a ghastly afterlife in a new place, the place of eternal damnation, where they interacted with a new population of black-robed characters. The sprawling landscape measuring seven feet by fourteen feet is reminiscent of Hieronymus Bosch's *Garden of Earthly Delights*. It is filled with a passel of the pudgy guys in sweatsuits and a multitude of miniature monks, measuring half a fingernail. The 35,000 separate figures were cut out with tiny scissors and stored in Ziploc bags until they were needed like grains of pepper trapped in those tiny packets stacked up on lunch counters. The *Hell* piece took O'Neil two years to complete, working full-time. She delicately travelled with it from Texas to California to her gallery in New York.

In a strange twist of bad luck, several of O'Neil's artworks, including *Hell*, were destroyed in the fall of 2012 in the flooding of lower Manhattan that resulted from Hurricane Sandy. During and after the storm, throughout SoHo waters rushed in every which way, the insides and outsides of buildings became permeable borders, and almost as a rhyme to the artworks themselves, O'Neil's gallery became flooded and water invaded the storage rooms soaking and destroying their contents. *Hell* exists now only in digital images and in memory. It is remarkable how prophetic O'Neil's work was. She ended her series in hurricane waves of graphite, only to revive the men in *Hell*, which was then taken by Hurricane Sandy. The real-life disaster caused a rupture, a break, a point from which there was no going back. On losing *Hell*, O'Neil said: "I was obviously devastated ... but also I'll say this. Destruction is now my best friend. If I could go back in time and save all [my work] that was destroyed by hurricane waters, I would never dream of saving any of it. Truly."[32]

O'Neil's apocalyptic landscapes give us opportunities to pause, to summon a reckoning with the precariousness of contemporary life, and to acknowledge the fact, as Butler writes, "that we can be injured, that others can be injured, that we are subject to death at the whim of another." These moments can elicit "both fear and grief," but also give us a space to "begin the process of imagining" something else.[33]

ACKNOWLEDGMENTS

I would like to thank Robyn O'Neil for her generosity and her wild imagination.

NOTES

1 After a five-year hiatus from drawing the sweatpanted men, beginning in 2012, O'Neil started making them again in 2017. On her return to the men, she commented: "Now that I am working with the figure again it has become clear how vital these people are to what I do. The stories I've always wanted to tell have focused on the difficulties of being human, roaming this planet in our too human bodies. I'm back to pencil and paper, and I'm back to imagining the obstacles that my guys will overcome or not." Susan Inglett Gallery, *The Good Herd*, New York, 3 February–15 March 2017, press release, http://www.inglettgallery.com/exhibitions/robyn-o-neil#1-o-neil-installation-i.
2 Butler, "For and Against Precarity," 13.
3 Lefebvre, *Critique of Everyday Life*, 806.
4 Simmel, "The Metropolis and Mental Life," 324.
5 Williams, "Structures of Feeling."
6 All of the titles of the subsections come from the titles of Robyn O'Neil's works.
7 Carson, *The Beauty of the Husband*, 97.
8 Although the men consistently wear basic black sweatsuits throughout the series, there was a brief break in their uniform when the *New York Times* asked O'Neil to draw her men wearing Chanel. The artist decided to put only half in Chanel and the other half remained in their typical clothes. Of those figures wearing Chanel, some were dressed in womenswear, some in menswear, and some in gender-bending mix-and-match combinations. O'Neil told the *New York Times:* "The Chanel men represent individuality, while the other men have lost their identity. They're zombies" (Maura Egan, "High Art," т *Magazine, New York Times,* 28 August 2005, http://www.nytimes.com/2005/08/28/style/tmagazine/high-art.html). O'Neil referred to this play on her landscapes as a "fantasy drag/murder

scene in the woods" (Kate Donnelly, interview with Robyn O'Neil, *From Your Desks,* 12 July 2011, http://fromyourdesks.com/2011/07/12/robyn-oneil/). The clear winners in this scene were the Chanel clad, as the style reporter Maura Egan wrote: "in other words, high fashion (and cross-dressing) wins" (Egan, "High Art"). It is amazing how the change in the costuming of the figures alters the feeling of the work. As conformity dissipates and individuals with styles start to emerge, other ways of living seem possible and we can begin to see a way out of the zombification of the world.

9 Augé, *Non-places,* xii.

10 Charlotte Perkins Gilman's *Herland* was a novel of speculative fiction depicting a feminist utopia free from the patriarchy, but also absent of sexuality. The women of Herland reproduced through parthenogenesis. *Herland,* in particular, and Gilman's oeuvre, in general, have had a big effect on O'Neil. Email correspondence with the artist, 9 August 2014.

11 Email correspondence with the artist, 9 August 2014.

12 S. Stewart, *On Longing,* 67.

13 Simic, *The Lunatic,* 5.

14 Email correspondence with the artist, 9 August 2014.

15 Butler, *Precarious Life,* 20.

16 Donnelly, interview with Robyn O'Neil.

17 Williams, "Structures of Feeling."

18 Marchand, "Mankayia and the Kiowa Indians," 23.

19 Erikson, *Everything in Its Path,* 32.

20 An excerpt of Erikson, *Everything in Its Path,* can be found here: http://www.training.fema.gov.

21 Berlant, *Cruel Optimism,* and Butler, "For and Against Precarity," 13.

22 Butler, "For and Against Precarity," 13.

23 Ibid.

24 Proust, *Swann's Way,* 51.

25 For more on hoosh see Anthony, *Hoosh.*

26 Solnit, *Paradise in Hell,* 17.

27 Fritz, "Disasters and Mental Health," and Solnit, *Paradise in Hell,* 165.

28 Solnit, *Paradise in Hell,* 305.

29 Benjamin, "Theses on the Philosophy of History," 257.

30 Ibid., 262.

31 Berlant, *Cruel Optimism.*

32 Email correspondence with the artist, 9 August 2014.

33 Butler, *Precarious Life,* xii.

BIBLIOGRAPHY

ARCHIVES

Archives of American Art, Smithsonian Institution
Glenbow Archives
Mass Observation Archive, The Keep, Brighton, UK
Moose Jaw Public Library Archives

BOOKS AND ARTICLES

Abraham, Ayisha. "Deteriorating Memories: Blurring Fact and Fiction in Home Movies in India." In *Mining the Home Movie: Excavations in Histories and Memories*, edited by Karen L. Ishizuka and Patricia R. Zimmermann, 168–84. Berkeley: University of California Press, 2008.

Ahmed, Sara. "Happy Objects." In *The Affect Theory Reader*, edited by Melissa Gregg and Gregory J. Seigworth, 29–51. Durham and London: Duke University Press, 2010.

Alexander, Neta. "From Dust till Drone: Roomba Aesthetics and Non-Human Cinema." *Flow* 23, no. 5 (2017). https://www.flowjournal.org/2017/03/from-dust-till-drone/.

Anderson, David G. *Identity and Ecology in Arctic Siberia: The Number One Reindeer Brigade*. Oxford Studies in Social and Cultural Anthropology. Oxford: Oxford University Press, 2000.

– "Property Rights and Civil Society in Siberia: An Analysis of the Social Movements of the Zabaikal'skie Evenki." *Praxis International* 12, no. 1 (1992): 83–105.

Anderson, John. "Designs for Living." *Playboy*, July 1961.

Anderson, Kay. "The Idea of Chinatown: The Power of Place and Institutional Practice in the Making of a Racial Category." *Annals of the Association of American Geographers* 77, no. 4 (1987): 580–98.

– *Vancouver's Chinatown: Racial Discourse in Canada, 1875–1980*. Montreal and Kingston: McGill-Queen's University Press, 1995.

Anthony, Jason. *Hoosh: Roast Penguin, Scurvy Day, and Other Stories of Antarctic Cuisine.* Lincoln: University of Nebraska Press, 2012.

Apel, Dora. *Beautiful Terrible Ruins: Detroit and the Anxiety of Decline.* New Brunswick, NJ: Rutgers University Press, 2015.

Ashton, Dore. *Noguchi East and West.* Berkeley: University of California Press, 1992.

Atleo, E. Richard (Umeek). *Principles of Tsawalk: An Indigenous Approach to Global Crisis.* Vancouver: University of British Columbia Press, 2011.

Augé, Marc. *Non-places: An Introduction to Supermodernity.* New York: Verso, 1995.

Ayto, John, and Ian Crofton. *Brewer's Britain and Ireland: The History, Culture, Folklore and Etymology of 7500 Places in These Islands.* London: Weidenfeld & Nicolson, 2005.

Bachelard, Gaston. *The Poetics of Space: The Classic Look at How We Experience Intimate Places.* Translated by Maria Jolas. Boston: Beacon Press, 1994.

Barr, Nancy W. "Detroit after Dark: Photographers Take On the Night." In *Detroit after Dark: Photographs from the Collection of the Detroit Institute of Arts*, 8–19. Detroit: Detroit Institute of Arts, 2016.

Barthes, Roland. *Camera Lucida: Reflections on Photography.* Translated by Richard Howard. New York: Hill and Wang, 1981.

– "Eiffel Tower." In *A Barthes Reader*, edited by Susan Sontag, 236–50. New York: Hill & Wang, 1982.

– *Roland Barthes by Roland Barthes.* Translated by Richard Howard. New York: Hill and Wang, 2010.

– "The Third Meaning: Research Notes on Some Eisenstein Stills." In *Image Music Text*, translated by Stephen Heath, 52–68. London: Fontana, 1977.

Bastien, Betty. *Blackfoot Ways of Knowing: The Worldview of the Siksikaitsitapi.* Calgary: University of Calgary Press, 2004.

Bataille, Georges. *The Accursed Share: An Essay on General Economy.* New York: Zone Books, 1988.

– *Visions of Excess: Selected Writings, 1927–1939.* Translated by Allan Stoekl with Carl R. Lovitt and Donald M. Leslie Jr. Minneapolis: University of Minnesota Press, 1985.

Baucom, Ian. "History 4°: Postcolonial Method and Anthropocene Time." *Cambridge Journal of Postcolonial Literary Inquiry* 1, Special Issue 01 (March 2014): 123–42.

Bauman, Richard. "Verbal Art as Performance." *American Anthropologist* 77, no. 2 (1975): 290–311.

– *Story, Performance, and Event.* Cambridge: Cambridge University Press, 1986.

Bellour, Raymond. "The Film Stilled." *Camera Obscura* 8, no. 3 (1990): 98–124.

Benjamin, Walter. *The Arcades Project.* Translated by H. Eiland and K. McLaughlin. Cambridge, MA: Harvard University Press, 1999.

– *Berlin Childhood around 1900.* Translated by Howard Eiland. Cambridge, MA: Belknap Press, 2006.

– *Illuminations: Essays and Reflections.* Translated by Harry Zohn. New York: Schocken Books, 1968.

– "Review of the Mendelssohns' *Der Mensch in der Handschrift*." In *Selected Writings, Volume 2*, 131–4. Cambridge, MA: Belknap/Harvard Press, 1999.

- "Theses on the Philosophy of History." In *Illuminations*, 253–64. New York: Pantheon, 1968.
- *The Work of Art in the Age of Its Technological Reproducibility, and Other Writings on Media*. Edited by Michael W. Jennings, Brigid Doherty, and Thomas Y. Levin. Cambridge, MA: Harvard University Press, 2008.

Berg, Maxine. "Skill, Craft and Histories of Industrialisation in Europe and Asia." *Transactions of the Royal Historical Society* 24 (December 2014): 127–48.

Berlant, Lauren. *Cruel Optimism*. Durham: Duke University Press, 2011.
- "Structures of Unfeeling: *Mysterious Skin*." *International Journal of Politics, Culture, and Society* 28 (2015): 191–213.
- "Trump, or Political Emotions." *Supervalent Thought*, 4 August 2016. http://supervalentthought.com/2016/08/04/trump-or-political-emotions/.

Blanchfield, Brian. *Proxies: Essays Near Knowing*. Lebanon, NH: University Press of New England, 2016.

Blum, Alan. *The Imaginative Structure of the City*. Montreal and Kingston: McGill-Queen's University Press, 2003.

Bois, Yve-Alain, and Rosalind Krauss. *Formless*. Cambridge, MA: MIT Press, 1999.

Brett, Bill. *There Ain't No Such Animal and Other East Texas Tales*. College Station: Texas A & M University Press, 1979.
- *This Here's a Good'un*. College Station: Texas A & M University Press, 1983.

Bryan, Van. "Prometheus the Creation of Man and the History of Enlightenment." *Classical Wisdom Weekly*, 20 May 2013. http://classicalwisdom.com/prometheus-the-creation-of-man/.

Bunge, William. *Fitzgerald: Geography of a Revolution*. Athens: University of Georgia Press, 1971/2011.

Buñuel, Luis. *An Unspeakable Betrayal: Selected Writings of Luis Buñuel*. Translated by Garrett White. Berkeley and London: University of California Press, 2002.

Burgin, Victor. *In/Different Spaces: Place and Memory in Visual Culture*. Berkeley: University of California Press, 1996.

Butler, Judith. *Precarious Life: The Powers of Mourning and Violence*. New York: Verso, 2004.
- "For and Against Precarity." *Tidal: A Journal of Theory and Strategy for the Occupy Movement* 1 (2011): 12–13.

Campbell, Craig. "Contrails of Globalization and the View from the Ground: An Essay on Isolation in East-Central Siberia." *Polar Geography* 27, no. 2 (2003): 97–120.

Carroll, Lewis. *Through the Looking-Glass and What Alice Found There*. Scituate, MA: Digital Scanning, Inc., 2007.

Carson, Anne. *The Beauty of the Husband*. New York: Vintage, 2001.

Ceballos, Gerardo, Paul R. Ehrlich, Anthony D. Barnosky, Andrés García, Robert M. Pringle, and Todd M. Palmer. "Accelerated Modern Human–Induced Species Losses: Entering the Sixth Mass Extinction." *Science Advances* 1, no. 5 (1 June 2015). https://doi.org/10.1126/sciadv.1400253.

Chalfen, Richard. "Your Panopticon or Mine? Incorporating Wearable Technology's Glass and GoPro into Visual Social Science." *Visual Studies* 29, no. 3 (2014): 299–310.

Chambers, Glenn. "Goodbye God, I'm Going to Texas: The Migration of Louisiana Creoles of Colour and the Preservation of Black Catholic and Creole Traditions in Southeast Texas." *Journal of Religion and Popular Culture* 26, no. 1 (2014): 124–43.

Chan, Anthony B. *Gold Mountain: The Chinese in the New World*. Vancouver: New Star Books, 1983.

Chen, Mel Y. *Animacies: Biopolitics, Racial Mattering, and Queer Affect*. Durham and London: Duke University Press, 2012.

Cho, Lily. *Eating Chinese: Culture on the Menu in Small Town Canada*. Cultural Spaces. Toronto: University of Toronto Press, 2010.

Choi, Vivian Y. "Anticipatory States: Tsunami, War, and Insecurity in Sri Lanka." *Cultural Anthropology* 30, no.2 (2015): 286–309.

Choy, Timothy, and Jerry Zee. "Condition – Suspension." *Cultural Anthropology* 30, no. 2 (2015): 210–23.

Cixous, Hélène. *Ex-Cities*. Philadelphia: Slought Books, 2006.

Classen, Constance. "Museum Manners: The Sensory Life of the Early Museum." *Journal of Social History* 40, no. 4 (2007): 895–914.

Cole, Teju. *Blind Spot*. New York: Penguin Random House, 2017.

Colomina, Beatriz. *Domesticity at War*. Cambridge, MA: MIT Press, 2007.

– *Privacy and Publicity: Modern Architecture as Mass Media*. Cambridge, MA: MIT Press, 1994.

Connor, Steven. "Introduction." In *The Five Senses: A Philosophy of Mingled Bodies*, by Michel Serres, 1–16. London and New York: Continuum, 2008.

– "Michel Serres' Five Senses." In *Empire of the Senses: The Sensual Culture Reader*, edited by David Howes, 318–34. Oxford and New York: Berg, 2005.

– "Taking Pity on Things." Talk presented at the Festival of Ideas, Cambridge, 26 October 2012. Page numbers refer to pdf version: http://stevenconnor.com/wp-content/uploads/2014/09/pity.pdf.

Cook, James. *The Journals of Captain James Cook on His Voyages of Discovery: The Voyage of the Resolution and Discovery 1776–1780, Vol III, Part 2*. Edited by J.C. Beaglehole. Cambridge: Hakluyt Society, 1967.

Coulthard, Glen. *Red Skin, White Masks: Rejecting the Colonial Politics of Recognition*. Minneapolis: University of Minnesota Press, 2014.

Crate, Susan Alexandra. *Cows, Kin, and Globalization: An Ethnography of Sustainability*. Lanham, MD: Rowman Altamira, 2006.

Darroch, Michael. "Border Scenes: Detroit ± Windsor." *Cultural Studies* 29, no. 3 (2015): 298–325.

Darroch, Michael, and Kim Nelson. "Windsoria: Border / Screen / Environment." *Public* 40: "Screens" (2009): 56–65.

De Certeau, Michel. *The Writing of History*. New York: Columbia University Press, 1991.

Deleuze, Gilles. *Cinema 1: The Movement-Image*. Translated by Hugh Tomlinson and Barbara Habberjam. Minneapolis: University of Minnesota, 1989/1986.

- *Cinema 2: The Time-Image*. Translated by Hugh Tomlinson and Robert Galeta. Minneapolis: University of Minnesota, 1989.

Demetrios, Eames. *Beautiful Details*. Los Angeles: AMMO Books, 2014.

Derrida, Jacques. *Archive Fever: A Freudian Impression*. Translated by Eric Prenowitz. Chicago and London: University of Chicago Press, 1995.

- *Margins of Philosophy*. Translated by Alan Bass. Reprint edition. Chicago: University of Chicago Press, 1984.

- *Of Grammatology*. Edited by Gayatri Chakravorty Spivak. Corr. edition. Baltimore: Johns Hopkins University Press, 1998.

Descola, Philippe. *Beyond Nature and Culture*. Chicago and London: University of Chicago Press, 2013.

Detienne, Marcel, Jean-Pierre Vernant, Jean-Louis Durand, et al. *The Cuisine of Sacrifice among the Greeks*. Translated by Paula Wissing. 1st edition. Chicago: University of Chicago Press, 1998.

Dolphijn, Rick, and Iris van der Tuin. "'Matter Feels, Converses, Suffers, Desires, Yearns and Remembers': An Interview with Karen Barad." *New Materialism: Interviews and Cartographies*. Accessed 7 December 2017. https://quod.lib.umich.edu/o/ohp/11515701. 0001.001/1:4.3/--new-materialism-interviews-cartographies?rgn=div2;view=fulltext.

Dunn, Katherine. *Geek Love*. New York: Random House, 1989.

Durkheim, Emile. *The Elementary Forms of Religious Life*. Oxford: Oxford Paperbacks, 2008.

Duus, Masayo. *The Life of Isamu Noguchi: Journey without Borders*. Princeton, NJ: Princeton University Press, 2004.

Eames, Charles, and Ray Eames. *An Eames Anthology*. Edited by Daniel Ostroff. New Haven: Yale University Press, 2015.

Eames, Charles, and Eero Saarinen. "Case Study Houses 8 and 9." *Arts and Architecture*, December 1945, 44–51.

Edensor, Tim. "Illuminated Atmospheres: Anticipating and Reproducing the Flow of Affective Experience in Blackpool." *Environment and Planning D: Society and Space* 30 (2012): 1103–22.

- "Reconnecting with Darkness: Experiencing Landscapes and Sites of Gloom." *Social and Cultural Geography* 14, no. 4 (2013): 446–65.

- "The Gloomy City: Rethinking the Relationship between Light and Dark." *Urban Studies* 52, no. 3, special issue: "Geographies of the Urban Night" (2015): 422–38.

Erikson, Kai. *Everything in Its Path: Deconstruction of Community in the Buffalo Creek Flood*. New York: Simon & Schuster, 1978.

Esposito, Roberto. *Persons and Things*. Cambridge and Malden: Polity Press, 2015.

Fabian, Johannes. *Time and the Other: How Anthropology Makes Its Object*. New York: Columbia University Press, 1983.

Feenberg, Andrew. *Transforming Technology: A Critical Theory Revisited*. Oxford and New York: Oxford University Press, 2002.

Feld, Steven. "Places Sensed, Senses Placed: Toward a Sensuous Epistemology of Environments." In *Empire of the Senses: The Sensual Culture Reader*, edited by David Howes, 179–91. Oxford and New York: Berg, 2005.

Ferguson, Roderick A. "Sissies at the Picnic: The Subjugated Knowledges of a Black Rural Queer." In *Feminist Waves, Feminist Generations: Life Stories from the Academy*, edited by Hokulani K. Aiku, Karla A. Erickson, and Jennifer L. Pierce, 188–96. Minneapolis: University of Minnesota Press, 2007.

Fondahl, Gail. *Gaining Ground? Evenkis, Land and Reform in Southeastern Siberia*. Cultural Survival Studies in Ethnicity and Change. Boston: Allyn and Bacon, 1998.

Foucault, Michel. "Nietzsche, Genealogy, History." In *Language, Counter-Memory, Practice: Selected Essays and Interviews*, edited by D.F. Bouchard, 76–100. Ithaca: Cornell University Press, 1977.

Frankétienne. *Ready to Burst*. Translated by K.L. Glover. Brooklyn: Archipelago Books, 2014.

Freud, Sigmund. *Art and Literature*. New edition. London: Penguin UK, 1990.

– *On Metapsychology – the Theory of Psychoanalysis: Beyond the Pleasure Principle, Ego and the Id and Other Works*. Penguin Books, 1991.

Friedberg, Anne. *The Virtual Window: From Alberti to Microsoft*. Cambridge, MA: MIT Press, 2006.

Fritz, Charles. "Disasters and Mental Health: Therapeutic Principles Drawn from Disaster Studies." Washington, DC: Disaster Research Center, 1996.

Fromhold, Joachim. "Wizard Lake." *Indian Place Names of the West Part 1*. Blackfalds, AB: Self-published, 2001.

Fuss, Diana. *The Sense of an Interior: Four Writers and the Rooms That Shaped Them*. New York and London: Routledge, 2004.

Garrett, Bradley. "Assaying History: Creating Temporal Junctions through Urban Exploration." *Environment and Planning D: Society and Space* 29, no. 6 (2011): 378–80.

Gilman, Charlotte Perkins. *Herland*. Dover: New York, 1998.

Golovnev, Andrei V., and Gail Osherenko. *Siberian Survival: The Nenets and Their Story*. Ithaca, NY: Cornell University Press, 1999.

Gordon, Avery F. *Ghostly Matters: Haunting and the Sociological Imagination*. Minneapolis and London: University of Minnesota Press, 2008.

Gordon, Linda, and Gary Y. Okihiro, eds. *Impounded*. New York: W.W. Norton, 2006.

Government of Canada. "Copy of Treaty and Supplementary Treaty No. 7 between Her Majesty the Queen and the Blackfeet and Other Indian Tribes, at the Blackfoot Crossing of Bow River and Fort Macleod." 1877. Cat. No. Ci 72-0766, IAND Publication No. QS-0575-000-EE-A. Accessed 25 December 2016. http://www.aadnc-aandc.gc.ca/eng/1100100028793/1100100028803.

– "Copy of Treaty No. 6 between Her Majesty the Queen and the Plain and Wood Cree Indians and other Tribes of Indians at Fort Carlton, Fort Pitt and Battle River with Adhesions." 1964. Cat. No. R33-0664, IAND Publication No. QS0574-000-EE-A-1. Accessed 25 December 2016. http://www.aadnc-aandc.gc.ca/eng/1100100028710/1100100028783.

Gregson, Nicky, Alan Metcalfe, and Louise Crewe. "Identity, Mobility, and the Throwaway Society." *Environment and Planning D: Society and Space* 25 (2007): 682–700.

Guido, Laurent, and Olivier Lugon, eds. *Between Still and Moving Images: Photography and Cinema in the 20th Century*. New Barnet: John Libbey Publishing, 2012.

Hales, Peter Bacon. "Levittown: Documents of an Ideal American Suburb." Accessed 1 October 2016. http://websupport1.citytech.cuny.edu/Faculty/pcatapano/US2/US %20Documents/Levittown%20Documents%20of%20an%20Ideal%20American%20 Suburb.pdf.

Hamilton-Paterson, James. *Seven Tenths: The Sea and Its Thresholds*. New York: Europa Editions Inc., 2009.

Haraway, Donna. "Anthropocene, Capitalocene, Plantationocene, Chthulucene: Making Kin." *Environmental Humanities* 6 (2015): 159–65. http://environmentalhumanities.org/arch/vol6/6.7.pdf.

Harrison, Paul. "Corporeal Remains: Vulnerability, Proximity, and Living On after the End of the World." *Environment and Planning A* 40, no. 2 (2008): 423–45.

Hastrup, Kirsten. "The Ethnographic Present: A Reinvention." *Cultural Anthropology* 5, no. 1 (1990): 45–61.

Heavy Head, Ryan. "Feeding Sublimity: Embodiment in Blackfoot Experience." MA thesis, University of Lethbridge, 2005.

Hell, Julia, and Andreas Schönle. *The Ruins of Modernity*. Durham, NC: Duke University Press, 2010.

Herrera, Hayden. *Listening to Stone: The Art and Life of Isamu Noguchi*. New York: Farrar, Straus and Giroux, 2015.

Herring, Scott. *Another Country: Queer Anti-Urbanism*. New York: NYU Press, 2010.

Highmore, Ben. "Formations of Feelings, Constellations of Things." *Cultural Studies Review* 22, no. 1 (2016): 144–67.

– *Ordinary Lives: Studies in the Everyday*. London and New York: Routledge, 2011.

Hoffman, Ernst Theodor. *The Tales of Hoffmann*. Reprint edition. Harmondsworth and New York: Penguin Classics, 1982.

Howe, Cymene, and Anand Pandian. "Lexicon for an Anthropocene Yet Unseen." *Cultural Anthropology*, 28 June 2017. https://culanth.org/fieldsights/803-lexicon-for-an-anthropocene-yet-unseen.

Huber, Matthew. *Lifeblood: Oil, Freedom, and the Forces of Capital*. Minneapolis and London: University of Minnesota Press, 2013.

Ince, Catherine, and Lotte Johnson, eds. *The World of Charles and Ray Eames*. London: Thames and Hudson, 2015.

Jordan, Larry. *Jim Reeves: His Untold Story*. Page Turner Books International, 2011.

Karibo, Holly. "Ambassadors of Pleasure: Illicit Economies in the Detroit-Windsor Borderland, 1945–1960." PhD diss., University of Toronto, 2012.

Kepes, György. "Notes on Expression and Communication in the Cityscape." *Daedalus* 90, no. 1, "The Future Metropolis" (1961): 147–65.

Keyte, Julia. "Objects in Purgatory: How We Live with Uncherished Gifts." *Interiors* 4, no. 3 (2013): 315–37.

Kirkham, Pat. "'At Home' with the Eameses: Performance, Hosting and Hospitality." In *The World of Charles and Ray Eames*, edited by Catherine Ince and Lotte Johnson, 112–28. London: Thames and Hudson, 2015.

– *Charles and Ray Eames: Designers of the Twentieth Century*. Cambridge, MA: MIT Press, 1995.

Kirksey, Eben. *Freedom in Entangled Worlds: West Papua and the Architecture of Global Power*. Durham: Duke University Press, 2012.

Kirshenblatt-Gimblett, Barbara. *Destination Culture: Tourism, Museums, and Heritage*. Berkeley: University of California Press, 1998.

Klein, Christina. *Cold War Orientalism: Asia in the Middlebrow Imagination, 1945–1961*. Berkeley: University of California Press, 2003.

Klokov, K.B. "Northern Reindeer of Taymyr Okrug as the Focus of Economic Activity: Contemporary Problems of Reindeer Husbandry and the Wild Reindeer Hunt." *Polar Geography* 21, no. 4 (1 October 1997): 233–71.

Kohn, Eduardo. *How Forests Think: Towards an Anthropology beyond the Human*. Berkeley: University of California Press, 2013.

Kolpaschikov, Leonid, Vladimir Makhailov, and Don Russell. "The Role of Harvest, Predators, and Socio-Political Environment in the Dynamics of the Taimyr Wild Reindeer Herd with Some Lessons for North America." *Ecology and Society* 20, no. 1 (23 January 2015). http://dx.doi.org/10.5751/ES-07129-200109.

Koptseva, Natalia P., and Vladimir I. Kirko. "Post-Soviet Practice of Preserving Ethnocultural Identity of Indigenous Peoples of the North and Siberia in Krasnoyarsk Region of the Russian Federation." *Life Science Journal* 11, no. 7 (2014): 180–5.

Koptseva, Natalia P., Kseniya V. Reznikova, and Vladimir I. Kirko. "The Political Struggle for Evenkia's 'Special Status' within Krasnoyarsk Krai (Central Siberia)." *Asian Politics & Policy* 9, no. 1 (2017): 99–121.

Koshelev, Michael P., and Anatolyi D. Mukhachev. "Development of the Technology for Producing Reindeer in the USSR." *Rangifer* 6, no. 2 (1 June 1986): 341–3.

Kovyazin, N.M., and K.G. Kuzakov. *Sovetskaya Evenkia (ekonomiko-Geograficheskiy Ocherk) (Soviet Evenkia [An Economic-Geographic Essay])*. Moscow; Leningrad: Izdatel'stvo Akademii Nauk SSSR, 1963.

Krausse, Joachim, and Claude Lichtenstein. *Your Private Sky: R. Buckminster Fuller*. Germany: Lars Müller Publishers, 1999.

Kundera, Milan. *Testaments Betrayed*. New York: Harper Collins, 1995.

Kuoljok, Kerstin Eidlitz. *The Revolution in the North: Soviet Ethnography and Nationality Policy*. Vol. 1. Almqvist och Wiksell, 1985.

Kwon, Heonik. "Maps and Actions: Nomadic and Sedimentary Space in a Siberian Reindeer Farm." PhD thesis, University of Cambridge, 1993, http://ethos.bl.uk/Order Details.do?uin=uk.bl.ethos.284243.

Landes, David S. *The Unbound Prometheus: Technological Change and Industrial Development in Western Europe from 1750 to the Present*. Cambridge: Cambridge University Press, 2003.

Larsen, John, and Maurice Richard Libby. *Moose Jaw: People, Places, History*. Regina: Coteau Books, 2001.

Laruelle, Marlene. *New Mobilities and Social Changes in Russia's Arctic Regions*. New York: Routledge, 2016.

Latour, Bruno. "Anthropology at the Time of the Anthropocene – A Personal View of What Is to Be Studied." Distinguished lecture, American Association of Anthropologists, Washington, DC, December 2014.

Lavery, Carl, and Richard Gough. "Introduction." *Performance Research: A Journal of the Performing Arts* 20, no. 3 (2015): 1–8.

Lefebvre, Henri. *Critique of Everyday Life*. New York: Verso, 2014.

Lepselter, Susan. *The Resonance of Unseen Things*. Ann Arbor: University of Michigan Press, 2016.

Lokensgard, Kenneth Hayes. *Blackfoot Religion and the Cultural Consequences of Commoditization*. Abingdon: Routledge, 2016.

Lonsdale, Steven H. "Attitudes towards Animals in Ancient Greece." *Greece & Rome* 26, no. 2 (1979): 146–59.

Lyford, Amy. *Isamu Noguchi's Modernism, Negotiating Race, Labor, and Nation, 1930–1950*. Berkeley: University of California Press, 2013.

– "Noguchi, Sculptural Abstraction, and the Politics of Japanese American Internment." *MutualArt*, March 2003. https://www.mutualart.com/Article/Noguchi--sculptural-abstraction--and-the/94A84070D73470C6.

Maldonado-Torres, Nelson. "On the Coloniality of Being: Contributions to the Development of a Concept." *Cultural Studies* 21, nos. 2–3 (2007): 240–70.

Malm, Andreas. "The Anthropocene Myth." *Jacobin*, 30 March 2015. http://jacobinmag.com/2015/03/anthropocene-capitalism-climate-change/.

Marchand, Michael. "Mankayia and the Kiowa Indians: Survival, Myth, and the Tornado." *Heritage of the Great Plains* 26, no. 2 (1993): 19–29.

Mars, Roman. "A Sweet Surprise Awaits You." *99% Invisible*, 22 September 2015.

Marshall, Alison. *Cultivating Connections: The Making of Chinese Prairie Canada*. Vancouver: UBC Press, 2014.

– *The Way of the Bachelor: Early Chinese Settlement in Manitoba*. Vancouver: UBC Press, 2011.

Martin, Terry. *The Affirmative Action Empire: Nations and Nationalism in the Soviet Union, 1923–1939*. Ithaca and London: Cornell University Press, 2001.

Mason, Philip Parker. *The Ambassador Bridge: A Monument to Progress*. Detroit: Wayne State University Press, 1987.

Mauss, Marcel. *The Gift: The Form and Reason for Exchange in Archaic Societies*. London: Routledge, 2001.

Mavor, Carol. *Reading Boyishly: Roland Barthes, J.M. Barrie, Jacques Henri Lartigue, Marcel Proust, and D.W. Winnicott*. Durham and London: Duke University Press, 2007.

McSweeney, Joyelle. *The Necropastoral: Poetry, Media, Occults*. Ann Arbor: University of Michigan Press, 2014.

– "What Is the Necropastoral?" Poetry Foundation, 29 April 2014. https://www.poetryfoundation.org/harriet/2014/04/what-is-the-necropastoral/.

Merton, Robert K. *On the Shoulders of Giants: A Shandean Postscript*. New York: Harcourt Brace, 1985.

Mirzoeff, Nicholas. "The Right to Look." *Critical Inquiry* 37, no. 3 (2011): 473–96.

Mitchell, W.J.T. *Landscape and Power*. Chicago: University of Chicago Press, 2002.

Moore, P.F. "Devonian Reefs in Canada and Some Adjacent Areas." In *Reefs: Canada and Adjacent Areas*, edited by Helmut H.J. Geldsetzer, Noel R. James, and Gordon E. Tebbutt, 367–90. Memoir 13. Canadian Society of Petroleum Geologists, 1988. Accessed

31 December 2016. http://archives.datapages.com/data/cspg_sp/data/013/013001/367_cspgsp0130367.htm.

Mulvey, Laura. *Death 24x a Second: Stillness and the Moving Image*. Edinburgh: Reaktion Books, 2006.

Nabokov, Peter. *A Forest of Time: American Indian Ways of History*. Cambridge: Cambridge University Press, 2002.

Nancy, Jean-Luc. *The Fall of Sleep*. Translated by Charlotte Mandell. New York: Fordham University Press, 2009.

Ngai, Sianne. *Our Aesthetic Categories: Zany, Cute, Interesting*. Cambridge, MA, and London: Harvard University Press, 2012.

Nixon, Rob. "The Anthropocene: The Promise and Pitfalls of an Epochal Idea." In *Future Remains: A Cabinet of Curiosities for the Anthropocene*, edited by Gregg Mitman, Marco Armiero, and Robert Emmett, 1–18. Chicago and London: University of Chicago Press, 2018.

– *Slow Violence and the Environmentalism of the Poor*. Cambridge, MA: Harvard University Press, 2011.

Noguchi, Isamu. "I Became a Nisei." Letter, October 1942. http://www.noguchi.org/sites/default/files/Isamu-Noguchi-I-Become-A-Nisei-Noguchi-Museum.pdf.

– "An Interview with Katherine Kuh, 1962." In Noguchi, *Isamu Noguchi: Essays and Conversations*, 130–5.

– *Isamu Noguchi: Essays and Conversations*. Edited by Diane Apostolos-Cappadona and Bruce Altshuler. New York: Harry N. Abrams, Inc., 1994.

– "Japanese Akari Lamps, 1954." In Noguchi, *Isamu Noguchi: Essays and Conversations*, 102–4.

– *A Sculptor's World*. Göttingen: Steidl, 2004.

– *Space of Akari and Stone*. San Francisco: Chronicle Books, 1986.

Nye, David. "The Transformation of American Urban Space: Early Electrical Lighting 1875–1915." In *Urban Lighting, Light Pollution, and Society*, edited by Josiane Meier, Ute Hasenöhrl, Katharina Krause, and Merle Pottharst, 30–45. New York: Routledge, 2015.

Ogden, Laura. *Swamplife: People, Gators, and Mangroves Entangled in the Everglades*. Minneapolis: University of Minnesota Press, 2011.

O'Gorman, Marcel. "Bernard Stiegler's Pharmacy: A Conversation." *Configurations* 18, no. 3 (2010): 459–76.

– "Detroit Digital." *CTheory*, 29 November 2007. http://ctheory.net/ctheory_wp/detroit-digital-on-tourists-in-the-apocalypse/.

Painter, George D. *Marcel Proust: A Biography*. Vol. 2. New York: Random House, 1959.

Panofsky, Erwin. *Perspective as Symbolic Form*. Translated by Christopher S. Wood. New York: Zone Books, 1991.

Pelto, Pertti J. *The Snowmobile Revolution: Technology and Social Change in the Arctic*. Kiste and Ogan Social Change Series in Anthropology. Menlo Park, CA: Cummings, 1973.

Phelan, Peggy. *Unmarked: The Politics of Performance*. New York: Routledge, 1993.

Pika, Alexander, and Bruce Grant, eds. *Neotraditionalism in the Russian North: Indigenous Peoples and the Legacy of Perestroika*. Circumpolar Research Series, No. 6. Edmonton and Seattle: Canadian Circumpolar Institute and University of Washington Press, 1999.

Pittman, Blair. *The Stories of I.C. Eason, King of the Dog People*. Denton: University of North Texas Press, 1996.

Plotz, John. "Can the Sofa Speak? A Look at Thing Theory." *Criticism* 47, no. 1 (2005): 109–18.

Povinelli, Elizabeth. *The Cunning of Recognition: Indigenous Alterities and the Making of Australian Multiculturalism*. Durham and London: Duke University Press, 2002.

Povoroznyuk, Olga. "Belonging to the Land in Tura: Reforms, Migrations, and Identity Politics in Evenkia." *Journal of Ethnology and Folkloristics* 8, no. 2 (2014): 33–51.

Povoroznyuk, Olga, Joachim Otto Habeck, and Virginie Vaté. "Introduction: On the Definition, Theory, and Practice of Gender Shift in the North of Russia." *Anthropology of East Europe Review* 28, no. 2 (9 December 2010): 1–37.

Powell, Douglas Reichert. *Critical Regionalism: Connecting Politics and Culture in the American Landscape*. Chapel Hill: University of North Carolina Press, 2007.

Pringle, Patricia. "Scampering Sofas and 'Skuttling' Tables: The Entertaining Interior." *Interiors* 1, no. 3 (2010): 219–44.

Proust, Marcel. *Remembrance of Things Past*. Vol. 1. Translated by C.K. Moncrieff and Terence Kilmartin. New York: Random House, 1981.

– *Swann's Way*. New York: Penguin, 2002.

Public Lighting Commission of Detroit. *First Annual Report of the Public Lighting Commission of the City of Detroit, for the Fiscal Year Ending June 30th 1896*. Detroit: The Thos. Smith Press, 1896.

Reichlin, Bruno. "The Pros and Cons of the Horizontal Window: The Perret-Le Corbusier Controversy." *Daidalos* 13 (1984): 65–78.

Ridington, Robin. "From Artifice to Artifact: Stages in the Industrialization of a Northern Hunting People." *Journal of Canadian Studies* 18, no. 3 (August 1983): 55–66.

Riskin, Jessica. *Genesis Redux: Essays in the History and Philosophy of Artificial Life*. Chicago: University of Chicago Press, 2007.

Rodney, Lee. "Art and the Post-Urban Condition." In *Cartographies of Place: Navigating the Urban*, edited by Michael Darroch and Janine Marchessault, 253–69. Montreal and Kingston: McGill-Queen's University Press, 2014.

Romero, Andrés, and Toby Austin Locke. "Words in Worlds: An Interview with Kathleen Stewart." *Dialogues*, Cultural Anthropology website, 20 July 2017. https://culanth.org/fieldsights/1160-words-in-worlds-an-interview-with-kathleen-stewart.

Sayer, Derek. *Making Trouble*. Chicago: Prickly Paradigm Press, 2017.

Schauer, Julie. "Isamu Noguchi, Biomorphic Art and Design." *Artventures*, 12 February 2016. http://artvent-artventures.blogspot.ca/2016/02/isamu-noguchi-biomorphic-art-and-design.html.

Schivelbusch, Wolfgang. *Disenchanted Night: The Industrialization of Light in the Nineteenth Century*. Berkeley and Los Angeles: University of California Press, 1988.

Schwartz, Hillel. *The Culture of the Copy: Striking Likenesses, Unreasonable Facsimiles.* New York: Zone, 1996.

Scott, Joan. "The Incommensurability of Psychoanalysis and History." *History and Theory* 51, no. 1 (2012): 63–83.

Serres, Michel. *The Five Senses: A Philosophy of Mingled Bodies.* Translated by Margaret Sankey and Peter Cowley. London and New York: Continuum, 2008.

Shelley, Mary Wollstonecraft, and Barry Moser. *Frankenstein, or, The Modern Prometheus: The 1818 Text in Three Volumes.* Berkeley: University of California Press, 1984.

Shelley, Percy Bysshe, and Lawrence John Zillman. *Prometheus Unbound, a Variorum Edition.* Seattle: University of Washington Press, 1959.

Shirokogoroff, S.M. *Social Organization of the Northern Tungus, with Introductory Chapters concerning Geographical Distribution and History of the Groups.* Shanghai, China: The Commercial Press Limited, 1929.

Simic, Charles. "The Lunatic." In *The Lunatic: Poems,* 5. New York: Ecco, 2015.

Simmel, Georg. "The Metropolis and Mental Life." In *On Individuality and Social Forms,* 324–39. Chicago: University of Chicago Press, 1971.

Simpson, David. "Raymond Williams: Feeling for Structures, Voicing 'History.'" *Social Text* 30 (1992): 9–26.

Simpson, Leanne Betasamosake. *As We Have Always Done: Indigenous Freedom through Radical Resistance.* Minneapolis: University of Minnesota Press, 2017.

Solnit, Rebecca. *Paradise in Hell: The Extraordinary Communities That Arise in Disasters.* New York: Penguin, 2010.

Sontag, Susan. *On Photography.* London: Penguin, 1975.

Spender, Matthew. *From a High Place: A Life of Arshile Gorky.* Berkeley: University of California Press, 2001.

Ssorin-Chaikov, Nikolai. "Soviet Debris: Failure and the Poetics of Unfinished Construction in Northern Siberia." *Social Research: An International Quarterly* 83, no. 3 (2016): 689–721.

Starobinski, Jean, and Richard Pevear. "Windows: From Rousseau to Baudelaire." *The Hudson Review* 40, no. 4 (1988): 551–60.

Stewart, Garrett. *Between Film and Screen: Modernism's Photo Synthesis.* Chicago: University of Chicago Press, 1999.

Stewart, Kathleen. "Atmospheric Attunements." *Rubric* 1 (2010). http://rubric.org.au/wp-content/uploads/2010/05/Atmospheric-Attunements.pdf.

– *Ordinary Affects.* Durham: Duke University Press, 2007.

– "Regionality." *Geographical Review* 103, no. 2 (2013): 275–84.

– "Weak Theory in an Unfinished World." *Journal of Folklore Research* 45, no. 1 (2008): 71–82.

– "Worlding Refrains." In *The Affect Theory Reader,* edited by Melissa Gregg and Gregory J. Seigworth. Durham and London: Duke University Press, 2010.

Stewart, Susan. *On Longing: Narratives of the Miniature, the Gigantic, the Souvenir, the Collection.* Durham: Duke University Press, 1992.

Steyerl, Hito. "In Defense of the Poor Image." *e-flux journal*, no. 10 (2009). http://www.e-flux.com/journal/10/61362/in-defense-of-the-poor-image/.

Straw, Will. "The Urban Night." In *Cartographies of Place: Navigating the Urban*, edited by Michael Darroch and Janine Marchessault, 185–200. Montreal and Kingston: McGill-Queen's University Press, 2014.

Sugrue, Thomas. *The Origins of the Urban Crisis: Race and Inequality in Postwar Detroit*. Princeton, NJ: Princeton University Press, 2005.

Tagg, John. *The Burden of Representation: Essays on Photographies and Histories*. Minneapolis: University of Minnesota Press, 1993.

Talbot, Deborah. *Regulating the Night: Race, Culture and Exclusion in the Making of the Night-Time Economy*. Aldershot, UK: Ashgate, 2007.

Tanizaki, Junichiro. *In Praise of Shadows*. Leete's Island Books, 1977. http://dcrit.sva.edu/wp-content/uploads/2010/10/In-Praise-of-Shadows-Junichiro-Tanizaki.pdf.

Taussig, Michael. "Tactility and Distraction." In *The Sixth Sense Reader*, edited by David Howes, 267–74. Oxford and New York: Berg, 2009.

Thacker, Eugene. *In the Dust of This Planet: Horror of Philosophy Vol. 1*. Zero Books, 2011.

Tovias, Blanca. "The Right to Possess Memory: Winter Counts of the Blackfoot, 1830–1937." *Ethnohistory* 61, no. 1 (2014): 99–122.

Uvachan, V.N. *Put´ Narodov Severa K Sotsializmu. Opyt Sots. Str-va Na Eniseĭskom Severe. (Ist. Ocherk)*. Moscow: Mysl´, 1971.

Vivieros de Castro, Eduardo. *The Relative Native: Essays on Indigenous Conceptual Worlds*. Chicago: HAU Books, 2015.

Wark, McKenzie. *Molecular Red: Theory for the Anthropocene*. Verso Books, 2015.

Weber, Max. *The Protestant Ethic and the Spirit of Capitalism: And Other Writings*. Translated by Stephen Karlberg. Third Roxbury Edition. Los Angeles: Roxbury Publishing, 2002.

Weiner, Douglas R. *Models of Nature: Ecology, Conservation, and Cultural Revolution in Soviet Russia*. Bloomington: Indiana University Press, 1988.

– "The Predatory Tribute-Taking State: A Framework for Understanding Russian Environmental History." In *The Environment and World History*, edited by Edmund Burke and Kenneth Pomeranz, 276–316. Berkeley: University of California Press, 2009.

Whipple, Fred. H. *Municipal Lighting*. Detroit: Free Press Print, 1888.

Wiles, Will. *Care of Wooden Floors: A Novel*. Boston and New York: New Harvest Houghton Mifflin Harcourt, 2012.

Wilkinson, Alex. "All Things Thrown and Wonderful, All Memories Great and Small." *Journal of Historical Sociology* 27, no. 4 (2014): 579–99.

Williams, Linda. *Hard Core: Power, Pleasure and the Frenzy of the Visible*. Berkeley: University of California Press, 1989.

Williams, Raymond. "Base and Superstructure in Marxist Cultural Theory." *New Left Review* 82 (1973): 3–16.

– *The Long Revolution*. Westport, CT: Greenwood Press, 1975.

– *Marxism and Literature*. London: Oxford University Press, 1977.

- *Politics and Letters.* London: NLB, 1979.
- "Structures of Feeling." In *Marxism and Literature,* 128–35. New York: Oxford University Press, 1977.

Williams, Raymond, and Michael Orrom. *Preface to Film.* London: Film Drama, 1954.

Winter, John. "Eames House." In *The World of Charles and Ray Eames,* edited by Catherine Ince and Lotte Johnson, 85–97. London: Thames and Hudson, 2015.

Witmore, Christopher. "Landscape, Time, Topology: An Archeological Account of the Southern Argolid, Greece." In *Envisioning Landscape: Situations and Standpoints in Archaeology and Heritage,* edited by Laura McAtackney, Graham Fairclough, and Dan Hicks, 194–225. Walnut Creek, CA: Routledge, 2009.

Wittgenstein, Ludwig. *Philosophical Investigations.* Translated by G.E.M. Anscombe. Oxford: Basil Blackwell, 1986.

Woolf, Virginia. "The Cinema." In *Selected Essays,* 175. Oxford: Oxford University Press, 2009.
- *Jacob's Room.* Oxford: Oxford University Press, 1999.

Woolgar, Steve. "Configuring the User: The Case of Usability Trials." In *A Sociology of Monsters: Essays on Power, Technology and Domination,* edited by John Law, 57–99. London and New York: Routledge, 1991.

Wynter, Sylvia. "Towards the Sociogenic Principle: Fanon, Identity, the Puzzle of Conscious Experience, and What It Is Like to Be 'Black.'" In *National Identities and Sociopolitical Changes in Latin America,* edited by Mercedes Durán-Cogan and Antonio Gómez-Moriana, 30–66. New York and London: Routledge, 2001.

Yamaguchi, Yoshiko, with Fujiwara Sakuya. *Fragrant Orchid.* Translated with an introduction by Chia-Ning Chang. Honolulu: University of Hawaii Press, 2015.

Yates, Frances A. *The Art of Memory.* Chicago: University of Chicago Press, 2001.

Zardini, Mirko. "Toward a Sensorial Urbanism." In *Sense of the City: An Alternate Approach to Urbanism,* edited by Mirko Zardini, 19–27. Montreal: Canadian Centre for Architecture, 2005.

Zee, Jerry C. "Holding Patterns: Sand and Political Time at China's Desert Shores." *Cultural Anthropology* 32, no. 2 (2017): 215–41.

CONTRIBUTORS

Craig Campbell is associate professor of anthropology at the University of Texas at Austin. He is currently working on a book titled *In the Shadow of a Dam: The Future of River Life on the Industrial Edgelands of Siberia.*

Michael Darroch is associate professor of media art histories and visual culture in the School of Creative Arts, University of Windsor. He was founding director (2010–16) and is now co-director of the IN/TERMINUS Creative Research Collective. He co-edited *Cartographies of Place: Navigating the Urban* (McGill-Queen's University Press, 2014), an interdisciplinary collection that situates different historical and methodological currents in urban media studies. Recent essays engage with histories of communication and media studies, urban media cultures, and borderlands studies.

Karen Engle is associate professor of media art histories and visual culture in the School of Creative Arts, University of Windsor. Recent publications include "Fragments of Desire" with Trudi-Lynn Smith in *Imaginations: Journal of Cross-Cultural Image Studies* 7, no. 1 (2016), and "The Boondoggle: Lee Miller and the Vicissitudes of Private Archives," *Photographies* 8, no. 1 (2015). She is author of the book *Seeing Ghosts: 9/11 and the Visual Imagination* (McGill-Queen's University Press, 2009).

Lindsey A. Freeman, assistant professor of sociology at Simon Fraser University, is the author of *Longing for the Bomb: Oak Ridge and Atomic Nostalgia* (University of North Carolina Press, 2015), and *This Atom Bomb in Me* (Stanford University Press, 2017).

Christien Garcia is a Social Sciences and Humanities Research Council post-doctoral fellow at the University of Cambridge's Centre for Screen and Film. He recently received his PhD in English and cultural studies from McMaster University.

Adam Kaasa is senior tutor in architecture, Royal College of Art, London. Recent publications include the book co-edited with Honor Gavin *Uncommon Building: A Collective Excavation of a Fictional Structure* (Spirit Duplicator, 2017).

Mark Jackson is senior lecturer in postcolonial geographies in the School of Geographical Sciences at the University of Bristol, UK. Recent publications include papers in *Geohumanities*, *Progress in Human Geography*, and *The Sage Handbook of Nature*, 3rd ed. His new book is *Coloniality, Ontology, and the Question of the Posthuman* (Routledge, 2018). He is also the series editor for Routledge Research in New Postcolonialisms.

Adam Lauder is an SSHRC postdoctoral fellow at York University, Toronto. Lauder's current research explores Canadian artists' shifting engagements with information technologies and changing concepts of "information" in the 1970s.

Kimberly Mair is associate professor of sociology at the University of Lethbridge and author of the book *Guerrilla Aesthetics: Art, Memory, and the West German Urban Guerrilla* (McGill-Queen's University Press, 2016).

Lee Rodney is associate professor of media art history and visual culture in the School of Creative Arts at the University of Windsor where she is co-director (with Michael Darroch) of the IN/TERMINUS Research Group. She also curates the Frontier Files, an online archive of visual and material culture relating to geographic borders in North America and elsewhere. Her book *Looking beyond Borderlines: North America's Frontier Imagination* was published by Routledge in 2017.

Joey Russo received his PhD in anthropology at University of Texas at Austin, where he was an ACLS/Mellon Fellow. Recent publications include "Casino Light," *Capricious: Journal for Emerging Affect Inquiry* 1, no. 1 (2016).

Lesley Stern is professor emerita in visual arts at the University of California, San Diego. She is currently working on and writing about the relationship between gardens and the larger world.

Yoke-Sum Wong is the managing editor of *The Journal of Historical Sociology* (Wiley). She recently returned to Canada after over a dozen years in the UK and is now teaching at the Alberta College of Art and Design, Calgary. She is a research affiliate with the Anthropology Department at the University of Texas at Austin.

INDEX